THE DANCE OF THE
DISSIDENT DAUGHTER

The Dance of the Dissident Daughter

A Woman's Journey from Christian Tradition to the Sacred Feminine

Sue Monk Kidd

HarperSanFrancisco
An Imprint of HarperCollins*Publishers*

Excerpt from *Women Who Run with the Wolves* by Clarissa Pinkola Estés, Ph.D.,
copyright © 1992, 1995. Reprinted by kind permission of the author, Dr. Estés,
and Ballantine Books, a division of Random House, Inc.

HarperCollins books may be purchased for educational, business, or sales
promotional use. For information please write: Special Markets Department,
HarperCollins Publishers Inc., 10 East 53rd Street, New York, NY 10022.

HarperCollins Web site: http://www.harpercollins.com
HarperCollins®, ☙®, and HarperSanFrancisco,™ are trademarks of
HarperCollins Publishers Inc.

FIRST HARPERCOLLINS PAPERBACK EDITION PUBLISHED IN 2002
Book design by Ralph Fowler
Set in Adobe Garamond

Library of Congress Cataloging-in-Publication Data
Kidd, Sue Monk.
The dance of the dissident daughter :
a woman's journey from Christian tradition
to the sacred feminine / Sue Monk Kidd. — 1st ed.
p.   cm.
Includes bibliographical references.
ISBN 0–06–064588–1 (cloth)
ISBN 0–06–064589–X (pbk.)
1. Kidd, Sue Monk. 2. Spiritual biography—United States.
3. Feminism—United States—Biography.
4. Feminism—Religious aspects.
I. Title.
BL73 .K53A3 1996
291.2'114'092—dc20   [B]   95–26603

05 06 ❖/RRD 18 17 16 15

This book is dedicated
to my daughter, Ann,
who is also my friend,
and Betty and Terry,
friends who became
my sisters, with love
and gratitude.

Women will starve in
silence until new stories
are created which confer
on them the power of
naming themselves.

Sarah Gilbert
Susan Gubar

CONTENTS

ACKNOWLEDGMENTS

This book is rooted in my relationships and interactions with many people.

I want to begin with the outstanding women whose sharing, presence, and support have enriched my life and therefore these pages. To Betty Blackerby, Terry Helwig, Anita Stenz Chapman, Ramona McLeland, Terri Castillo, Kathleen Bohn, Djohariah Toor, Robin Williams, Melanie Britt, Lisa Isenhower, Betty Cockrell, Mary Page Sims, Mitzi Winesett, and Elizabeth Canham, deep thanks and love.

I also want to mention the fourteen women who were my companions during the pilgrimage through Crete: Carol Christ, Terry Helwig, Karen McFarland, Marian Nuckolls, Patricia Silbert, Jana Ruble, Carol Wilken, Jaime Shvey, Jan McCormick, Cathleen Peterson, Deborah Howard, Jane Steed, Robin Sotire, and Martha Ann. The impact they had on my life as we journeyed together urged me on, and ultimately their presence is part of this work.

I owe much to the people at HarperSanFrancisco who have stuck with me now through three books. Kandace Hawkinson, my editor for this book, provided the kind of insight, availability, support, and encouragement every author wishes for. Her knowledge about the subject and her wisdom about communicating the material have made this a better book. Her able assistant, Erica Smith, was also helpful and appreciated. My new editor, Barbara Moulton, guided this book through the final stages with wonderful suggestions and gifted hands, and I am grateful for her considerable gifts and experience. It also could not have been done without associate editor Lisa Bach, who provided continuous help and encouragement. And to Tom Grady, my publisher, who has given me enormous support and room to grow, I offer deepest thanks. I also offer my sincere appreciation to Mary Peelen and Steve Hanselman in the marketing department, whose openness and expertise have never failed to impress me, to Mimi Kusch, my able production editor, and to Priscilla Stuckey for her brilliant copyediting.

Three friends and colleagues gave generously of their time to read the entire manuscript, offering their considerable gifts to this work. Anita Stenz Chapman offered not only creative insights and clarity, but also ongoing nurture as I wrote. Roy M. Carlisle provided expert advice and comments and solid belief in this work. Karen McFarland also made many valuable suggestions, opened up new ideas, and was a source of sisterly encouragement.

Dr. Beatrice Bruteau, philosopher of great measure and a long-time mentor, discussed portions of the manuscript with me, and I'm grateful for her presence in my life and work. My friend Lois McAfee went an extra mile in gathering material. Another friend, Nancy Hardesty, offered helpful ideas. And computer genius Chris Goforth helped me with the rigors of technology throughout the writing.

I want to especially acknowledge Springbank Retreat Center, a beautiful and uniquely sacred place, and all the women who make it so. Its impact on me at a crucial time was transformative.

Portions of this work in progress were presented at Journey into Wholeness, Anderson Lay School of Theology, and the Academy of Spiritual Formation. I am grateful for those opportunities and the feedback they provided as I wrote.

I want to acknowledge the generations of women in my family, particularly my mother and grandmother, whose lives are part of me and whose love I constantly feel. To my children, Bob and Ann, I offer thanks and love for their blessing on this work. And most important is my husband, Sandy, whose support for me, for my journey, and for this book indicates the kind of sensitive, enlightened, and extraordinary man he is.

THE DANCE OF THE
DISSIDENT DAUGHTER

I was listening to National Public Radio the other day when someone asked the question: "Once you wake up, can you wake up any more?"

Yes, I thought. In a way my whole life has been about waking up and then waking up some more.

This book is about waking up some more.

In these pages I've tried to tell you about the deep and immense journey a woman makes as she searches for and finds a feminine spirituality that affirms her life. It's about the quest for the female soul, the missing Feminine Divine, and the wholeness women have lost within patriarchy. It's also about the fear, anger, pain, questions, healing, transformation, bliss, power, and freedom that come with such journeys.

I never thought I would write this book. That's because this journey is one I never imagined myself taking.

I was going along doing everything I "should" have been doing, and then, unexpectedly, I woke up. I collided with the patriarchy within my culture, my church, my faith tradition, my marriage, and also within myself. And this collision changed everything. I began to wake up to a whole new way of being a woman. I took what seemed to me then, and seems to me now, an immense journey.

It was true: There had been other awakenings in my life, but no waking experience had been as passionate and life altering as this one, nor had there been another where I felt more was at stake. The female soul is no small thing. Neither is a woman's right to define the sacred from a woman's perspective.

Still, the initial idea of telling my story in this book gave me pause. The hardest thing about writing is telling the truth. Maybe it's the hardest thing about being a woman, too. I think of Nisa, an old African woman who was telling her story for the tape recorder of a writer. She said, "Fix my voice on the machine so that my words come out clear.

I am an old person who has experienced many things and I have much to talk about. I will tell my talk . . . but don't let the people I live with hear what I have to say."[1] I love Nisa for that. I know that feeling. But in the end, Nisa and I told our truth anyway.

The reason I went ahead and wrote this book is difficult to express, so I will try to explain it this way. While I was writing it, a nature show came on television, a special about whales. I watched them on the screen as they flung themselves out of the sea, arced into the air, then fell back into the water. The behavior, the narrator said, is called breaching. He also said it may be the whales' way of communicating when the seas get high and wild. He speculated it was a tracking system for rough weather, some kind of urgent and powerful ballet that allowed the whales to follow one another's vibrations and not get lost. With each lunge, the whales marked their course, letting the others know where they were.

I thought to myself that women must have the whale's instinct. When we set out on a woman's journey, we are often swimming a high and unruly sea, and we seem to know that the important thing is to swim together—to send out our vibrations, our stories, so that no one gets lost. I realized that writing my book was an act of breaching. I hoped my story might help you find or keep your bearings or encourage you to send out your own vibrations.

In Etty Hillesum's journal, which chronicles her life before and during her imprisonment in a Nazi concentration camp, I came upon a few sentences that touched me very much. Hillesum wrote,

There is nothing else for it, I shall have to solve my own problems. I always get the feeling that when I solve them for myself I shall have solved them for a thousand other women. For that very reason I must come to grips with myself.[2]

We tell our stories for ourselves, of course. But there are also those thousand other women. And yet I'm aware that no two women's journeys into the Sacred Feminine are the same. Nor is this book, by any means, a complete picture of that journey. It is one woman sending out her own unique vibration.

Still it's true, I think, that when a woman offers the truth about her struggle to wake up, to grow beyond old models of womanhood and old spiritualities that no longer sustain, when she expresses what it was *really* like to discover and relate to the Feminine Divine, to heal feminine wounds, to unearth courage, and to reclaim her power, then women's differences tend to give way to something more universal. Often in such stories we find a deep sameness beneath our dissimilarities. We find we are all women, and down deep we ache for what has been lost to us. We want to tell the truth about our lives, to see the truth through other women's lives. We want to trust a Feminine Source of wisdom. We long for the whole, empowered woman who wants to be born in us.

When we start on this journey, we discover a couple of things right away. First, the way is largely uncharted, and second, we are all we've got. If women don't tell our stories and utter our truths in order to chart ways into sacred feminine experience, who will? It is stories women need. Stories give us hope, a little guidance, and a lot of bravery. That's why I "tell my talk," as Nisa says.

Such journeys may be new for you; you may want to launch out into women's spirituality, but at the same time you may feel terribly hesitant. I can only tell you, I understand this. When I began, such journeys were painfully new to me, too. You could hardly have found a more hesitant beginner or, paradoxically, a more eager one. This book will walk you through the journey. It will illumine the passages. It may even hold your hand a little. My hope is that the book will be an opening for you, that it will reassure and challenge you at the same time. I even dare to hope that something in these pages will make a tiny explosion in your heart and that you will see the thing you've hungered for all along as a woman. Above all, take what seems yours to take, and leave the rest.

Or, such journeys may not be new to you. You may be in the midst of your own transformation. You may already be exploring a Sacred Feminine dimension. You may be fully engaged in a struggle to exit patriarchy and come into your own as a woman, grappling with how your life is changed. In that case, this book is meant to offer you clarity and nurture. It is meant to be a companion to you. It should provide new markers, passages, insights, questions, motivations, inspiration, boldness, and meaning.

And there may be some of you who have already made your great transition. Maybe you have journeyed deep and long to the Sacred Feminine. I'm hoping that this book will open up some new avenues of experience and empowerment, just as I'm sure—if I were able to hear your story—that your journey would give me brand new ways of expanding and understanding my own. I hope, too, that the book will encourage you to find new ways to offer your experience to other women.

In the end, no matter where you are in the spectrum of women's spirituality, I invite you to weave new connections to your female soul. For always, always, we are waking up and then waking up some more.

SUE MONK KIDD

PART ONE
Awakening

I was trying . . . to lead a conventional life, for that was how I was brought up, and it was what my husband wanted of me. But one can't build little white picket fences to keep the nightmares out.

Anne Sexton

If we do not want to change and develop, then we might as well remain in a deathlike sleep.

Bruno Bettelheim

Woman is as common as a loaf of bread, and like a loaf of bread will rise.

From a wall poster

"THAT'S HOW I LIKE TO SEE A WOMAN"

It was autumn, and everything was turning loose. I was running errands that afternoon. Rain had fallen earlier, but now the sun was out, shining on the tiny beads of water that clung to trees and sidewalks. The whole world seemed red and yellow and rinsed with light. I parked in front of the drugstore where my daughter, Ann, fourteen, had an after-school job. Leaping a puddle, I went inside.

I spotted her right away kneeling on the floor in the toothpaste section, stocking a bottom shelf. I was about to walk over and say hello when I noticed two middle-aged men walking along the aisle toward her. They looked like everybody's father. They had moussed hair, and they wore knit sportshirts the color of Easter eggs, the kind of shirts with tiny alligators sewn at the chest. It was a detail I would remember later as having ironic symbolism.

My daughter did not see them coming. Kneeling on the floor, she was intent on getting the boxes of Crest lined up evenly. The men stopped, peering down at her. One man nudged the other. He said, "Now that's how I like to see a woman—on her knees."

The other man laughed.

Standing in the next aisle, I froze. I watched the expression that crept into my daughter's eyes as she looked up. I watched her chin drop and her hair fall across her face.

Seeing her kneel at these men's feet while they laughed at her subordinate posture pierced me through.

For the previous couple of years I had been in the midst of a tumultuous awakening. I had been struggling to come to terms with my life as a woman—in my culture, my marriage, my faith, my church, and deep inside myself. It was a process not unlike the experience of conception and labor. There had been a moment, many moments really, when truth seized me and I "conceived" myself as woman. Or maybe I reconceived myself. At any rate, it had been extraordinary and surprising to find myself—a conventionally religious woman in my late thirties—suddenly struck pregnant with a new consciousness, with an unfolding new awareness of what it means to be a woman and what it means to be spiritual *as a woman.*

Hard labor had followed. For months I'd inched along, but lately I'd been stuck. I'd awakened enough to know that I couldn't go back to my old way of being a woman, but the fear of going forward was paralyzing. So I'd plodded along, trying to make room for the new consciousness that was unfolding in my life but without really risking change.

I have a friend, a nurse on the obstetrical floor at a hospital, who says that sometimes a woman's labor simply stalls. The contractions grow weak, and the new life, now quite distressed, hangs precariously. The day I walked into the drugstore, I was experiencing something like that. A stalled awakening.

Who knows, I may have stalled interminably if I had not seen my daughter on her knees before those laughing men. I cannot to this day explain why the sight of it hit me so forcibly. But to borrow Kafka's image, it came like an ice ax upon a frozen sea, and suddenly all my hesitancy was shattered. Just like that.

The men's laughter seemed to go on and on. I felt like a small animal in the road, blinded by the light of a truck, knowing some terrible collision is coming but unable to move. I stared at my daughter on her knees before these men and could not look away. Somehow she seemed more than my daughter; she was my mother, my grandmother, and myself. She was every woman ever born, bent and contained in a small, ageless cameo that bore the truth about "a woman's place."

In the profile of my daughter I saw the suffering of women, the confining of the feminine to places of inferiority, and I experienced a collision of love and pain so great I had to reach for the counter to brace myself.

This posture will not perpetuate itself in her life, I thought.

Still I didn't know what to do. When I was growing up, if my mother had told me once, she'd told me a thousand times, "If you can't say something nice, don't say anything at all." I'd heard this from nearly everybody. It was the kind of thing that got cross-stitched and hung in kitchens all over my native South.

I'd grown up to be a soft-voiced, sweet-mouthed woman who, no matter how assailing the behavior before me or how much I disagreed with it, responded nicely or else zip-locked my mouth shut. I had swallowed enough defiant, disputatious words in my life to fill a shelf of books.

But it occurred to me that if I abandoned my daughter at that moment, if I simply walked away and was silent, the feminine spirit unfolding inside her might also become crouched and silent. Perhaps she would learn the *internal* posture of being on her knees.

The men with their blithe joke had no idea they had tapped a reservoir of pain and defiance in me. It was rising now, unstoppable by any earthly force.

I walked toward them. "I have something to say to you, and I want you to hear it," I said.

They stopped laughing. Ann looked up.

"This is my daughter," I said, pointing to her, my finger shaking with anger. "You may like to see her and other women on their knees, but we don't belong there. *We don't belong there!*"

Ann rose to her feet. She glanced sideways at me, sheer amazement spread over her face, then turned and faced the men. I could hear her breath rise and fall with her chest as we stood there shoulder to shoulder, staring at their faces.

"Women," one of them said. They walked away, leaving Ann and me staring at each other among the toothpaste and dental floss.

I smiled at her. She smiled back. And though we didn't say a word, more was spoken between us in that moment than perhaps in our whole lives.

I left the drugstore that day so internally jolted by the experience that everything in me began to shift. I sat in the car feeling like a newborn, dangled upside down and slapped.

Throughout my awakening, I'd grown increasingly aware of certain attitudes that existed in our culture, a culture long dominated by men. The men in the drugstore had mirrored one attitude in particular, that of seeking power over another, of staying up by keeping others down.

Sitting in my car replaying my statement back to those men—that women did not belong on their knees—I knew I had uttered my declaration of intent.

That night Ann came to my room. I was sitting in bed reading. She climbed up beside me and said, "Mama, about this afternoon in the drugstore . . ."

"Yeah?"

"I just wanted to say, thanks."

CONCEIVING THE FEMININE SELF

Poet Maxine Kumin wrote, "When Sleeping Beauty wakes up, she is almost fifty years old."[1] I wasn't fifty when my awakening began, but I was nearing forty. I'd lived just long enough for the bottom to start falling out of my notions of womanhood.

It all started when I was thirty-eight, two years before I walked into the drugstore. I was a full-time writer, spending many hours immersed in books. I lived in a nice house with a man I'd been married to for eighteen years, and we had two children, Bob and Ann, both in early adolescence. I went to church regularly and was involved in the social life of the small, Southern town where we lived. The last thing I expected was an encounter with feminist spirituality.

Feminist. What a word to deal with. I felt a secret sympathy for the underlying cause of feminism—what it might do for women—but I was uncomfortable with the word, uncomfortable with the images it carried. Overall, I'd kept a discreet distance from it. In fact, if there had been a contest for Least Likely to Become a Feminist, I probably could have made the finals on image alone.

But then one September night, I fell asleep and dreamed a momentous dream:

While sitting on the sand at the edge of the ocean, I am amazed to see that I am nine months pregnant and starting labor. I look around for help, but I am on an island by myself. Well, I think, I'll just deliver the baby myself. As the labor begins, I rub my abdomen and breathe deeply. I scoop up water as the waves flow ashore and bathe my abdomen and face. The pain comes and goes. Sometimes I cry and feel I might faint, but then the pain subsides. Finally I start to push. I give birth to a healthy baby girl. I hold her up, laughing with joy. I bring her close and look into her eyes. I am shocked to see I have given birth to myself, that I am the baby and the mother both.

I woke abruptly. You know how some dreams are so vivid you have to spend a few moments after you wake assuring yourself it didn't really happen? That's how I felt, like I needed to look around in the sheets for a newborn. I felt awed, like something of import and worthy of great reverence had taken place.

For years I'd written down my dreams, believing, as I still do, that one of the purest sources of knowledge about our lives comes from the symbols and images deep within. So, being careful not to wake my husband, I slipped out of bed, crept through the darkness into my study, and wrote down the dream.

At breakfast I took my tea to the patio and stared at the morning, wondering about this baby girl who was myself. What new potential did she represent? Who would she grow up to be? The dream was a mystery in many ways, but somehow I knew clearly that it was about my life as a woman.

Despite that realization, it didn't quite sink in that this dream was signaling the beginning of a profound new journey. I didn't know then that the child in the dream would turn my world upside down. That she would eventually change every fundamental relationship in my life: my way of being religious and spiritual, my way of being a woman in the world, my marriage, my career, and my way of relating to other women, to the earth, and even to myself.

At forty (or sometimes thirty or sixty), women grow ripe for feminist spiritual conception. By then we've been around long enough to grow disenchanted with traditional female existence, with the religious experience women have been given to live out.

Nearing forty, I needed to rethink my life as a "man-made woman." To take back my soul. Gradually I began to see what I hadn't seen before, to feel things that until then had never dared to enter my heart. I became aware that as a woman I'd been on my knees my whole life and not really known it. Most of all, I ached for the woman in me who had not yet been born, though I couldn't have told you then the reason for the ache.

When this disenchantment, this ripeness, begins, a woman's task is to conceive herself. If she does, the spark of her awakening is struck. And if she can give that awakening a tiny space in her life, it will develop into a full-blown experience that one day she will want to mark and celebrate.

Conception, labor, and birthing—metaphors thick with the image and experiences of women—offer a body parable of the process of awakening. The parable tells us things we need to know about the way awakening works—the slow, unfolding, sometimes hidden, always expanding nature of it, the inevitable queasiness, the need to nurture and attend to what inhabits us, the uncertainty about the outcome, the fearful knowing that once we bring the new consciousness forth, our lives will never be the same. It tells us that and more.

I've given birth to two children, but bringing them into the world was a breeze compared to birthing myself as woman. Bringing forth a true, instinctual, powerful woman who is rooted in her own feminine center, who honors the sacredness of the feminine, and who speaks the feminine language of her own soul is never easy. Neither is it always welcomed. I discovered that few people will rush over to tie a big pink bow on your mailbox.

Yet there is no place so awake and alive as the edge of becoming. But more than that, birthing the kind of woman who can authentically say, "My soul is my own," and then embody it in her life, her spirituality, and her community is worth the risk and hardship.

Today, eight years after my waking began, I realize that the women who are bringing about this kind of new female life are brand new beings among us. I keep meeting them; I keep hearing their stories. They confirm my own experience, that somewhere along the course of a woman's life, usually when she has lived just long enough to see through some of the cherished notions of femininity that culture holds out to her, when she finally lets herself *feel* the limits and injustices of the female life and admits how her own faith tradition has contributed to that, when she at last stumbles in the dark hole made by the absence of a Divine Feminine presence, then the extraordinary thing I've been telling you about will happen. This woman will become pregnant with herself, with the symbolic female-child who will, if given the chance, grow up to reinvent the woman's life.

This female-child is the new potential we all have to become women grounded in our own souls, women who discover the Sacred Feminine way, women who let loose their strength. In the end we will reinvent not only ourselves, but also religion and spirituality as they have been handed down to us.

Nobel Prize–winning novelist Toni Morrison wrote of her character Pilate that "when she realized what her situation in the world was . . . she threw away every assumption she had learned and began at zero."[2] With her new awareness, Pilate conceived herself and birthed a new way of being woman.

When my dream came, the potential to do the same rose up. Only it would take a long time to shed my old assumptions and begin at zero.

THE DEEP SLEEP

The dream left me with a vague kind of anticipation, a sense of restlessness. Two things happened as a result. First, I made plans to go away two months later for a solitary retreat at a Benedictine monastery, which I typically did when something was stirring inside. The second thing involved a journal.

Writing is not only my career, it's my compulsion. I keep voluminous journals, normally beginning a new one each January, so it was revealing that soon after the dream, even though it was September, even though I already had a nice journal with months of pages left, I went out and bought a new one. I bought a pink one.

Many mornings throughout October, I sat by the windows in the den before the children awoke, before my husband, Sandy, came in and started the coffee ritual. I sat there thinking about my life as a woman.

So much of it had been spent trying to live up to the stereotypical formula of what a woman should be—the Good Christian Woman, the Good Wife, the Good Mother, the Good Daughter—pursuing those things that have always been held out to women as ideals of femininity.

One morning I wrote about something that had happened several months earlier. I'd been inducted into a group of women known as the Gracious Ladies. I'm not exactly sure what the criteria was, except one needed to portray certain ideals of womanhood, which included being gracious and giving of oneself unselfishly. During a high-lace ceremony, standing backstage waiting to be inducted, I felt a stab of discomfort. I thought about the meticulous way we were coiffed and dressed, the continuous smiling, the charm that fairly dripped off us, the sweet, demure way we behaved, like we were all there to audition for the Emily Post-er Child. We looked like the world's most proper women.

What am I doing here? I thought. Lines from the poem "Warning," by Jenny Joseph, popped into my head and began to recite themselves.

When I am an old woman, I shall wear purple / with a red hat that doesn't go, and doesn't suit me, . . . / I shall go out in my slippers in the rain / And pick the flowers in other people's gardens / And learn to spit.[3]

I turned to a woman beside me and said, "After we're Gracious Ladies, does that mean we can't wear purple with a red hat or spit?" She smiled but appeared vaguely dismayed that someone who'd managed to get into the group had just said the word *spit*.

"It's from a poem," I explained.

"I see," she said. Still smiling.

It occurred to me on that October morning that living the female life under the archetype of Gracious Lady narrowed down the scope of it considerably. It scoured away a woman's natural self, all the untamed juices of the female life. It would be many years before I read Clarissa Pinkola Estés's words, "When a woman is cut away from her basic source, she is sanitized,"[4] but somehow even then, in the most rudimentary way, I was starting to know it.

In my spiritual life I was also a sanitized woman. I had always been very spiritual and very religious, too, so as I wrote in my journal I began trying to put my womanhood together with my spirituality and religion.

I wrote that I was mainstream orthodox. It sounded very dull, but actually it hadn't been dull at all. I'd pursued a spiritual journey of depth and meaning, but—and this was the big realization for me—I'd done so safely within the circle of Christian orthodoxy. I would no more have veered out of that circle than a child would have purposely drawn outside the lines in her coloring book.

I had been raised in the Southern Baptist Church, and I was still a rather exemplary member of one, but beginning in my early thirties I'd become immersed in a journey that was rooted in contemplative spirituality. It was the spirituality of the "church fathers," of the monks I'd come to know as I made regular retreats in their monasteries. I was influenced by Meister Eckhart and Julian of Norwich, who did, now and then, refer to "God our Mother," but this had never really sunk in. It was nice poetry. Now I wondered: What did "God our Mother" really mean?

Morning after morning I wrote, starting to realize how my inner journey had taken me into the airy world of intellect and the fiery realm of spirit, places that suddenly seemed very removed. I thrived on solitude, routinely practicing silent meditation as taught by the monks Basil Pennington and Thomas Keating. Because I visited monasteries and practiced the spirituality they were built upon, people often asked me,

"Why do you like monasteries so much?" I would grin and say, "Well, what do you expect? My middle name *is* Monk." Like the Gracious Lady, Monk was an archetype—a guiding inner principle—I lived by.

I'd read many of the classics of Christian contemplative literature, the church fathers and the great mystics of the church. For years I'd studied Thomas Merton, John of the Cross, Augustine, Bernard, Bonaventure, Ignatius, Eckhart, Luther, Teilhard de Chardin, *The Cloud of Unknowing,* and others. Why had it never seemed peculiar that they were all men?

I often went to Catholic mass or Eucharist at the Episcopal church, nourished by the symbol and power of this profound feeding ritual. It never occurred to me how odd it was that women, who have presided over the domain of food and feeding for thousands of years, were historically and routinely barred from presiding over it in a spiritual context. And when the priest held out the host and said, "This is my body, given for you," not once did I recognize that it is women in the act of breastfeeding who most truly embody those words and who are also most excluded from ritually saying them.

When those particular thoughts struck me one morning as I was writing, they pricked a bubble of anger I didn't know I had, and I surprised myself by throwing my pen across the room. It landed inside the fireplace in a pile of soot. I had to go get the pen and clean it off. There had been so many things I hadn't allowed myself to see, because if I fully woke to the truth, then what would I do? How would I be able to reconcile myself to it? The truth may set you free, but first it will shatter the safe, sweet way you live.

The thoughts and memories I was collecting in the journal were random, disjointed. Frankly, I couldn't see what any of them had to do with the dream. It was as if I were walking around and around some secret enclosure, trying to find a way into it. I sometimes wondered what good my pacing was doing.

But after leaving the process for a few days, I would be back in the den, picking up where I'd left off, trying to make sense of things. I wrote about how odd it was that at the same time I was making these retreats in monasteries, going to Eucharist, and meditating on the words of Merton and St. Francis, I was going to a Baptist church—not just on Sunday mornings, but also on Sunday and Wednesday evenings—where the emphasis was not on symbol and silence and God in the soul but on evangelizing and preaching and God in the word. I was a contemplative in an evangelical church, which is sort of like trying to squeeze a round soul into a square slot. It was all I could do to hold the tension between them. I had one foot on shore and the other in a boat that had started to drift.

But despite the inner tension, I kept trying to adapt. The Southern Baptist Church had been the fabric of my religious existence since childhood. And if that wasn't enough, I was married to a Southern Baptist minister who was a religion teacher and chaplain on a Baptist college campus. That alone was enough to keep me securely tethered to the flock. So I taught Sunday school and brought dishes to all manner of potlucks and tried to adjust the things I heard from the pulpit to my increasingly incongruent faith.

I filled pages about my life as a Baptist.

I recorded the time Ann, then eight, tugged on my dress during a church service while the minister was ordaining a new set of deacons. "When are they going to do the women?" she asked.

"The women?" I echoed.

She nodded. Her assumption of equality was earnest and endearing. These days you will find a few female deacons in the more moderate Southern Baptist churches, but not so much then. I'd felt like a harbinger of cruel truth when I told her, "They don't ordain women, honey. Only men."

She had frowned, truly puzzled.

That day in church, the words *only men, only men, only men* went on echoing in my head for a good five minutes, but it soon passed. With a little more ripeness, I might have conceived a new female life that long-ago day, but then I was too consumed with staying in line and being a good and proper woman, something that renders you fairly sterile as far as feminine journeys go.

Writing down that memory reminded me of the time *I* was eight and had my own first encounter with "cruel truth." I was in the church yard during Vacation Bible School. It was hot. Georgia hot. The girls sat under a tree, making tissue paper corsages, while the boys climbed the limbs above us. I could not remember how it started, only that a quarrel broke out—one of those heated boys-are-better-than-girls or girls-are-better-than-boys arguments that eight year olds have with such verve. Finally one of the boys told us to shut up, and, of course, we wanted to know who'd made him our boss. "God!" he said. "God made *us* the boss."

So we girls marched inside to the teacher and asked her point-blank if this was so. We asked her with the same earnest and endearing assumption of equality with which Ann had posed her question to me. And, like me, the teacher was slow to answer. "Well . . . actually . . . technically, I guess I have to say the Bible does make men the head."

"The head?" we asked.

"That means in charge," she said and looked at us as if to say, I know, I know, it's a blow, but that's the way it is.

I stared at her, amazed. I had never heard anything like this before, and I was sure it had to be a mistake. A *big* mistake. I mean, if this were true, then women, girls, me—we were not at all what I thought. At eight I couldn't have expressed it fully, but on some level I knew what this meant. That we were less than males and that we were going to spend the rest of our lives obeying and asking permission or worrying if we didn't. That event and others like it would eventually limit everything I ever thought about freedom and dreams and going where they took me. But worse, those events said something about the female gender itself—that it simply wasn't up to par. It had to be subdued, controlled, ruled over.

For girls there is always a moment when the earnest, endearing assumption of equality is lost, and writing about it in my journal thirty years later made me want to take those two eight year olds into my arms—myself and Ann, both.

October was nearly spent before I finally got around to reflecting on my life as a "Christian writer," which was how I was often identified. I'd been a prolific contributor to an inspirational magazine with millions of readers. I'd written articles for religious journals and magazines, books about my contemplative spirituality. It always surprised me where my readers turned up. One time I called L. L. Bean to order Sandy a denim shirt, and the operator said she was reading one of my books. I got lots of mail from readers. I spoke at Christian conferences, in churches. As a result, it seemed people expected me to be a certain way. Of course, I expected me to be a certain way, too. And that way had nothing remotely to do with feminist spirituality.

After a month of journal writing, one morning I sat as usual in the den. The light was coming up in the backyard, and the maple, at the height of fall color, appeared to be on fire. As I gazed at it, I understood that while I had gone through a lot of spiritual transformation and written about it, my changes had not deviated much from what were considered safe, standard, accepted Christian tenets. I had never imagined any kind of internal reformation that would call into question the Orthodox Christian Woman, the Good Daughter to the Church, or the Monk who lived high in the spiritual tower of her head. The risk of doing so seemed much too high for lots of reasons, but certainly paramount among them was that it might jeopardize my marriage and my career. I finally came to this:

As a woman, I've been asleep. The knowing rose in me, fast and brilliant, like the light coming now across the grass. I closed the journal and put it away.

A woman in Deep Sleep is one who goes about in an unconscious state. She seems unaware or unfazed by the truth of her own female life, the truth about women in general, the way women and the feminine have been wounded, devalued, and limited within culture, churches, and families. She cannot see the wound or feel the pain. She has never acknowledged, much less confronted, sexism within the church, biblical interpretations, or Christian doctrine. Okay, so women have been largely missing from positions of church power, we've been silenced and relegated to positions of subordination by biblical interpretations and doctrine, and God has been represented to us as exclusively male. So what? The woman in Deep Sleep is oblivious to the psychological and spiritual impact this has had on her. Or maybe she has some awareness of it all but keeps it sequestered nicely in her head, rarely allowing it to move down into her heart or into the politics of her spirituality.

The awarenesses about my female life that emerged during that month were sketchy, thin, and incomplete. A memory here, a thought there, a recognition, an insight—all of them sifting around like vapor. I knew as a woman I'd been asleep, but I had no idea exactly how. I knew I was waking up, but I didn't possess a clue about what I might be waking up to. All I knew was that there was this tiny female life inside, some part of me waking up and wanting to be born. She was rousing me out of years of somnambulance, and something had to be done with her.

An Unambiguous Woman

All in all I had been what some have called an "unambiguous woman." I didn't know this term at the time. It was coined by feminist theorist Deborah Cameron and later referred to by author Carolyn Heilbrun in her book *Writing a Woman's Life.* "What does it mean to be unambiguously a woman?" writes Heilbrun. "It means to put a man at the center of one's life and to allow to occur only what honors his prime position. One's own desires and quests are always secondary."[5]

For me the "man" was sometimes my husband, at other times my father, male colleagues, clergy, or God. But at its most basic, this "man" was symbolic of male authority itself, the cultural father or the collective rule of men in general.

I didn't consciously recognize when I was being unambiguously woman; I'd been blind to it. Before October, I would have denied it vehemently, as we are apt to do when something true is unconscious to us.

I had truly thought of myself as an independent woman. Certainly I was not outwardly submissive. I had my career, my own life, ideas, and plans. I behaved in seemingly independent ways, but inside I was still caught in daughterhood. I was deferring to the father at the center. I operated out of a lot of assumptions and ideas, but I had no idea the extent to which my ideas were really the internalized notions of a culture that put men at the center. My independent forays and outspokenness came at emotional cost and required excessive expenditures of energy. They engendered uneasy feelings, after-the-fact worry, second-guessing, and the habit of looking over my shoulder.

Living without real inner authority, without access to my deep feminine strength, I carried around a fear of dissension, confrontation, backlash, a fear of not pleasing, not living up to sanctioned models of femininity.

Such ideas may have been barely forming in me, but they still packed a lot of feeling. A lot of confused feeling. One evening in early November while the family was eating dinner, I reminded Sandy I was going away soon to the monastery for a retreat. With me gone, he had it all—work, kids, meals, house, laundry, the whole thing.

He grimaced. He said, "I wish you weren't going." That's what he said. Here's what I heard: Stay home. Stay put. Put me at the center of the universe and allow to happen only what honors my prime position.

"You know what?" I shouted. "I am fed up. I am just plain fed up!" Then I left the table, with Sandy, Ann, and Bob all staring at me, their forks poised in the air.

Sandy followed me into the bedroom, full of concern. "What is it? What's wrong?"

I wish I could have explained it to him then in a neat, coherent fashion, but it was so new and such a jumble inside. "I don't know," I said. "I don't know."

When a woman wakes up, it's not experienced in isolation. Her family, the people she's closest to, will be thrust into the experience as well, because it's not just the woman who's expecting a new life. In a way, the whole family is pregnant.

Broken Connection to the Feminine Soul

I had always prayed, though much of my prayer in the last few years had been silent meditation. One morning, though, I tried to get talkative with God, to talk to "him" about the things in my journal, the fed-up feeling, the realization that a new way of being a woman wanted to be born in me. I got nowhere. I kept wondering how "he" was going to understand this distinctly feminine experience.

I tried briefly to imagine a God like me. God as female. But it was such a foreign notion.

Now with the wisdom of hindsight, I can look back and understand what I could not really see then—that as a woman I was severed from something deep inside myself, something purely and powerfully feminine. Steeped in a faith tradition that men had named, shaped, and directed, I had no alliance with what might be called the Sacred Feminine. I had lost my connection to feminine soul.

When I use the term *feminine soul,* I'm referring to a woman's inner repository of the Divine Feminine, her deep source, her natural instinct, guiding wisdom, and power. It is everything that keeps a woman powerful and grounded in herself, complete in herself, belonging to herself, and yet connected to all that is. Connection with this inner reality is a woman's most priceless experience.

I wish someone had told me this that autumn, and I suppose that's why I'm saying it at the outset. We need to know the root problem when the awakening begins, when all is fuzzy and the feelings are confused and we find ourselves suddenly yelling across the dinner table that we are fed up. We need to know what has happened to women and to ourselves so we can find our way back to our feminine souls with as much purpose and clarity as possible.

With the connection to my feminine soul broken, I had no idea how to unfold my spiritual life in a way that was natural and genuine for women. I didn't even know there was a feminine way of being spiritual. If I had, I probably couldn't have given myself permission to embrace it. Not then.

Disconnected from my feminine soul, I had also unknowingly forfeited my power to name sacred reality. I had simply accepted what men had named. Neither had I noticed that when women give this power away, it is rarely used to liberate and restore value to women. More often it is used to shore up and enhance the privileged position of men.

In the beginnings of Christianity, church fathers debated whether women had souls at all. Later the issue became whether or not a woman's soul could be saved. Today the issue is one of women reconnecting with their souls.

To reconnect with our souls we need to claim the freedom and power to shed our conditioning, to tear out the stitches from the old fabric, and to define for ourselves who we are as women, what is sacred, and how we relate to sacred experience. When we finally do that, we will weave new lives and a new era. We will take back our souls once and for all.

This shedding and defining, this tearing out stitches and reweaving new ones became the essential work of my journey. But as author Madonna Kolbenschlag wrote, "Much testing, much reflecting, much living must intervene before we can say, 'My soul is my own.'"[6]

Sleep Dust

Like the Sandman from the nursery tale, who stole into children's rooms and put them to sleep by sprinkling sleep dust over them, our culture, even the culture of our faith, has helped anesthetize the feminine spirit.

I like the way Clarissa Pinkola Estés says it:

When a woman is exhorted to be compliant, cooperative, and quiet, to not make upset or go against the old guard, she is pressed into living a most unnatural life—a life that is self-blinding . . . without innovation. The world-wide issue for women is that under such conditions they are not only silenced, they are put to sleep. Their concerns, their viewpoints, their own truths are vaporized.[7]

The sleep seems to descend on females early in life. Studies conducted by Harvard professor Carol Gilligan and Colby College professor Lyn Mikel Brown from 1986 to 1990 have revealed that something truly phenomenal happens to girls around adolescence.[8] They undergo a gradual change in which they lose their feisty spirit, courage, and willingness to speak out—qualities they had known in girlhood. Around this time their truth becomes silenced, held back. They become afraid of conflict with males, because they know on some level that males hold the power. They become—perhaps forever—good little girls, settling into the clichés and limits imposed on their gender.

So sleep begins. For some it can extend throughout life as unconsciousness deepens and numbness sets in. These women lose all memory of the problem they once saw. For other women the sleep is more fitful; they sometimes glimpse the truth, but it never seems to rouse them fully. These women tend to fall back asleep when the waking state becomes threatening.

But whether our sleep is sound or partial, when we are cut off from our feminine source, from the Feminine Divine, symptoms inevitably break through.

Although outwardly appearing stable and satisfied, inwardly we may feel silenced, afraid, stuck, self-doubtful, unable to carry through with things, angry but unable to express it directly. We may grow perfectionistic and driven, but strangely at the same time we may feel powerless, without boundaries, overwhelmed with the roles we are expected to carry out. Moreover, we may harbor fears of being left alone, of risking ourselves, of conflict.

In my mid- to late thirties, before my awakening began, I was experiencing many of these symptoms. Yet I was unable to see that they were trying to tell me something, that they were voices urging me to drop deep into my own feminine nature.

Wake-Up Calls

Even on the literal level, waking was always hard for me. I have had only one nickname in my life, given to me by my brother, eleven years younger than I. He called me Sue-up, a name he made up for me when he was a toddler and I a young adolescent. At that time I'd sleep so soundly that alarm clocks could not get through to me, and I would wake only after being shaken a half-dozen times. Each morning people in my family would go around asking, "Is Sue up?" My little brother, who was learning to speak, thought this was my name.

Now beginning to wake up at thirty-eight, I realized that once again I'd been living up to my old nickname. As a woman I'd slept so soundly that wake-up calls had not really gotten through to me. Not the feminist movement, not the marginalization of women in the church, not exclusive male language in scripture and liturgy. I had been upset and alarmed by the staggering assault on women through rape, spousal abuse, sexual abuse, harassment, and genital mutilation, but somehow this didn't initiate a full-blown awakening.

I'd been disturbed by a stream of statistics, such as four times as many girls die worldwide of malnutrition as boys because boys are preferred and given more food. Or the fact that women do two-thirds of the work in the world and receive one-tenth of the world's wages.[9] Or that American women earn 75 percent of what similarly employed men do and comprise only 2 percent of top management. But neither did this rouse my feminine heart in the sort of way that propels one into a life-changing journey.

The first fictional story I ever wrote was about a woman who walked in her sleep nearly every night.[10] "People deposit their misery somewhere in their body," the character Hallie says. "Mine apparently is the sleep center of my brain." But despite her awareness that her sleepwalking signals something wrong in her life, she refuses to face her life or her problems.

Then one night she sleepwalks outside and climbs a ladder that has been left leaning against the house. She wakes three rungs from the top, everything around her darkness and air. Frightened, she backs down and returns to her room, where she ties her arm to the bedpost, afraid she'll sleep again and wake on the roof, this time stepping off into thin air.

But even then she doesn't confront the changes she needs to make. So she walks in her sleep again, this time backing the car down the driveway and crashing into a Japanese elm. It takes the crash to wake her. She sits at the wheel, stunned, a trickle of blood on her forehead, knowing finally that she must alter the direction of her life.

Here is one of the principles of women waking: If you don't respond to the first gentle nudges, they will increase in intensity. Next you will wake up on the roof. And if you do not respond to that, there will likely be a crash. There are women who sleep through the crashes, too. I imagine by then the impulse to wake gives up and they drift into permanent hibernation.

Why in the world do women sleep through all manner of wake-up calls? I think part of it is because we use psychological sleep as a way of avoiding pain. Our choice, as Florence Nightingale put it, is between pain and paralysis. A hard one. But it's only when we are willing to see the truth about our lives as women, however painful that truth might be, that we enter the portal of the journey.

That November, two months after the dream of giving birth to myself, I had a real collision with the truth. It would be my "driveway crash."

THE NEST OF YELLOW LEAVES

The monastery visit I'd planned was supposed to be just another routine retreat.

When I arrived dusk was falling. I strolled to the church along a sidewalk covered with so many fallen leaves that it was like walking on one long yellow carpet. I sat through vespers, listening to the monks chant the office, hopelessly trying to follow them in the prayer book but nevertheless swept into the strange beauty of the chant.

Afterward I waited outside the church for a monk named Father Paschal, who was to be my spiritual director during the retreat. Standing ankle-deep in leaves, I watched the monks file out in their black, hooded robes, and I wondered which one Father Paschal might be. He would have no problem spotting me; I was the only female in the whole place.

Suddenly I heard a little cough behind me and, turning, saw a smiling man with shaven dark hair and round glasses. "I'm Father Paschal," he said.

At that moment I opened my mouth and uttered what is undoubtedly the most embarrassing Freudian slip of my life. I said, "Hello, I'm Father Sue."

He got a funny look on his face. Heat flared in my cheeks.

"Are you feeling nervous about being here?" he asked, attributing my word slip to anxiousness.

I hated to tell him that no, actually I was an old hand at monasteries. "I must be," I said.

We chatted a while longer, though I don't recall a thing we said after that. My face stayed warm a good half hour.

Back in my room, I thought about my strange slip of the tongue. It hadn't come from nervousness like Father Paschal suggested, so why did

I say that? Maybe it was an indication of just how at home I felt in monastic places, that I had become "one of them." Sure, that's got to be it, I thought.

But some other part of me suspected the real truth, one too bitter to let in. That part in my unconscious, knowing and wise, was telling me exactly who I was identified with. It was telling me that my values, my spirituality, my way of being a woman in the world were masculine through and through. I was immersed in the world of the father.

Father Sue. I wanted to cry.

The next morning I rose and went for a walk, taking pen and journal. I walked toward a small stand of trees at the edge of the monastery, where I picked my way through young pines, half-bare maples, and bramble until I came to a small, hidden clearing.

It was wall-to-wall yellow leaves and dappled light. Impulsively I took armfuls of leaves and plumped them into a big pile to sit on. When I finished, the mound resembled the kind of nest Big Bird of Sesame Street would require. Almost laughing, I wrote in my journal, "I'm here in the woods sitting on a big nest of leaves."

I laid down my pen. You know what, I thought, maybe I made this big nest because I'm here to hatch my new life, to give birth to something. I remembered the dream of giving birth to myself, to the female life that wanted to come into being, and immediately, surprisingly, my eyes filled with tears.

I sat still. I wrote, "So then, what's standing in the way of this new life being born?" And it came to me all at once. *For one thing, you're going to have to forgive yourself for not being born male. You're going to have to learn to love your real female life.*

I sat there open-mouthed. What? That was ridiculous. Of course I loved being a woman. I reveled in my femaleness.

But the inner voice was not talking about my surface revelings in being feminine. It was telling me something much more complex. It was telling me that I'd lost the voice of my native soul, or as novelist Ursula K. Le Guin put it, the innate mother tongue. I had learned instead to speak the father tongue, the dominant cultural language.[11]

Inside I felt like something submerged in me from the beginning of time had slit the surface. Some awful, sunken truth I didn't want to acknowledge had floated up to awareness. Maybe that humiliating Father Sue comment had dislodged it. Or maybe the comment was merely the debris of a truth already rising. For a moment I tried to pretend the thought hadn't come, but it was too late. My body had recognized it as the truth even before my mind could allow it. My heart was thudding, and my stomach was doing slow rolls into my chest.

Next I was crying one of those shoulder-shaking cries. A girl, I thought. I was born a girl with three brothers. I felt utterly cheated. My anguish was so intense it shocked me. It was as if I felt inferior simply for being female—that as a woman I was damaged goods or at least "seconds."

I had somehow never known this about myself. It was terrible to admit, but even worse was feeling the pain that came with it. I thought, If I'd been born male, dear God! the things I could have done! I longed for parity with men, the freedom and choices of men, the ability to quest without worrying about who would cook dinner or pick up the children. I longed for the power men had to name the world, for the world had been largely male defined. Even God "himself" was defined by men and envisioned in their image.

Being female had always seemed vaguely limiting, confining, lacking in power, second-class. As I tried to understand why, I found myself thinking about Eve. Some words played in my head, the old litany about women I'd heard in church: "second in creation and first to sin." Some years before, the Southern Baptist denomination had passed a resolution saying that women should not have a place of authority over men in church because of this. It had come straight out of the epistle of 1 Timothy (2:11–14) written in the second century:

Let a woman learn in silence with all submissiveness. I permit no woman to teach or to have authority over men; she is to keep silent. For Adam was formed first, then Eve; and Adam was not deceived, but the woman was deceived and became a transgressor. (RSV)

As I brooded over this, I remembered the first time I'd heard the words *first to sin, second in creation*. The memory was still vivid, un-dulled after more than twenty-five years.

It was a Sunday morning, and I was around twelve. I sat in church in my childhood Georgia with my mother and father and two of my three younger brothers. We were listening to a visiting preacher give a ser-mon. It had to do with the "God-ordained family." The preacher had a portable chalkboard beside the pulpit, and on it he diagrammed the family for us. He wrote *God* at the top, then in a descending chain of command he wrote *husband, wife, children.*

I remembered the downward-pointing arrows he drew between each word, showing us the line of authority. When he got to the part about why wives were below husbands, I was on the edge of my pew. "Woman was the first to sin and the second to be created," he said. Then he went on to talk about Eve, how she was created for man's benefit, that she was unworthy because she disobeyed God and offered Adam the forbidden fruit.

It was just like that day in Vacation Bible School when the teacher had informed us the Bible put men in charge. I felt the same rush of disbelief and betrayal.

By then I'd heard the message many times, but that day it fell like the proverbial last straw, the one that breaks the female camel's back. I listened to this "man of God" taking his message right out of what we considered to be the truest book of all. A feeling of pressure built in my chest, almost the same feeling I got at the city pool when I stayed underwater too long. I looked down the pew at my mother to get her reaction. Her eyes had glazed over; she looked like she'd heard it at least five hundred times before. I looked at the other women. Same there. I wanted them to stand up and say indignantly that this wasn't so, but none of them looked the least bit perturbed.

My heart sank. If I could have put the feeling into words, I would have said, "God, how *could* you?"

The so-called God-ordained image of female as under male, incapable, disobedient, unworthy—all of which added up to inferior—was a devastating notion to me as a girl. It snuffed out something vital, some hope for my female life.

When I left church that day, real doubt had set in about the value of being a girl.

Years later when I came upon some words by theologian Elizabeth A. Johnson, I felt the deep click of truth inside. She said that experiences like the one I had "give girl children from the beginning the experience of a world where the male is the norm from which her own self deviates."[12] Over the years the idea of being "other," of being the lesser sex, had continued to seep into me. I saw now it had penetrated the marrow of my tiniest bones. That day in the nest of leaves outside the monastery

I came to know this for the first time. It was a moment of awakening. I had touched the wound of my feminine life.

THE FEMININE WOUND

When I returned home from the monastery, I wasn't quite the same. Oh, I tried to be. The holiday season was coming, and I thought if I dived into it full force the pain would be forgotten. I shelved my journal. The children and I went shopping. We dragged out decorations, drove to the country, and cut greenery. We put so much evergreen in the house Sandy said it looked like we were celebrating Arbor Day. I went crazy baking things, and I don't even like to bake. I also created new writing projects for myself. I did what I could to blot out the recognition that there was a feminine journey to be made and it was probably going to be the most arduous, most revolutionary experience of my life.

Feminist theologian Carol P. Christ states that a woman's awakening begins with an "experience of nothingness."[13] It comes as she experiences emptiness, self-negation, disillusionment, a deep-felt recognition of the limitation placed on women's lives, especially her own.

An experience of nothingness was what I encountered at the monastery. In tasting what it meant to be female in my culture and faith, I felt, for the first time, a hidden despair lodged inside.

At the time I had delusions that I was probably the only woman in the world with a wound like that. Later I would be surprised to discover that most women carry this wound, though it is usually buried and unnamed. Psychotherapist Anne Wilson Schaef's name for this wound is "the original sin of being born female." She writes,

To be born female in this culture means that you are born "tainted," that there is something intrinsically wrong with you that you can never change, that your birthright is one of innate inferiority. I am not implying that this must remain so. I do believe that we must know this and understand it as a given before it can be worked through.[14]

Of course, being female is not inferior at all, but that doesn't change the fact that women have often experienced it that way. Messages of inferiority and self-denial are passed to us all our lives, messages that we should deny our own experiences, feelings, and needs. We absorb them in an ongoing process of osmosis that creates and enlarges the wound's core.

Early on a girl starts to soak up the idea that she is less than boys. Not long ago my friend Betty told me about the day she and her husband walked beside the rapids of the Chatooga River and came upon a young family. Betty watched as the father took the boy, who looked about four years old, down to the water's edge so he could dip his hands into the surging water and feel the spray on his face. The boy's sister, slightly older, begged her mother to take her to the edge, too. "No," the mother told her. "It's too dangerous there."

A small incident, but when multiplied a hundred, a thousand times in a little girl's life, she learns that she's not as capable as a boy of handling life on the edge. She learns to hang back.

Peggy Orenstein's 1994 book, *Schoolgirls*,[15] draws on a 1991 survey by the American Association of University Women, which suggests that parents and teachers seem to have lesser expectations for girls than for boys. Orenstein showed that girls' self-esteem is lost as they "dumb themselves down" and conform to lesser expectations to avoid being threatening. The girls in her study learned by adolescence not to be too outspoken, too aggressive, or too smart. They learned to balance drive with deference. The boys, by contrast, were rewarded for their drive and discouraged from showing deference. Girls learned to negate themselves through simple experiences: On the playground calling a boy "a girl" was the worst slur possible.

Orenstein also found that boys received more attention from teachers than did girls. In many of the classrooms she visited, boys were called on more often. Even at home many of the schoolgirls felt their brothers were favored, that the boys were, in fact, listened to more than they.

At church girls fare no better. A young girl learns Bible stories in which vital women are generally absent, in the background, or devoid of power. She learns that men go on quests, encounter God, and change history, while women support and wait for them. She hears sermons where traditional (nonthreatening) feminine roles are lifted up as God's ideal. A girl is likely to see only a few women in the higher echelons of church power.

And what does a girl, who is forming her identity, do with all the scriptures admonishing women to submission and silence? Having them "explained away" as the product of an ancient time does not entirely erase her unease. She also experiences herself missing from pronouns in scripture, hymns, and prayers. And most of all, as long as God "himself" is exclusively male, she will experience the otherness, the lessness, of herself; all the pious talk in the world about females being equal to males will fail to compute in the deeper places inside her.

As a girl absorbs her culture, for instance as she watches movies and television, she may also come to understand that her real importance derives from her relationship with men and boys, by how good she looks for them or how well she takes care of them. She will notice the things traditionally assigned to women—keeping a home, cleaning, cooking, laundry, child rearing—and grow aware of how little value these things seem to have in the world compared to things men typically do.

When she grows up and enters the workplace, she will likely plunge into the staggering dilemma that is often hers alone—working while caring for children and keeping a house. She'll likely encounter ceilings, networks, and traditional assumptions that work against her as a woman. She will arrive at the disconcerting realization that success comes only as she learns to modulate and adapt her feminine self to a man's world.

If she sees few women in places of real power, hears few female voices of strength, and witnesses little female creativity, then despite what is said to her about women's equality, she experiences women (and herself) as absent and silent.

The feminine wound is created as we *internalize* all these experiences—the voices we hear at church, school, home, work, and within the culture at large suggesting (in ways both bold and subtle) that women and feminine experience are "less than."

If you receive often enough the message that women are inferior and secondary, you will soon believe you *are* inferior and secondary. As a matter of fact, many experts tell us that "all women in our society arrive at adulthood with significant feelings of inadequacy."[16]

Once on an airplane I sat beside a thirty-year-old woman with a briefcase. As we chatted, a female voice came over the loudspeaker and said, "This is your captain."

The woman stopped midsentence. "Oh no," she said, "a woman pilot."

"I'm sure she's well trained," I said.

"Right," she said, "but she's still a woman."

Her feminine wound—her personal concentration of female inferiority—had made a brief appearance.

As time went on, I would grasp how deep such wounds go. For we carry not only our own wounding experiences, but the inherited wounds of our mothers and grandmothers as well. "We think back through our mothers and grandmothers, if we are women," Virginia Woolf said.[17]

This statement is not mere poetry. We carry something ancient inside us, an aspect of the psyche that Carl Jung called the collective unconscious. Containing river beds of collective experience, the collective unconscious is the place where preexisting traces of ancestral experience are encoded.[18] Thousands of years of feminine rejection reside there, and it can rise up to do a dark dance with our conscious beliefs.

I read a moving example of this interplay in physician Christiane Northrup's book, *Women's Bodies, Women's Wisdom*. She recounted being in the delivery room countless times, hearing new mothers apologize to their husbands when the baby was not male. She described the experience as staggering to her. But, she writes,

When my own second daughter was born, I was shocked to hear those very words of apology come into my brain from the collective unconscious of the human race. I never said them out loud, and yet they were there in my head—completely unbidden. I realized then how old and ingrained is this rejection of the female by men and women alike.[19]

For Northrup, as for me, recognizing this wound in herself was a pivotal moment in her growth as a woman.

There's always the danger, though, that as we open our eyes to the social, physical, psychological, and spiritual violence done to women throughout history, not to mention the wounding in our own personal histories, we will become paralyzed by a sense of victimization. For me, opening my eyes to the feminine wound was rather like getting hit by a stun gun. I felt knocked down by the force of it, and for a short while I didn't get up. On some level, I felt overwhelmed by the depth of the feminine wound, which I was uncovering, not only in myself, but all around.

The danger of getting stuck in feelings of victimization is real, but nevertheless, recognizing the feminine wound is important because in the end it's the only way we can stop being victims. We can't change anything until we acknowledge the problem. I'd been an *unconscious* victim before my awakening began. Discovering the truth was waking me up to my victimization, but it was also making it possible for me to move beyond it.

Feminist writer Naomi Wolf has especially cautioned women not to shape our identity as victims. Yet shaping our identity as victims is quite different from naming the truth of our victimization in order to work against it and live into our power. If women don't document and protest the harm done to us, who will? As Wolf says, "Women are not natural victims, but they sure *are* victimized."[20]

While holding onto the awareness, then, that we must not fall into shaping our identity as victims, we have to tell ourselves the "flat-out truth," as my grandmother used to call it. And the flat-out truth is that we have come into a world, into a church or faith tradition, that for millennia has believed us inferior. It is a tradition permeated by an authoritarian attitude that devalues, diminishes, rejects, and limits women and the feminine.

But seeing such truth can be dangerous. Philosopher Mary Daly reminds us, "It isn't prudent for women to see all of this. Seeing means that everything changes: the old identifications and the old securities are gone."[21]

The question, she says, is whether women can forgo prudence in favor of courage. That was the question that followed me as I made my way into the new year.

Winter of Resistance

I call the first winter of my awakening the winter of resistance. It was marked by persistent attempts to ignore the groundswell of pain and awareness that had erupted at the monastery and the new consciousness that wanted in.

One day I pulled the slender volume *Children's Letters to God* from a bookshelf and came upon this letter from a little girl named Sylvia: "Dear God, Are boys better than girls, I know you are one but try to be fair. Sylvia."[22]

Tears floated to my eyes. Why did questions like these inhabit little girls and grown women, and when did we lose our courage to confront God with them? I threw on a coat and left the house, hoping a walk would offer diversion. Outside it was cold and bright with winter sun.

I walked to a neighborhood lake, sat on the grass, and watched a flotilla of ducks glide across the water in a perfect V.

I'd told no one about my experience at the monastery or the things it was kindling inside me. I wondered now if I should find someone trusted and pour out my experience. But did I really want to open up that hidden pocket of pain? Expressing it aloud to someone would hold me accountable to it in a whole new way, and frankly, I didn't know yet if I wanted to own up to the wound I'd vividly uncovered.

Mostly, I didn't want to believe I could have been wounded by my own faith. I didn't want to acknowledge how it had relegated half the human population to secondary status and invisible places. I didn't want any of this to be true.

The ground was starting to feel cold. Out on the lake, wind made scalloped patterns in the water. I drew my knees to my chin trying to muffle a throbbing space in my chest. I felt alone and unequipped for upheavals such as this. If I pursued this journey there would be so much to unravel, so much to unlearn.

Later I would read Ursula K. Le Guin's comment: "I am a slow un-learner. But I love my unteachers."[23]

I, too, was a slow unlearner. The problem was I didn't have any un-teachers. I didn't personally know anyone close at hand who'd gone through a feminist spiritual awakening. How did one do it? Did I dare step over the boundaries church and convention had drawn for women? Did I dare venture beyond the place where my mother had stopped?

No, no, no.

I got up from the edge of the water and walked home. It was the prudence-or-courage question again. That day I chose prudence.

In the following weeks, I tried to ignore the monastery experience al-together, but as the days grew darker and the trees barer, it pushed un-bidden into my thoughts. I could not seem to banish my awakening, so I did the next best thing. I trivialized it.

One of the primary forms that resistance takes is trivialization. Surely I was making a big deal out of this, I began to tell myself. So maybe there is a feminine wound in me, in women, in the church, in the earth, but what about all those other major problems I should be concerned about—the environment, crime, war, homelessness? What is a little fem-inine wound by comparison?

Yet the truth is, as long as one woman is dehumanized, none of us can be fully human.

Once during that time I abandoned prudence for courage. While at a party, the subject of women's dedication to the church came up. "But for all our dedication, we've certainly gotten a rotten deal," I said. It is the sort of thing waking women blurt almost without realizing it.

A man rolled his eyes at the ceiling. "Oh no," he said. "You're not one of *those* women, are you?"

"What women?" I asked.

"You know, those screaming feminists who are always yelling about how bad women have been treated."

"No," I told him fast as I could. "I'm not one of those." And I dropped the subject as if it was toxic waste.

He had effectively dismissed my voice and experience. But then it hit me: Wasn't that what I'd been doing to myself—dismissing my own experience, the voice speaking deep inside?

Trivializing our experience is a very old and shrewd way of controlling ourselves. We do it by censoring our expressions of truth or viewing them as inconsequential. We learned the technique from a culture that has practiced it like an art form.

The trick works like this. An image is created of a "screaming feminist" with an ax to grind. The image takes on enormous negative energy in the church and culture. Branding a woman with this image effectively belittles her opinion and discredits it. So rather than risk the image being attached to her, a woman will often back quickly away. I later realized that's what I'd done when the man threatened to attach the label to me. It is a rare and strong woman who has enough inner substance to face the ridicule and pain that can come from expressing feminism.

The church itself has used this negative image as a way of controlling women and discouraging them from challenging the status quo. Once when I suggested to a woman that she stand up for women in a church situation, she said, "I really want to, but I'd hate to look like one of those fanatical feminists our minister preaches about."

Sometimes, though, others' attempts to control and trivialize don't work. Once when I led a discussion at a mixed-gender retreat, a couple of women began to express their pain as women within Christianity. A male clergyman, who I suspect was feeling uncomfortable, said, "Oh, come on, the church is human, it makes mistakes. Why can't you just forgive and be done with it?"

I'm not sure he realized what he'd done—brilliantly trivializing and dismissing their feelings. I mean, who could argue with what he said? Yes, the church is human. Yes, it makes mistakes. Yes, forgiveness is good.

There is a time to be gentle and a time to be fierce, and each of the two women managed to be both at the same time. Each spoke fierce things with a tone of gentleness. One said, "Must you focus on *my* need to forgive and let go? I'm not yet at a place where I can do that. I really need to express what's inside me, and I need the church to listen. Why not go to the heart of it and focus on the church's need to repent and change?"

The other woman said, "Think a moment. If men were at the bottom and women were the ones in charge, if our theology tended to give us the power and excluded you, if it deified the feminine only, would you still be saying, 'The church is only human, why don't you just let it go?' "

She brought to my mind the comment by Nelle Morton, one of the grandmothers of feminist spirituality, who said things are always different when you are looking "from the bottom up." This looking from the bottom up is the catalyst for a reversal of consciousness, not only for ourselves but also for the most resistant among us. For when we stop perceiving, assuming, and theorizing from the top, the dominant view, and instead go to the bottom of the social pyramid and identify with those who are oppressed and disenfranchised, a whole new way of relating opens up. Until we look from the bottom up we have seen nothing.

Maybe that's what happened to the man. Maybe the women's gentleness opened his eyes and their fierceness forced him to perceive from the bottom up, because he was quiet for a while. Then he said, "I think I see what you mean."

As the first spring of my awakening approached and I struggled to see, I grew less and less prudent. I would look at my daughter and think how I didn't want her female life wounded. I didn't want it wounded by the church or my own unconsciousness. Neither did I want my husband or my son to remain unconscious. And how would the cycle be broken, how would patterns be redeemed, if I kept resisting?

And I couldn't help feeling a growing discontent with my female life, flashes of anger and sadness about the "way it is." My attention was being drawn more and more to symptoms that cropped up inside me from time to time. I began to ask myself: Why do I sometimes feel tentative and self-doubtful? Why do I silence my real self? Why do I fall into driven and perfectionistic patterns? Why do I occasionally lapse into passivity, afraid to rock the boat? Why do I work so hard to fulfill outward expectations? Why does it matter that I please everyone? Are these things emanating from the feminine wound? And how can I keep ignoring them?

My dreams were full of earthquakes and floods. Old buildings crumbling and washing away. I was still reluctant to open myself up to the quaking and torrents inside, but the dream voice was telling me that whether I chose to recognize it or not, I was in the midst of upheaval. Something was toppling, and I'd better pay attention.

Dancing Women

In May I attended a Journey into Wholeness Conference on St. Simon Island off the coast of Georgia, a conference that explored the concepts of C. G. Jung. Toward the end of the conference week, around forty or fifty women decided to go to the beach and have something they were calling a full moon celebration. I don't know what possessed me to go along. I suppose curiosity. Maybe some intuition that this was a moment to be seized, a now-or-never moment.

So I found myself following a long line of women winding through the sand dunes, walking by the light of a large moon suspended over the ocean. As the sound of the surf swelled in the distance, I felt the urge to turn back. But we'd all come together in several cars and a couple of vans; there was nothing to do now but get through it.

Someone had brought along a Native American drum, and she began to beat it as we wound through sea oats and darkness. On the beach we gathered driftwood and built a fire, then sat around it. The women began to sing, laugh, tell stories. They talked about their lives as women, their struggles to "bring forth an authentic female life." There was an awful lot of talk about the "Great Mother" (whoever she was) and being connected to the earth and the moon (whatever that meant). I hugged my knees tight and didn't say a word.

As their sense of feminine celebration rose, and since these women were being their instinctual selves and nothing else, a whole lot of them got up and danced. They twirled and swayed along the border of waves.

Treading into the water, they dipped it up with their hands and tossed it toward the sky, letting it fall around them like wedding rice.

Playing and dancing, casting fluid shadows on the beach, they looked half-real to me, like mermaids who'd swum ashore and found their legs. I sat dazed by the whole thing. It was like landing on Venus.

I don't think I'd ever felt so awkward, bewildered, or unsettled in my life, yet I was mesmerized. These women were embodying an experience of their femininity I knew nothing about. They seemed to truly love their womanhood. They didn't appear to doubt their thoughts and feelings as women. Instead they seemed naturally themselves, self-defined, self-connected.

Then almost against my will I flashed back to that day at the monastery six months earlier. Father Sue, I thought. It had never been so clear to me as then how far I had drifted from my feminine instinct, how much I had lost my way as a woman.

I remembered recognizing at the time that I needed to birth a new life, one that had something to do with loving my female self and finding my way back to the deep authenticity of it. I'd tried over the last few months to suppress the memory, but here on the beach with these women the need to suppress it left me completely. I knew I could not ignore this journey. I did not want to.

Someone who'd danced far down the beach found a huge sea turtle shell that had washed ashore, and she came back to share her find. I trekked down with a small group to inspect it. We stared at the hulk of shell while water lapped around our bare ankles. "I feel like the shell is a gift to us," a woman said. "A sign."

Another woman who was a student of ancient mythology told us that the turtle was a feminine symbol of strength and wisdom. "Did you know that in some ancient cultures the turtle shell was considered the base and support of the universe? It was said the whole world axis sat on her back."

Silence fell as we stared at the carapace, ink-gold beneath the moon. One by one the women began to dance again, dipping to brush their hands across the shell as they circled it, as if they were touching the source of feminine support, wisdom, and strength.

It was a ritual of deep beauty that I could only watch from the edge. But when the women finally walked back up the beach, I lagged behind just long enough to brush my hand across the shell.

Acts of Naming

After I returned home from the conference, I had a talk with my friend Betty. We'd met at a women's luncheon five years earlier and had become good friends. That evening I poured out my story to her: the awakening that was trying to unfold in me, the resistance I'd felt, the experience at the monastery, what had happened to me on the beach. I said it *out loud to another woman*. Besides scrawling words in my journal, this was my first real act of naming my experience.

She listened, nodding. Finally she said, "I don't know why we haven't talked about this sooner. My awakening began over a year ago." As we talked we discovered we had something profound in common: a journey to find our female souls.

After that we began to meet regularly to talk about our lives as women. We met all summer and into the fall and on and on. It became a mutual process of self-discovery. We debated ideas in books we were reading, pondered new contexts of spiritual meaning for women. Together, over time, we named our lives as women, named our wounds, named our sacred realities. To say it very simply, we helped each other.

Going to another woman for help can be a breakthrough act, because throughout history women have been programmed to turn to men for help. We might go to other women for solace, for "domestic wisdom," but for solutions and insight, to find out how the world works and how to name reality, many women tend to go to men. To male experts, teachers, fathers, husbands, older brothers, priests, and ministers. Certainly we can find real help there. I have been encouraged and blessed by enlightened men. But it alters something inside a woman when she begins to turn *also* to women, to see women, and therefore herself, as namers of reality.

My experience on the beach and my discussions with Betty gave me the courage to begin to see myself and other women this way.

To name is to define and shape reality. For eons women have accepted male naming as a given, especially in the spiritual realm. The fact is, for a long time now men have been naming the world, God, sacred reality, and even women from their own masculine perspective and experience and then calling it universal experience. As feminist culture critic Elizabeth Dodson Gray points out, this naming tended to benefit men's needs and concerns and in lots of cases to oppress women. Was it such a wild thought that women might start naming God, sacred reality, and their own lives *themselves?*

I wondered how the world might have been different if women had been equally involved in the act of naming. How might sacred experience be different? How might we as women be different? Would there be a feminine wound for us to name and heal?

Naming allows a woman to embrace her own experience, to utter her female truth, perhaps for the first time. Since my waking had been precipitated by an encounter with feminine woundedness (as it frequently is for women), that summer I began the process of naming by acknowledging and expressing the feminine wound in myself.

In an interview, novelist Alice Walker says,

You think you can avoid [pain], but actually you can't. If you do, you just get sicker, or you feel more pain. But if you can speak it, if you can write it, if you can paint it, it is very healing.[24]

I began to paint pictures of my wounded female life. Through the summer I painted images that were painful and even startling to me. As I painted, deeply buried emotions boiled to the surface.

They were emotions that for many years had influenced my behavior in unconscious but profound ways. Unacknowledged feelings about our womanhood operate like the so-called wizard in Oz who sits hidden behind the curtain pulling strings, creating large, unwanted, sometimes frightening effects. Not only do they control our lives in unwanted ways, but unfelt feelings stay in the body "like small ticking time bombs," says Christiane Northrup. "They are illnesses in incubation."[25]

A lot of women have told me, "I don't really know what I'm feeling half the time." Perhaps that's because when uncomfortable feelings come, we push them aside. After a while, we've blocked them so well, for so long, that they no longer get through at all.

Once we begin to acknowledge wounded feelings, though, it's almost a relief. We may feel like Dorothy when her dog, Toto, drew aside the curtain, exposing the man who was scaring everyone with his behind-the-scenes machinations. We can see then what has been controlling a lot of our life. We can see where the self-doubt, the silencing, the drivenness, the need to fulfill collective expectations come from. But most of all, in seeing the wound for what it is, we take charge, just as Dorothy, seeing the Wizard for what he was, mobilized herself to stand up to him.

I found myself painting a woman without feet, a woman without a mouth, a woman without hands.

Why these mutilated women?

In painting my female life without feet, I was uncovering an inability to "stand" firmly on my own feminine ground, to "stand up to others" or "stand up for" myself. Several years after I painted those images, I was visiting the High Museum in Atlanta when I came upon a striking sculpture of a pair of feet. Just feet from the ankles down. They were surrounded by a field of large glass spheres that appeared to be oversized teardrops. The title of the work was *Mother*.

So there are our feet, I thought, in this bed of tears. I felt the artist Kiki Smith had captured the universal severing of women from their female "standpoint."

In painting a woman without a mouth, I was revealing to myself a female life unable to adequately voice the Feminine Self, which is always a woman's truest voice.

The woman without hands spoke to me about a life severed from the power to grasp one's deep life as woman, to hold onto one's inherent power. One day that summer while browsing in a small shop, I happened upon an illustration of the Virgin Mary drawn in detail except for one thing. She had no hands.

As I looked at the print, I realized that over the long course of church history, Mary had been the closest thing Christianity had to an archetype of the Feminine Divine. For many she filled the vacuum in the divine image and came to represent the feminine "side." She was referred to as Queen of Heaven, Lady All Holy, Sovereign Mistress of the World.[26]

Yet at the same time Mary was portrayed as a humble, submissive, untainted virgin, the lowliest of handmaids whose compliant response was, "Let it be done to me according to your word," a response women have mirrored in virtually every relationship in their lives.

In the Baptist tradition we'd prefaced most conversations about Mary by saying, "She was *just a woman*," emphasizing her lesser place. In fact, if the Christmas story hadn't been read once a year in the Baptist churches I'd attended, it would have been easy to forget Jesus had a mother at all.

In the shop that day, I remembered the one and only experience with Mary I'd had as a child. I was spending the night at the home of a Catholic family, and on the mantle in the guest bedroom was a porcelain statue of Mary. Standing upon a sliver of crescent moon, she was a mystery that called up an inexplicable rush of feeling. I experienced what I suppose could be called the magnetic pull to the Feminine

Divine. With a gesture of spontaneous adoration, I reached out and touched her, whispering the only words for her I knew: "Hail, Mary."

Later I questioned my veneration of the feminine figure. I felt as though I'd eaten a forbidden fruit.[27]

As the memory faded, I stared at the handless Mary in the picture. The omission of her hands made me wonder: Was the handless Sue I'd been drawing connected to the handless Mary? Did a wounded and diminished feminine life emerge in part from a wounded and diminished Feminine Divine? Did reclaiming my feminine hands have something to do with reclaiming a feminine divinity? It was a thought wildly new to me. I could do nothing at the time but tuck it quietly away.

I simply went on doing the only things I knew to do at this point in my waking—acknowledge and express my feminine experience as best as I could, mostly through art and journaling. And I went on saying it out loud to Betty, who received it with the tender words, "I know, Sue. All of us down deep know."

FACES OF DAUGHTERHOOD

One morning when summer had nearly burned itself out, I woke to the sound of rain. I went to my study and sat before my sketches and paintings of the wounded female life—the handless, footless, mouthless women. For months I'd been acknowledging my feminine wound, but now I felt a need to let it go or at least symbolize its going in a ritual of foretelling.

When the rain stopped, I burned the drawings one by one on the patio then stared at the heap of cinder left behind. It was this sight—the small lump of cinder and aftermath—that filled me suddenly with a need to understand how the feminine wound had affected my life. What sort of ash and fallout had it deposited? What patterns had it instilled?

I bent down and touched the cooled cinders, letting them move through the sieve of my fingers, aware that the next part of my awakening lay in probing those questions, going even deeper into the act of naming myself. Or was it an unnaming I was about to take up? Sometimes you have to unname something before you can define it for yourself.

The morning after I burned my pictures marked a pivotal moment in my unnaming. As I stood in the garden picking what was left of the tomatoes, an awareness splintered into my thoughts: *I am grown, with children of my own. But inside I am still a daughter.* A daughter is a woman who remains internally dependent, who does not shape her identity and direction as a woman, but tends to accept the identity and direction projected onto her. She tends to become the image of woman that the cultural father idealizes.

My simple self-confession was a deceptively powerful one, for in making it I took my first distinct, albeit tiny, step away from identifying myself as a dependent person. I began to observe myself as daughter instead of merely being one.

After that it became increasingly clear to me that much of the way I lived and related as a woman and many of the female patterns in my life were, in fact, hidden adaptations to the feminine wound. They were the many faces of my daughterhood.

A wound to the psyche often causes the same response as a wound to the body: compensation. For example, if you severely injure an ankle, the connective tissue or fascia in that area will remold around the trauma, trying to compensate for the damage. You may begin to walk a little differently, to favor the other side ever so slightly. If this keeps up, over time your posture will change. Whole new patterns of maintaining your structure will emerge as bones, soft tissues, and tendons realign themselves.

We respond to the feminine wound in a similar way—by making subtle but in the long run profound postural shifts in the psyche. Our psyches begin to realign and remold to compensate for the damage, usually favoring the "other side." For instance, if the feminine "ankle" is crippled, we learn to shift our weight to the "standpoint" of strength. That is, we compensate by identifying with and supporting male dominance. We become good daughters to the cultural father.

One of the more delicate phases in the waking process is accepting how we've been complicit. Simone de Beauvoir pointed out, for instance, that women themselves condition their daughters to serve the system of male primacy. If a daughter challenges it, the mother will generally defend the system rather than her daughter.[28] These mothers, victims themselves, have unwittingly become wounded wounders.

Women need to attack culture's oppression of women, for there truly is a godlike socializing power that induces women to "buy in" or collude, but we also need to confront our own part in accepting male dominance and take responsibility where appropriate. I knew I would have to come to grips with how I'd bought into patriarchy. I would have to look hard at my own daughterhood.

Cultural Blueprints

Early that autumn, my husband and I traveled to New York, where we visited an exhibition of Magritte's paintings. In one painting an ordinary-looking man in a suit was holding a brush and painting an actual woman into existence in his living room. It was as if he were God and she were Eve at the moment of creation. Almost completed, she stood there waiting for the next stroke of creation.

Wait a minute, I thought. Just how *is* Everywoman's life created? How much of my life did I allow to be painted into existence by church, culture, and male attitudes? Down deep, was my life as woman self-conceived and self-created as an original and unfolding work from my own hands, or was it contrived according to hidden blueprints?

Carolyn Heilbrun has written about the "scripts" for womanhood that are handed to women to live out, culturally defined scripts that are written in advance and passed to females from birth.[29] And historian Gerda Lerner writes that men and women live on a stage, acting out their assigned roles. The play can't go on without both of them, she says, *but*

the stage set is conceived, painted and defined by men. Men have written the play, have directed the show, interpreted the meanings of the action. They have assigned themselves the most interesting, the most heroic parts.[30]

By blindly following the script, we tend to become what Ursula K. Le Guin calls "male constructs" or, in Madonna Kolbenschlag's words, "formula females."[31] It is sort of like filling in a paint-by-number canvas, creating ourselves within the outline of stories, wishes, and mindsets projected onto us by a faith and culture that have been shaped and regulated by men. By blindly following the script, we forfeit the power to shape our own lives and identities.

I studied Magritte's painting. It all went back, of course, to Adam and Eve, to the idea of woman being fashioned out of man or out of the male rib. If woman was formed from man, in his image, to be his helper, then her life and roles emerged from him and revolved around him—or so said this mindset.

Sandy moved on to the next painting, but I remained. After a while he came back. "What's so fascinating about this one?" he asked.

"I was just wondering, when it comes to my life, who holds the brush?"

He looked at the picture, then back at me.

I hadn't said much to him about my awakening; I knew how uncomfortable, how resistant he might be. But standing in the middle of the museum, I told him a little of what was happening to me. That I was experiencing an awakening, that this awakening was spiritual, and that it was feminist.

There was a long pause. That may have been the first time I used the word *feminist* out loud in relation to myself. Along the way, I'd decided that I cared passionately about the essence behind the word, that being a feminist was nothing more than aligning myself with the cause of equality and justice and fullness of personhood for women.

"Feminist?" he asked.

I nodded.

"Well, I guess that will be okay," he said, sounding a little like he was talking to a teenager who'd just asked to take the car out for the first time. Sounding, too, like he was trying to convince himself. Then he asked me where I wanted to go for dinner.

I felt like I'd been given some kind of permission I hadn't asked for and then been dismissed. Right then I finally found the words to tell him why I was fed up.

The more I talked, the angrier I got. People were starting to stare, so we left and I got angry in the taxi. I railed about what had been done to women. He got defensive. He railed back. At some point I realized he'd become a target for my anger, an anger I had kept tightly bottled. It wasn't fair to him, and yet I needed him to hear me. I wanted so badly for him to understand, and I couldn't make it happen.

During awakening, volatility often lies just beneath the surface of a woman's relationship with her partner. In our case it was created by hurt and blaming on my part, fear and resistance on his. Men's resistance often grows out of their fear—fear that everything is going to change, that women's gain is their loss, that women will "turn the tables on them." Men need to become aware, but blaming them doesn't help. It only polarizes. Eventually I came to see that what's needed is to invite men into our struggle, to make them part of our quest.

If Sandy and I had been more sensitive to what lay behind the other's reaction, if we'd picked our time wisely and listened, *really* listened to the other, we may have avoided such scenes. But frankly, it may not be possible to completely avoid the clash of feelings that accompanies powerful transitions. Sometimes the exchange may be calm and fruitful, but often it's a wild taxi ride.

Sandy and I made our peace, but it would be a while before I mentioned my journey again.

Flying home from New York, I thought about the painting. I thought about it over and over. In that curious and exotic way that an "unteacher" appears only when the student is ready, the Magritte painting appeared and opened several revelations to me. First, our lives as women are not always as self-created as we might assume. And second, once we are caught in the pattern of creating ourselves from cultural blueprints, it becomes a primary way of receiving validation. We become unknowingly bound up in a need to please the cultural father—the man holding the brush—and live up to his images of what a woman should be and do. We're rewarded when we do; life gets difficult when we don't.

Back home, I read these words by Jungian analyst Sylvia Perera:

What has been valued in the West in women has too often been defined only in relation to the masculine: the good, nurturant mother and wife; the sweet, docile agreeable daughter; the gently supportive or bright achieving partner. This collective model is inadequate for life; we mutilate, depotentiate, silence and enrage ourselves trying to compress our souls into it just as surely as our grandmothers deformed their fully breathing bodies with corsets for the sake of an ideal.[32]

Over the next few months I began to probe the feminine scripts that had been imprinted on my life.

Gracious Lady

During a visit to my childhood home in Georgia, I bumped into a school friend, and we relived the time during our adolescence when we'd gone to charm school. It was taught by a dramatic woman we called Miss Belle. It was her task to teach us the art of the female life. This involved learning how to set a formal dinner table, use crystal salt bowls instead of shakers, sit in a chair with ankles crossed, walk and pivot in high heels—the beauty pageant walk, we called it. We learned to pour tea, we learned the proper way to take off a summer glove, and we learned a lot of things a lady would never say and do. We discovered how to win boys by letting them open the pickle jar, whether it was too hard for us or not, and by asking boys questions we already knew the answers to.

My friend and I recalled these things with a laugh. "I was at a luncheon once where the host actually used those crystal salt bowls," I told her. "I got confused, thought they were sugar bowls, and spooned salt into my iced tea. When I saw what I'd done, you know the first thing that came to my mind? Miss Belle."

"I know," my friend replied. "She's been looking over our shoulders our whole lives."

Later I came upon Gloria Steinem's oft-quoted line, "We are all trained to be female impersonators," and I thought again about those hours in charm school.[33]

Learning to play the Gracious Lady had started way back there with Miss Belle and probably even before her.

In the film *Fried Green Tomatoes,* Evelyn Couch lives out the Gracious Lady, though she's a little too dowdy to pull it off in the manner of crystal salt dishes and beauty pageant walks. Evelyn is a proper and passive woman who is forever accommodating and being sweet, trying to do the right thing and meticulously playing by the rules of culture.

In her perky curls and lace collars, she uses her girlish charm and laughter to glide past life's unpleasantness. She visits her husband's aunt at the nursing home, bringing candy, and her smile hardly wavers when the old woman throws it and her out of the room. At the grocery store, a young man runs into her, almost knocking her over, and *she* apologizes. When a driver usurps a parking space she has been waiting for, she courteously swallows back her anger and continues to circle the lot. When she makes a perfect meal for her husband, setting the table with flowers, she sighs but acquiesces when he takes his plate to the chair before the television.

In one of the film's more hilarious moments, Evelyn attends a women's consciousness-raising group at the insistence of a friend who hopes it will instill some power into Evelyn. The leader gives each woman a mirror and tells them they are going to explore their femaleness, the source of their strength and separateness—their vaginas. Falling back in her chair, shocked and flustered, Evelyn makes a nonoffending exit, offering her girdle as an excuse. (Indeed, wearing a girdle is an interesting metaphor of a woman tightly controlled by conventional expectations.)

It is not until she meets old Mrs. Threadgoode that she begins to question the stereotype she's living. No Gracious Lady herself, Mrs. Threadgoode dyes her hair lavender and tells Evelyn stories about a firebrand girl named Tawanda (actually Mrs. Threadgoode herself), who never put on airs and who broke every social rule that confined her true female self.

Inspired, Evelyn discards the lace collars and the Gracious Lady constraints. We witness her ram a car that has stolen her parking place, shouting, "Tawanda!"

While I don't recommend ramming cars, in lots of ways the energy of Tawanda is the cure for Gracious Ladies, those children of Miss Belle, whose real selves are suffocating inside strictures of properness, charm, sweetness, and social convention.

Church Handmaid

One afternoon during the same visit to my hometown, I drove by my childhood church, speculating on a certain question: What would happen if I brought feminism into my spiritual life?

On impulse, I parked the car beside the church and found a side door open. Maybe I was trying to understand why the question I'd asked turned my hands into warm puddles. Maybe I was trying to recapture an attachment to an old pattern of faith I could feel slipping away. To shore it up. To pat it like a child pats a sand castle at the first hint of tide.

I entered the sanctuary, hoping it would purify my doubts, but all I could seem to remember in there were sermons about the fatherhood of God and the brotherhood of man and especially that devastating sermon about Eve and the chalkboard with the downward-pointing arrows.

I wandered into the educational building, found a child's classroom, and sat in one of those miniature chairs. My knees pushed up toward my chin. I felt like Goldilocks in the chair that was too small.

I thought how I'd started out in a nursery down the hall. My grandfather and father were both Baptist deacons. My mother taught children Sunday school and headed the social committee, making sure there were platters of food for all our fellowships. My grandmother had given devotionals at the Women's Missionary Union. Growing up, I'd attended this church three times a week for services.

I think sometimes a childhood place can lean so heavily on your growing up that later, when you are grown, you find it has become part of your internal geography. This church was such a place. But it came to me suddenly and without question that I must leave the Baptist world. I sat still on the little chair and breathed in and out very slowly, taking this in.

A goldfish bowl sat on a piano across the room. It was empty of fish and water, but I saw almost immediately the metaphor it represented. For so long the Baptist world had been both my goldfish bowl and the water I swam in. I'd come to think of it as the whole realm. I'd grown used to seeing everything through that water. It had never occurred to me that it was possible to leave. At a deep level, I'd not known I could make such a large choice.

It sounds silly, but at the time leaving this realm seemed as daunting to me as leaving the goldfish tank might have seemed to a goldfish. I wondered if I could survive outside the safe perimeters I knew so well. And I was not even thinking at that point about taking my leave from the entire church. I wasn't yet thinking about learning how to breathe in brand new spiritual environs, in a feminine realm where the old breathing mechanisms don't work at all.

Despite the growing disenchantment women experience in the early stages of awakening, the idea of existing beyond the patriarchal institution of faith, of withdrawing our external projection of God onto the church, is almost always unfathomable. It's that old the-world-is-flat conviction, where we believe that if we sail out on the spiritual ocean beyond a certain point we will fall off the edge of the known world into a void. We think there's nothing beyond the edge. No real spirituality, no salvation, no community, no divine substance. We cannot see that the voyage will lead us to whole new continents of depth and meaning. That if we keep going, we might even come full circle, but with a whole new consciousness.

Operating with the world-is-flat mentality, I was only thinking at that moment of going over to the Episcopal Church, which seemed to me to be a much larger fish tank.

I tried to picture myself explaining to my husband, my family, my friends that I was exiting the Baptist Church. It was way too much for the imagination. Not remotely possible. I got up from the too-small chair and left.

The following Sunday, home again, I returned to my own church. The deacons sat together on the front pews. All of them, I noticed, were men. The ministers—three more men—sat in huge chairs up front. I looked from one stained glass window to another. Most of the figures were men.

As the service began, I became acutely aware that every hymn and biblical passage used only masculine pronouns, as if that was all there was. Until then I had accepted that when it said *men* and *brotherhood,* that somehow meant me, too. But now, in a place much deeper than my head, I didn't feel included at all.

I realized that lacking the feminine, the language had communicated to me in subtle ways that women were nonentities, that women counted mostly as they related to men.

Until that moment I'd had no idea just how important language is in forming our lives. What happens to a female when all her life she hears sacred language indirectly, filtered through male terms? What goes on deep inside her when decade after decade she must translate from male experience into female experience and then apply the message to herself? What does the experience imprint inside her? Does it keep exclusive maleness functioning inside her, at least at the level of experience and symbol?

Sitting there, I thought of all the times I'd listened to ministers and Sunday school teachers extol the virtues of women who were subject to men, extensions of men, helpmates to men—women who lived as pale shadows of their true selves.

"Women have not only been educationally deprived throughout historical time in every known society, they have been excluded from theory formation," Lerner writes in *The Creation of Patriarchy.*[34] That is, we've been excluded from creating symbol and myth, from the meaning-making process that explains and interprets reality.

This has been particularly true within the church. There women have reigned in the nurseries and the social halls but have been mostly absent from pulpits and places where theology, policy, and spiritual meaning are forged. Within the church, women have been more apt to polish the brass, arrange the flowers, put cookies on a plate, clean up, keep the nursery, be led, pass the credit, look pretty, and be supportive. In other words, women have frequently functioned more as church handmaids than religious meaning makers or symbol creators.

The Church Handmaid is a woman who tries to be a Good Daughter to the Church, trying to be everything it wants and expects her to be. Throughout my life I'd done this without question.

Now, sitting in church, I was full of questions. Why was God always the God of Abraham, never the God of Sarah? Why was it often impossible, rare, or difficult for a woman to hold real power in the church? Women had been the largest consumers of church, yet we'd held a vastly disproportionate amount of power compared to our numbers and commitment there. Why had my father always chaired the finance committee and my mother the social committee, even though my mother could manage household budgets and figures with the acumen of an accountant?

The congregation stood to sing. Unbelievably, as if all the irony in the world were crashing down at once, the hymn was "Faith of Our Fathers." I tried to sing, but I could not open my mouth. It was as if something had given way in my chest. I lowered the hymnbook and sat back down. I was fighting tears.

Sandy bent down and nudged me. "Are you okay?" he whispered. I nodded, but inside I felt too heavy to move. Until that moment I hadn't fully understood. *I was in a religion that celebrated fatherhood and sonship. I was in an institution created by men and for men.*

By the time I got home I felt disbelief that I'd not seen all this before—that the church, my church, was not just a part of the male-dominant system I was waking up to, but a prime legitimizer of it.

I was too dazed to be angry. Mostly I felt disillusioned, sad, betrayed. I stood in front of the closet in the bedroom hanging up my dress, thinking, But women have been so loyal to the church, so supportive. How could it negate and exclude us this way? How had this happened?

That afternoon I opened a book I'd recently brought home, Simone de Beauvoir's *The Second Sex*. I read all afternoon. I read how religion had given authority to men. As de Beauvoir put it, religion had given men a God like themselves—a God exclusively male in imagery, which legitimized and sealed their power. How fortunate for men, she said, that their sovereign authority has been vested in them by the Supreme Being.

That night I couldn't sleep. I slipped out of bed and went to my study. I stood by the window, looking out at the night. The tears I'd suppressed that morning in church finally rolled down my face.

The Secondary Partner

I woke one morning and looked over at Sandy, still asleep on the pillow beside me. We had been married for nineteen years.

I thought about those years when I was a young wife starting my family, how the newly launched women's movement blew by me with hardly a rustle. Instead of meeting with a consciousness-raising group, I attended marriage and family programs at church. There I learned worthwhile things like communication skills, but I also learned a model of relating that unwittingly promoted women's psychological dependence on men and male authority. Women's personal journeys, goals, and quests were encouraged only to the extent that they didn't interfere with those of husband or children. A woman's surrender of herself on behalf of the rest of the family was (and often still is) extolled as the highest virtue.

In the world where I'd grown up, marriage for women had meant revolving around men like planets around the sun. As everyone knows, planets don't question their orbits; they just revolve. An enormous gravitational pull holds a woman in this orbit; it comes from finding approval and a sense of identity in her orbit, since finding these things within her feminine self is difficult in a culture where attitudes and conditioning are ranged against her.

I leaned up on my elbow and studied the tilt of Sandy's nose. In some way we did operate as if the husband's life was the sun while the wife's was the revolving planet. I began to wonder how a woman defies gravity and changes heavenly courses. What would happen if I actually brought feminism into my marriage?

Not that Sandy was a dogmatically rigid or authoritarian person. He'd never demanded that I should "submit" to him. On the contrary, he was kind and fun and loving and shared decision making with me. His resistance to my journey (which he didn't verbalize so much as I intuited) came from his own fears about how that would change our relationship. I wasn't sure, but I did know one thing—introducing feminism into the orbits of our life would make me about as popular with my husband as Galileo and Copernicus had been with the Catholic Church. Bringing feminism into my marriage would turn our little universe on its head.

Gazing at him, I realized that the model of the revolving wife was an old model of marriage we'd both inherited—one in which the wife holds a key, though secondary, position. It was the model of the Secondary Partner.

In the model of the Secondary Partner, the woman may run things at home and have her career, her pursuits, and her quests, but there is a gradation of power in the relationship. As Jungian analyst June Singer points out, when a girl is growing up, it is *not taken for granted,* as it is with boys, that her life and needs will be primary, that she will have access to places of authority and power like her brothers or father. What *is* taken for granted is that she will find her main source of fulfillment through her husband and family, that she will be secondary to them.[35]

A man assumes certain entitlements simply because he's male. For instance, Sandy was entitled to go and come in the world as he pleased. If he had a business trip, he simply went, no questions asked. And lots of times I packed the bag. But if I should have a writer's conference or a speaking engagement, it was a big deal, something that needed to be discussed. How long would I be gone? Could he manage the children without me? What about meals? How many times a day is the dog fed?

At times like those I felt a nebulous guilt for pursuing my own life.

When a woman lives out the Secondary Partner, she tends to believe, not so much consciously but deep inside, that she is there to be of service to her partner. She might become his inspiration, investing herself in his creativity and work rather than her own. She may become the "woman behind the man," the hostess who initiates dinner parties for his associates, the one who makes sure his clients get Christmas cards. In the extreme she may become completely deferential and adaptable where he's concerned, shaping herself to his opinions, beliefs, and wishes or, as a friend of mine says, "being wax to his flame."

While I didn't go quite that far, I realized that I did often look to Sandy for identity, approval, and validation. I depended on this the way he depended on my being in the self-sacrificing role.

Another film comes to mind, this one portraying a forty-two-year-old London housewife who is living the Secondary Partner to such a degree it has taken on the overtones of parody. *Shirley Valentine* opens with the soundtrack singing, "I'd like the chance to be the girl who used to be me." The recurring question in the film is: What happened to Shirley Valentine? Shirley Valentine was her maiden name, the name she had when she lived from her own center, when she was daring and stuffed full of passion for life. Her quest is to recover her essential self, her Shirley Valentine self.

With her children grown and her marriage settled into deep, deadening ruts, her existence is like modeling clay, stretching and molding itself to her husband's life. He wants chips and eggs on Monday, steak on Thursday. He wants his wife always nearby to meet his needs but not too intrusive; she should be just there, available and useful like an umbrella in its stand.

When Shirley gets a chance to go to Greece with a friend, she seizes the trip as part of her quest, though her husband forbids her to leave. One night sitting beside the Greek shore, Shirley thinks to herself, "I've allowed myself to lead this little life when inside me there is so much more. . . . That's where Shirley Valentine disappeared to. She got lost in all this unused life."

She meets Costas, a fun-loving Greek restaurant owner who takes her out on a boat. She tells him that when she was a girl—when she was Shirley Valentine—she used to be daring. She used to jump off the roof. Encouraged by Costas, she begins to recover this lost self as the two of them jump off the boat into water that, he tells her, is as deep as forever.

When the vacation is over, Shirley stays on, working in Costas's restaurant, waking up with the sea outside her window, soaking up life in the tiny, sun-drenched village, learning to laugh and dare again, and gradually reclaiming herself. She blossoms, ignoring all her husband's angry orders to come home.

My favorite scene is when her husband arrives in Greece in order to try to reconcile their lives. She waits for him at a table by the sea, watching him trudge up the hill. He passes her, then turns back. "I didn't recognize you," he said.

"I know," she tells him. "I used to be the mother. I used to be the wife. But now I'm Shirley Valentine."

That morning as I lay in bed watching my husband sleep, I yearned to transform the model of our marriage, to find my unused life, which is the work a Secondary Partner will need to do. I needed to find the woman I'd left behind and to challenge the conventional orbits of my relationship. But if I did all that, what would happen to my marriage? Could it sustain that sort of transformation? I had my qualms about it.

The Many-Breasted Mother

Another blueprint given to women, the Many-Breasted Mother, is one of the more revered. The image came to me as I watched a peculiar sight on the television news, an overwhelmed mother dog nursing a small litter of newborn kittens along with her own brood of pups. The kittens had been brought to her when their mother died. The mother dog lay sprawled on her side overrun with mouths, some that naturally belonged to her and some that didn't. "Poor thing, all she seems to do all day long is nurse something," said the owner.

Women have been encouraged to embrace the all-nurturing (many-breasted) role of womanhood as the jewel in the female crown. And while mothering can be a deeply beautiful role, it can also become distorted by self-negation. The Many-Breasted Mother ends up caring for an array of children, including projects, needs, groups, and persons, that may not even belong at her breast.

I remembered a verse I'd scrawled once when my children were small and I was feeling engulfed by the role of mother:

Priestess of dutiful sacrament,
You knead your soul into bread.
You serve it on a silver tray,
Bright morsels for your family to eat.
Aren't you hungry too?

Even as my children grew and became teens, many times my role as nurturer allowed the very essence of my life to be overrun and eaten away. Sadly, I know women who keep doing this even after their children have grown and left home.

When my Many-Breasted Mother really kicked in, I even found myself taking care of my husband. I would be sure he ate well, encourage him to exercise, make sure he had a shirt ironed for his meeting, table my issues to soothe his bad mood.

Women have been trained to be deeply relational creatures with "permeable boundaries," which make us vulnerable to the needs of others.[36]

This permeability, this compelling need to connect, is one of our greatest gifts, but without balance it can mean living out the role of the servant who nurtures at the cost of herself.

Referring to this feminine script in her essay "Professions for Women," Virginia Woolf describes the syndrome and offers a drastic remedy:

She was intensely sympathetic. She was immensely charming. She was utterly unselfish. She excelled in the difficult arts of family life. She sacrificed herself daily. If there was chicken, she took the leg; if there was a draft she sat in it—in short she was so constituted that she never had a mind or wish of her own, but preferred to sympathize always with the minds and wishes of others. . . . I did my best to kill her. My excuse, if I were to be had up in a court of law, would be that I acted in self-defense. Had I not killed her, she would have killed me.[37]

At the very least we need to disempower this part of ourselves, to relieve ourselves of the internal drive to forfeit our souls as food for others.

The Favored Daughter

One of the more uncomfortable discoveries I made about myself during this time was a need to prove myself to the father-world—my own father, the cultural father, the church father. The powerful male presence. I began to recognize how important it was to me that he be aware of my accomplishments. The need surfaced from a deep place in my feminine wound.

I'd grown up the firstborn in a field of bright, athletic brothers, unconsciously trying to convince everyone that being a girl was every bit as worthy. Certainly no one ever said to me that girlhood was less valuable. I simply picked it up by virtue of being female on the planet. And I set out to prove it wrong. I tried through a blaze of achievement: A's on the report card, school honors, swimming trophies, cheerleading trophies, church awards. I did it through compliance. I did it by being everything I imagined a good girl should be.

It had been a core pattern of my life, this attempt to be a Favored Daughter.

Favored Daughters are women who, carrying the wound of feminine inferiority, try to make up for it by seeking the blessing of the cultural father. Through accomplishments and perfectionism we hope to atone for the "original sin" of being born female. We are hoping that Father God will finally see our worth.

Even as an adult woman, I'd set up perfectionist standards, which kept me striving. I pursued a thin body, happy children, an impressive speech, and a perfectly written article with determination to succeed, but also with an internal voice that led me to feel whatever I did wasn't quite enough. I worried about not measuring up.

Herein lies the torment of it: Favored Daughters strive for their worth, piling up external validations, but inside they are most often plagued by self-doubt, wondering if their work or their efforts are good enough.

I met a Favored Daughter at a conference in Atlanta. A successful businesswoman, she told me her story one afternoon over coffee. "All my life I've been internally driven to succeed at things," she said, "even things that don't matter all that much. I had to be a star at everything. When I finally asked myself why, what came to me was the time my father took me to a Braves baseball game.

"I got the chance only because my brother was sick that day. I was a daydreamy girl who didn't care much for baseball, but I tried to like it to make my father happy. He loved the game almost irrationally. And he loved my brother the same way, I think, because he was a boy. My father loved me, too, but he didn't value me the way he did my brother. I always had the feeling that if I'd been a boy, he would have loved me in that same irrational way."

Suddenly her eyes grew teary. She said, "That day at the ballpark I was looking up at the sky counting the clouds, which was this thing I did. And here comes a foul ball flying into the stands, landing right at my feet.

"I was so lost in the clouds I didn't hear my father shouting at me to pick up the ball. By the time I realized what was happening, someone else had grabbed it. What I remember most is my father's reaction. He said, 'Geez, you girls. You think your brother would have lost the ball like that?'

"I've spent my whole life since trying hard not to drop the ball, trying to make it up to my father for being nothing but a girl, hoping I could finally get him to prize me like he did my brother. The crazy thing is, I have this nineteen-page résumé, but still there's a voice inside telling me I'm going to mess up."

I didn't know what to say to her except that I understood, that undoubtedly we were looking for validation in the wrong place. That we needed to quit trying and go recover the primacy of our feminine souls. Then maybe our sense of worth and confidence as women in the world would flow to us fully and naturally.

I've met so many of these women, heard so many stories like this. They are all different, and yet they are all the same. In every one the woman is sitting in the bleacher (or the pew, the school desk, wherever) just being her girl-self when the moment of truth descends kerplunk! at her feet—that in this family, this church, this culture, female is the less-prized gender. She starts to feel that her gender has somehow "dropped the ball." And without even being aware of what she's doing, she may try to make up for it by going through life trying to win love, validation, and esteem from the father-world.

The Silent Woman

Throughout all this unnaming I was doing, I kept thinking back to the sketches I'd drawn of the mouthless woman. I knew they were attempts to capture the pattern of the Silent Woman in myself.

I began to reflect on the ways I'd withheld my opinions, muzzled disconcerting truths, refrained from expressing my true feelings, squelched my riskier ideas, or thwarted my creativity. When I did that, I was living out the script of the Silent Woman. Being a Silent Woman is not about being quiet and reticent, it's about stifling our truth. Our *real* truth.

I wondered, Had silence encroached as I internalized the message of inferiority? Had I learned that silence was a safe place?

Some of the scripting concerning silence has come from the church, from Bible verses like this one: "Let a woman learn in silence, with all submissiveness" (1 Timothy 2:11, RSV). We may not claim this verse as a guiding principle, but it's there inside us nonetheless.

Overall, women's voices have not been encouraged unless they spoke as mouthpieces for the party line. Quiet ladies who held their tongues were loved and lauded. Uppity, pioneering women who spoke their minds and said bold things were attacked and sanctioned. "And that plays into our greatest fear, which is going against convention and having love and approval taken away," says writer Erica Jong.[38]

Very often silence becomes the female drug of choice.

I grew aware that while I spoke a lot, much of the time my deepest words, my outrage, the voice of my feminine soul, were silent. For the first time I began to feel the confinement of my creative voice. There were things I wanted to say, needed to say, yet they didn't lie within the boundaries of "Christian writing." In Gail Godwin's novel, *A Southern Family,* one of her characters, a writer, wonders if she writes "to satisfy the tastes of the culture that shaped me."[39] Now I wondered, Had I? Where had I hedged, pulled back, or diluted my truth?

As I reflected on these questions, I stumbled by chance upon the Greek myth of Philomela. It is the story behind the Silent Woman, and it goes like this: While traveling to see her sister, Philomela was raped by her brother-in-law, Tereus. Outraged, she threatened to tell her sister and the world what he'd done to her. He responded by cutting out her tongue and banishing her to a guarded tower where she was forced to live in silence.

Eventually, though, she seemed to know that if she continued to be silent she would die. So Philomela began to weave a series of tapestries that became her voice and told her story. She then enlisted an old woman to take them to her sister, who came and liberated her.

The myth is about the loss of women's voices. It suggests that the source of female silence is the rape of the feminine—the devaluation and violation of femaleness. It suggests that when women protest this violation, their voices are frequently squelched through ridicule, sanction, and fear of reprisal. In the public arena, at church, work, and home, women's tongues are often silenced when we dare to speak our anger, truths, and visions.

In 1993 the Councils of Churches in the Twin Cities and Minnesota sponsored a Re-imagining Conference. I didn't attend but I read about the multiplicity of women's voices that were raised there expressing women's truths, imagining bold feminine images of God, and presenting new challenges to the church. I also read dozens of editorials and letters to denominational papers by church traditionalists who reacted to these voices by castigating, repudiating, and calling for denunciation, full-scale church inquiries, and resignations.

Poet Muriel Rukeyser writes, "What would happen if one woman told the truth about her life? / The world would split open."[40]

Today the world is starting to split open with women's truths. The fear of voicing ourselves still runs deep, but women are still weaving their truths into a tapestry of stories and sending them out into the world.

In the end, speaking out would become the cure for my feminine silence. It would not necessarily banish my fear and reluctance, but I would learn to voice my soul in spite of it. To speak as if my life depended on it.

FORMING A FEMINIST CRITIQUE

By now more than a year had passed since my dream of giving birth to myself. I went about my routine—writing, being mother to my teenaged children, seeing friends, jogging, reading a lot, painting a little, serving on an occasional committee, going methodically to church, and, through it all, keeping my awakening mostly secret.

Part of it was because I was afraid of the response I might get. But secluding my experience during that early period was both cowardly *and* wise. Some things are too fragile, too vulnerable to bring into the public eye. Tender things with tiny roots tend to wither in the glare of public scrutiny. By holding my awakening within, I contained the energy of it, and it fed me the way blood feeds muscle. It fed me a certain propelling energy, and I kept moving forward.

I had finally told myself the truth about the presence of the feminine wound and the way I'd adapted to it. Now I began to tell myself the truth about how this wound came to be inflicted. I began to form what I called my feminist critique.

Forming a critique is essential to the birth and development of a spiritual feminist consciousness. Until a woman is willing to set aside her unquestioned loyalty and look critically at the tradition and convention of her faith, her awakening will never fully emerge. The extent of her healing, autonomy, and power is related to the depth of the critique she is able to integrate into her life.

As I formed my critique, I came face to face with a system of social governance, a vast complex of patterns and attitudes within culture, religion, and family. The name of the system is patriarchy. It's important to emphasize that patriarchy is neither men nor the masculine principle; it is rather a *system* in which that principle has become distorted.

The word *patriarchy* comes from the Greek word *pater*, which means father, and *archein*, which means rule. It has come to mean a way of social organization marked by the authority or supremacy of men and fathers. Western civilization has been organized this way since its prehistory, though patriarchy is now showing signs of real demise.

Learning to see patriarchy, not as I was conditioned to see it, but as it actually is—a wounder of women and feminine life—was not easy. One reason is that since patriarchy is so pervasive and familiar, it becomes invisible.

Psychotherapist Anne Wilson Schaef compares living in patriarchy to living in polluted air. "When you are in the middle of pollution, you are usually unaware of it. You eat in it, sleep in it, work in it, and sooner or later start believing that is just the way the air is," she writes.[41]

In a similar way we've accepted the widespread attitudes and effects of patriarchy as givens. They are so much a part of the world, we start to think that's just the way reality is.

In the play *The Search for Signs of Intelligent Life in the Universe,* a deceptively wise bag lady named Trudy mutters, "What is reality anyway? Nothin' but a collective hunch."[42]

Far from being the sole reality, patriarchy is actually nothing but a collective hunch. For women, making this fine distinction—that it is only one way of viewing reality and not reality itself—is crucial in helping us see patriarchy clearly.

The Hierarchy

As I began to observe the patriarchal world around me with more clarity, one of the first things I noticed was a principle that seemed to lie at the very heart of it: Life is a hierarchy with men and so-called masculine values at the top.

The hierarchy goes like this: at the top God, then men, then women, children, animals, plants, and minerals. (Of course there are also hierarchies within hierarchies as we consider issues of race, culture, and economic status.) Embedded in the human psyche, this hierarchal view has been passed on as the natural and "divinely created" order of life.

Once I perceived the truth of this, I began to see how subtly (and not so subtly) hierarchies were ingrained in church, family, marriage, workplaces, politics, and all kinds of systems of thought.

With men at the top (or at least with a sense of entitlement about being at top) and women below (or at least with a sense of belonging below), a way of relating was put into place based on dominance and dependence. The role of the one above was to dominate and oversee the ones below. The role of the one below was to answer to and depend on the one above. In addition, the one above learned how to protect his prestigious place at the top. He learned to stay up by keeping her down, that is, by insisting she be content with things as they are.

Theologian Anne E. Carr relates that this hierarchy issues forth in a whole series of "unequal power relations; God as father rules over the world, holy fathers rule over the church, clergy fathers over laity, males over females, husbands over wives and children, men over the created world."[43] The pattern even extends to our relationship to nature and how countries seek dominance over each other.

I was intrigued with an exercise Anne Wilson Schaef performed with mixed-gender groups.[44] She asked them to list on one half of a sheet of paper the characteristics of God and on the other half the characteristics of humans. Invariably the list for God was: omnipotent (all-powerful), omniscient (all-knowing), omnipresent, and eternal. The list for humans typically read: childlike, sinful, weak, stupid, and mortal.

At this point the exercise got more interesting. On a different sheet of paper she asked the group to list characteristics of males on one half and females on the other. The consensus list for male was: intelligent, powerful, brave, good, strong. The list for female fell into this general pattern: emotional, weak, fearful, sinful, dependent.

When Wilson Schaef asked the group to set all four lists side by side, they were surprised but had to conclude that according to their perceptions, male is to female as God is to humans.

The Great Imbalance

One of the more destructive consequences this hierarchy sets in motion is a pattern of imbalanced valuing, in which the masculine is valued over the feminine.

That autumn as I looked at the world with new eyes, asked new questions, and thought new thoughts, I was also reading new books. While reading feminist culture critic Elizabeth Dodson Gray's work, I was struck by her definition of patriarchy as "a culture that is slanted so that men are valued a lot and women are valued less; or in which men's prestige is up and women's prestige is down."[45] She followed her definition with a story about Margaret Mead. When Mead journeyed from tribe to tribe on her anthropological studies, she stumbled upon a discovery: It did not matter what work was done in a particular tribe but rather who did it. If weaving was done in one tribe by men, it was considered a high-prestige occupation. Twenty miles away, if weaving was done in a different tribe by women, it had low prestige.

The anecdote reminded me of a story a woman told about the time she tried to introduce a novel idea to a church committee where she was the only female member. She insisted the idea would save the church money. "It's unreasonable," she was told. "You just don't understand the way the real world works."

After she rotated off the committee, a new male member came on and presented the identical idea. It was resoundingly adopted. One wonders if perhaps it was not what was said but who said it.

HEAD OVER HEART I also began to notice that the imbalance of valuing was not confined to actual men and women. People also placed a greater value on men's experience or things associated with the masculine than on women's experience or things associated with the feminine.

A large amount of women's experience has been concentrated in nurturing roles, in matters of relationship. As we evolved these skills, we even came to carry or reflect relational, nurturing values for the culture at large. Likewise, men's traditional focus of experience in the public arena has conditioned them toward the values prized in that sphere—autonomy, reason, individuality, and competitiveness.

That women are connected with matters of "heart" and men with matters of "head" are distinctions entrenched in our culture, psyches, myths, and symbols. In fact, psychologists Jean Baker Miller, Carol Gilligan, and others have documented that certain differences do exist in the way men and women relate, know, and make moral choices. Gilligan found, for instance, that girls tend to relate from a web model, preferring interconnections and the centrality of relationships. Boys tend to relate from a hierarchal model that prefers autonomy, individualism, and competition.[46]

Some of these differences may be due to biology,[47] but much of it has come through historical conditioning. My personal belief is that while differences exist, women and men both have an innate and equal ability to engage in the full range of human experiences. (Men can nurture and women can quest for autonomy.) Neither men nor women should be limited to a narrow category of what's considered feminine if you're female or masculine if you're male. I also believe that men and women contain both "masculine" and "feminine" qualities and that the goal is to *balance, blend, and honor both* within the individual and the culture.

The point, however, is that women have been socialized toward certain choices and experiences, and these experiences need to be *valued in a way that is not inferior* to men's experiences. Indeed, as I made my critique, the problem seemed to me not that there are differences but rather how we value these differences.

It seemed clear that patriarchy has valued rationality, independence, competitiveness, efficiency, stoicism, mechanical forms, and militarism— things traditionally associated with the "masculine." Less valued are beingness, feeling, art, listening, intuition, nurturing, and attachment— things traditionally associated with the "feminine."

As a patriarchal institution, Christianity has tended to value "masculine" attributes more than those connected with the "feminine." Author Margaret Starbird put it succinctly: "Institutional Christianity, which has nurtured Western civilization for nearly two thousand years, may have been built over a gigantic flaw in doctrine—a theological 'San Andreas Fault': the denial of the feminine."[48]

Often competitiveness, logic, objectivity, and matters of the head have found preeminence over concerns with inclusiveness, relatedness, or matters of the heart. I recognized the imbalance in the way dogma, theological rightness, triumph of the "Christian way," oratorical sermons, church business, nationalism, individual pursuit, conversion figures, and breaking scripture down into its various hermeneutics have frequently been valued over feelings, tears, peace, gentleness, group consciousness, and gathering humanity together as a family.

I tried to picture a culture where the valuing was equal. In my wilder moments I imagined a society that paid child care workers, teachers, homeless advocates, poets, and bird-watchers as much as it paid professional football players, generals, and corporate CEOs. I tried to imagine a church where it mattered less what your beliefs and practices were and more how relationships were nurtured and healed. I tried to imagine a church that did not support its country's wars as a matter of patriotic course and instead stood against the devastation and suffering they caused in people's lives.

One day I spotted an elderly, white-haired woman wearing a T-shirt that read, "What if the military had to have bake sales to raise money and the PTA got the Pentagon budget?" I walked over and told her how wonderful it was, her wearing a shirt like that. She laughed and said, "Some people have called me subversive for wearing it. But I don't care. One day we may owe our survival to subversive women."

I decided maybe it was a good thing to be subversive when it comes to the heart.

One night as Ann and I watched a video of *The Wizard of Oz,* I realized that the Tin Man character, at least in the early part of the movie, seemed an apt symbol of patriarchal consciousness. He is a frozen figure, standing with his ax, his blade of power, in the air.

The story tells us he's lost his heart. He's lost the "juices" of life. Even his tears are frozen on his face. His ability to feel and relate at a deep empathetic level is gone.

Have you ever wondered how the Tin Man got into such a deplorable, frozen state? The book says the Tin Man was a woodsman whose ax became cursed, causing him to cut away his own body, piece by piece, including his heart, until he was no longer covered in warm flesh but encased in an armor of tin.

Through our lopsided valuing, we have come to labor under a "cursed ax," under a patriarchal system that has cut away the body, including the heart, replacing it with technological tin. And like the Tin Man we find ourselves trapped in our own heartlessness.

SPIRIT OVER NATURE   I also began to recognize another imbalance in the values that women and men carry for society. For thousands of years the "feminine" has been deeply associated with the body, flesh, sensuality, earth, and nature, while the "masculine" has been associated with spirit, heaven, and transcendence over nature. Actually men are no more connected to spirit than women, and women no more connected to nature than men. The perception may have arisen from women's closeness to fertility, procreation, and the rhythms of nature. Women are tied to these cycles in a way men are not. Women go through the monthly cycle of menstruation, just as the moon goes through a monthly cycle of waxing and waning. Through pregnancy, childbirth, and nursing we grow life inside our bodies, deliver life through our bodies, and feed life from our bodies. It has also been left to women to care for other bodies, tending the young, sick, and dying.

For these reasons, perhaps, women have represented flesh and embodied the earthly, and in doing so we've come to be identified with nature. Conversely, nature is thought of as feminine. We speak of Mother Earth and virgin forests. The connection is even entwined in the roots of our language. The word *mother* comes from the Latin word *mater,* which means matter. Mother and matter are both the stuff out of which everything is composed.

As I contemplated this profound connection, once again it became apparent to me which of the two polarities—nature/earth or spirit/heaven—was more valued. Both women and earth have been abused, raped, and disregarded.

The man's comment about my daughter in the drugstore—"That's how I like to see a woman, on her knees"—is not fundamentally different from a comment I've heard attributed to Francis Bacon, one of the fathers of the age of reason. Purportedly he said that the earth was a harlot and must be controlled. In other words, "That's how I like to see Mother Earth, on her knees."

In its flight from and fear of the "feminine," the church has failed to waken to its "ecological self"—a term author Joanna Macy uses to describe one who has conquered the personal ego and knows that she or he is not separate from anything else.

An awakened ecological self is someone like John Seed, director of the Rainforest Information Center, who says, "I try to remember that it's not me, John Seed, trying to protect the rainforest. Rather I am part of the rainforest protecting myself."[49]

This awakened self has been largely absent from the Christian tradition. In Christianity there is a deeply embedded separation between spirit and nature, a split apparent in this verse from Galatians 5:17: "The desires of the flesh are against the Spirit, and the desires of the Spirit are against the flesh; for these are opposed to each other . . ." (RSV).

Patriarchy has viewed the earth as a fallen creation and matter as inherently evil, and Christians have used and misused scriptures to drive the wedge deeper into the human psyche. "Do not love the world or the things in the world. If any one loves the world, love for the Father is not in him. For all that is in the world . . . is not of the Father but is of the world" (1 John 2:15, RSV).

Consequently, in Christianity nature is not a primary revelation of the divine. Rivers, trees, and stones are not perceived as alive and permeated with spirit but rather as dead matter. The earth, then, becomes something to be conquered, subdued, observed, and studied. It becomes a big science project.

Because of all this, we began to think of ourselves as separate from and innately superior to the rest of the planet. We lost the ability to identify with it at deep empathetic levels.

In Christianity this is even further undermined by a sacred intent to transcend the material earth and the flesh of our bodies, as is suggested in a verse from James 1:27: "Religion that is pure and undefiled before God and the Father is this: . . . to keep oneself unstained from the world" (RSV).

Often the earth seems to function like a mere way station where we can grapple with our redemption before going "up there" to the realm of the Father, who is viewed as totally other than the earth and high above it.

Christianity's unfortunate denial of matter (mother) also includes centuries of denial and hatred for the body with its cravings, instincts, and sexuality. In my early twenties, while at college in Texas, I went to church one Sunday and sat in the back row beside a woman who was holding a newborn baby in a pink bonnet. Halfway through the sermon, the baby got hungry. Babies do that. So the woman discreetly unbuttoned her dress and nursed the child beneath the bill of the pink bonnet. An usher noticed this, came over, and asked the woman to please leave. He was the picture of quiet indignance. He told her she could find a restroom down the hall. I can still remember the shame that spread over her face and the outraged scream the baby girl let out when the mother pulled her breast away.

Women with their incessant menstruation, conception, pregnancy, childbirth, and lactation have been too visceral for patriarchal religion. In the Bible, women involved in these womanly conditions were considered unclean and were separated from men. They had to go through purifications before being allowed near men or things religious. And since birth and menses were considered dirty, women were in constant need of being spiritualized and sanitized.

According to the attitude that sprang up, women could not be both holy *and* sexual. And as celibacy became a spiritual ideal in Christianity, men were more and more cast as spiritual and women as sexual. Woman's role was seen as the temptress, the *femme fatale,* who lured "good" men into the evils of flesh.

Theologian Rosemary Radford Ruether sums it up when she says that Christianity became "a body-fleeing, world-negating spirituality" that "projects upon the female all its abhorrence, hostility and fear of the bodily powers from which it has arisen and from which it wishes to be independent."[50]

Despair and Compassion

One day I was driving through town, my head full of the ideas and awarenesses I'd been gathering, when I saw a woman sitting on the steps of a business, her head in her hands. She wore a navy dress and brown coat, and she was crying. As I drove past her I, too, started to cry.

At first it made no sense that I was crying. I didn't know this woman. Then I realized I was not crying for her or for myself. I was crying for *women.* I was crying for the vast imbalance, the heart that had been lost, the rejection of the earth and body, the oppression and diminishment of things considered feminine. It was a suffering with, a despair I felt on behalf of something much larger than myself.

I don't know what it was about the woman that triggered my despair, but for weeks after that I went through a period of grief. This is the grief that comes when you leave the city limits of your own wound and step into the vastness of the *whole* feminine wound, which is ultimately a human wound.

Forming an honest feminist critique of our own faith tradition is not an easy thing to do. Betrayal of any kind is hard, but betrayal by one's religion is excruciating. It makes you want to rage and weep. It deposits a powerful energy inside.

Eventually that energy will flow out as either hostility or love. The energy must and will find a form, a shape, in our lives. It is now, as we wade into the secret distress of the feminine and encounter the largeness of the wound, that we need to be very conscious and keep the despair we might feel from becoming channeled into bitterness. We have to work very hard to keep it flowing toward compassion.

The Tamper-Proof Bottle

During those months when I was forming my feminist critique, I watched a friend struggle to open a tamper-proof bottle of medication. She gripped, pushed down, squeezed, and turned it many times without results. "You try," she said.

So I gripped, pushed, squeezed, turned, grunted. But I couldn't budge it either. "What's wrong with this thing?" I said.

"It's doing its job," she replied. "Only it's doing it a little too well."

Later I couldn't help but compare that bottle to Christianity's rigid tradition concerning women.

The words *tamper-proof* and *tradition* have similar intents.

Tradition comes from the Latin *traditio,* which means a delivery. The Christian tradition is a *delivery* of opinions, dogmas, rites, practices, and customs from one generation to the next. That delivery is its job. The essential intent within tradition is its need to perpetuate itself, to keep delivering, to remain untampered with. I thought to myself, When it comes to tradition, the church is certainly doing its job, but perhaps it's doing it a little too well.

Viewing tradition in this way, we can easily see why restricting women to narrowly defined and subordinate places reproduces itself, why change comes slowly or not at all or on the margins and not at the core.

Years earlier I'd taken a seminary course on church history, but nothing had been mentioned about its patriarchal underpinnings. Now I wanted to explore the tamper-proof traditions concerning women. Why hadn't the church accepted women as equal participants? How had all of this come to be?

Searching for answers, I turned to theologians Elisabeth Schüssler Fiorenza, Phyllis Trible, Elaine Pagels, Rosemary Radford Ruether, Mary Daly, and other women who were voicing truths that had once been unsayable. In the evenings I sometimes read a paragraph to my husband, just to test his response.

"Dr. Schüssler Fiorenza at Harvard says the intention of Jesus was feminist," I said to Sandy one evening.

"Mine, too," he said. He's a smart man, my husband.

I believe Sandy's intention *was* that, derived from a concept he held in his mind of equality and justice. But like me, like so many of us, he lived with an unconscious gap between concept and practice. Most "feminism" doesn't filter down into ways of relating, the way faith is practiced or votes are cast. I've seen churches give honest lip service to women's equality as a concept, while life and worship there go on in the same old patriarchal ways.

But Sandy was embracing the ideal, and I was glad at least for that.

After that night I began to mention other ideas from books I was reading. Sandy listened, nodded. When I began to weave in more personal fragments about the awakening I was experiencing, he listened then, too. But he didn't nod so much anymore.

One rain-soaked weekend when the children were off with friends and Sandy was away for a conference, I read practically nonstop, making a breathtaking discovery. I found that within early Christian history there had been two traditions regarding women. The first we could call the revolutionary tradition, which included Jesus' "feminist" and egalitarian intent and practice. This tradition, preaching a gospel of liberation and mutuality, treated women as equals. Evidence exists that Christian women carried out priestly functions—teaching, baptizing, and blessing the Eucharist—on a par with men.

But soon another tradition asserted itself, the patriarchal tradition with its antifemale, body-negating spirituality, insisting on the dominant cultural taboos and sanctions concerning women. This tradition, which had started long before Christianity, viewed women as naturally inferior and as the property of men, associating women with matter, flesh, evil, and sin.

For a while these two traditions—the revolutionary and the patriarchal—clashed, but soon the revolutionary tradition was stamped out, sealing an interpretation of women as inferior that has continued to this day. For a brief moment in history, a window of opportunity to reverse patriarchy opened, and then it was slammed shut. I can still remember the sense of loss that washed over me when I read Elaine Pagels's words:

Despite the previous activity of Christian women, by the year 200, the majority of Christian communities had endorsed as canonical the pseudo-Pauline letter of Timothy which stresses (and exaggerates) the anti-feminist element in Paul's views: "Let a woman learn in silence with all submissiveness. I permit no woman to teach or to have authority over men; she is to keep silent." . . . By the end of the second century women's participation in worship was explicitly condemned.[51]

After this Christianity became the official religion of the Roman Empire (in 312 C.E.), taking on even more patriarchal attitudes. The pattern of keeping women from full participation became set, uniform, and institutionalized in Christianity.

Because of women's so-called inherent sinfulness and the belief by church leaders that women did not even have souls to save, two methods were devised by which women could find salvation. One was submission in marriage and in child bearing; the other was virginity. "Both [models] involved roles of silence and subordination in which the stigma of being female could be overcome," writes Anne E. Carr.[52]

That same weekend I reread the parts of the Bible related specifically to women. If you do this all at once, it can be a shock. A number of years later I would come upon an article in the *Atlantic Monthly* on women and the Bible that summarized the kind of awareness I gained that weekend as I read through the scripture. The article said:

The Bible is no stranger to patriarchy. It was written mostly if not entirely by men. It was edited by men. It describes a succession of societies over a period of roughly 1200 years whose public life was dominated by men. . . . It talks almost only about men. In the Hebrew Bible as a whole, only 111 of the 1426 people who are given names are women. The proportion of women in the New Testament is about twice as great, but still leaves them a tiny minority.

As a prescriptive text, moreover, the Bible has been interpreted as justifying the subordination of women to men: "In pain you shall bring forth children, yet your desire shall be for your husband and he shall rule over you." "Wives, be subject to your husband as you are to the Lord." "Indeed, man was not made from woman, but woman from man. Neither was man created for the sake of woman but woman for the sake of man." As a text that has been presumed by hundreds of millions of people to speak with authority, moreover, the Bible has helped enforce what it prescribes.[53]

As I moved through the biblical material, I flipped over to Galatians 3:28, where Paul put forth a luminous statement, that in Christ there is no male or female. I thought, How unfortunate that *this* did not become the centerpiece for Christian tradition! What took hold more firmly were other statements attributed to Paul upholding male dominance and female subordinance, forbidding women from prophesying, demanding they cover their heads when they prayed in public (an outward sign they were under the authority of men).

At times I put the books down and paced in agitation. Other times I sat staring at sheets of water slide down the windows, too sad to turn the page. But I formed my consciousness by turning pages that weekend and for months to come. I found shocking statements about women by church fathers and leaders I'd once looked to for guidance—Jerome, Clement, Aquinas, Luther, Bonhoeffer, Teilhard de Chardin.

But perhaps no church father had such a profound and encompassing impact on shaping the foundations of Christian interpretation as Augustine, whose thinking, I discovered, was patriarchal in the extreme.

How odd, I kept thinking, that the same man who wrote "Our hearts were made for Thee, O Lord, and they are restless until they rest in Thee," also wrote, "Man but not woman is made in the image and likeness of God." In 1140, this actually became an official decree of the church.

Over the months the most amazing picture unfolded before me, a picture women have rarely glimpsed. Catholic theologian Elizabeth A. Johnson sums it up:

For most of [the church's] history women have been subordinated in theological theory and ecclesial practice at every turn. Until very recently they have been consistently defined as mentally, morally and physically inferior to men, created only partially in the image of God, even a degrading symbol of evil. Women's sexuality has been derided as unclean and its use governed by norms laid down by men. Conversely, they have been depersonalized as a romantic, unsexed ideal whose fulfillment lies mainly in motherhood. . . . They are called to honor a male savior sent by a male God whose legitimate representatives can only be male, all of which places their persons precisely as female in a peripheral role. Their femaleness is judged to be not suitable as metaphor for speech about God. In a word, women occupy a marginal place in the official life of the church.[54]

It was all a sobering indicator of the kind of soil in which Christianity grew. Even more sobering was the realization that after two thousand years so much was still being harvested from it.

Eden as Wounded Geography

On a day in early November while thumbing through a book, I came upon a picture of Eve being tempted by the serpent. I gazed at it a long time—the snake whispering in Eve's ear, her hand outstretched to receive the apple.

It brought to mind the classic interpretation that Adam, the symbolic man, was the superior one, the agent of God, while Eve, the symbolic woman, succumbed to evil because of her association with the snake. Woman was blamed for bringing evil into the world. Her punishment, we're told, was women's pain in childbirth and submission to man.

During my reading I'd come across a number of references concerning the symbolic history of the serpent. To my surprise, I'd learned that in ancient times the snake was not maligned or seen as evil but rather symbolized female wisdom, power, and regeneration. It was associated with the ancient Goddess and was portrayed as her companion. The snake was perhaps the central symbol of sacred feminine energy.

Frankly, at the time this made for uneasy reading. I glossed over those references. I think it was the word *Goddess*.

It's hard to describe the sort of anxiety the word created in me, as if the word itself were contraband. It seemed to violate a taboo so deep and ingrained, I felt stabs of irrational fear just reading about it, as if any minute witch burners from the sixteenth century might appear and carry me off.

An uneasy reaction to the word *Goddess* is common among women. Thousands of years of repression, hostility, and conditioning against a Divine Mother have made a deep impression on us. We've been conditioned to shrink back from the Sacred Feminine, to fear it, to think of it as sinful, even to revile it. And it would take a while for me to deprogram that reaction, to unpack the word and realize that in the end, *Goddess* is just a word. It simply means the divine in female form.

That day as I gazed at the picture of Eve and the serpent, I remembered Goddess and her connection to the snake, and inside I heard a resounding click. I remembered how Nelle Morton once described a moment of awareness in her feminist journey: "My whole life just fell open, and I began to see why things have happened as they have happened."[55] I began to understand what she meant.

Questions followed one another in rapid-fire succession: How had the snake, of all creatures—an animal no better or worse than other wild beings—come to embody the full projection of evil within the Jewish and Christian traditions? Why was the snake selected to represent Satan in the origin myth? Could it be that the patriarchal force chose the snake in hopes of diminishing women's connection to feminine wisdom, power, and regeneration? Was it a way of discrediting the Feminine Divine?

In the context of that time and history, the idea made gut-wrenching sense. In fact, later I would read many such theories by scholars, theologians, and historians.

To understand why the Eden story is so important we have to remember the extraordinary way origin myths operate in our psyches. In a way humans are not made of skin and bone as much as we're made of stories. The Eden myth perhaps more than any other floats in our cells, informing our vision of ourselves and the world.

Back when a battle for passage of the ERA was being waged in state legislatures, a man said to me, "You know what ERA stands for?"

"Equal Rights Amendment," I said.

"No," he said with a laugh. "It stands for Eve Ruined Adam." Interesting, isn't it, how Eden and women's struggle for rights get tangled?

Yet the impact the myth has on people today was brought home to me even more when I visited the High Museum of Art in Atlanta in 1994 to see an exhibition on the Civil Rights movement. The works portrayed the injustice and inhumanity inflicted on African Americans during the summer of 1964.

At the conclusion of the exhibit visitors were invited to pin their thoughts on a bulletin board. I was astonished to see one sheet of paper that said, "It's all women's fault, they brought evil into the world and continue to do so." Whether joke or serious statement, that worldview had come right out of Eden.

Holding the picture of Eve and the serpent that day, I realized how significant and sad it is that in the story Yahweh forever placed enmity between Eve and the snake. Taking symbolic history into account, we might say Yahweh placed enmity between Eve and her deep Feminine Source, her wisdom and power.

What did it mean spiritually and psychologically for a woman to be at odds with that source? Wasn't this another way of portraying women's severed connection with their feminine souls?

I came to realize that Eden is a wounded geography within women's lives, that part of my journey would be returning to this painful inner ground and redeeming the snake in my own psyche.

Recognizing Anger

Throughout this period of looking at Christian patriarchy for the first time, I felt deeply betrayed by a tradition I had served. I also became more aware of my anger.

In the beginning I'd felt the anger like a current, deep and distant, something molten and moving inexorably toward the surface. As it rose, I gave it few outlets. Except for a pen thrown across the room, an outburst in the taxicab, and a few other passing flashes, I'd kept a lid on it.

The church has been afraid of the power of anger. It has seemed to equate anger with sin. But was anger really sinful? What if the sin lies not in feeling the anger but in what one does with the feeling?

Most of my life I'd run from anger as something that good daughters and gracious ladies did not exhibit. Perhaps the thing most denied to women is anger. "Forbidden anger, women could find no voice in which publicly to complain; they took refuge in depression," writes Carolyn Heilbrun.[56] Her words came true for me. Without the ability to allow or the means to adequately express the anger, I began to slide into periods of depression.

There were days that autumn when I had little energy to write or paint or even read. On days like that I felt like somebody had switched off the lights inside. Part of the darkness was the grief that happens when you realize what's been done to women and what we've allowed to be done to us. Part of it was because I didn't know where this journey was taking me and I was scared, and part of it was due to the loss I was starting to feel inside, the loss of feminine soul. But certainly a lot of it came because betrayal and anger sat in me like boulders and I couldn't move them.

I desperately needed to give myself full permission to get angry. The permission finally happened in a most unexpected way. I was having lunch with a young woman who'd recently been ordained as a minister and was on the staff of a large church. When I asked about her work, she told me about one of the first Sundays she had been allowed to conduct the worship. Before the service she had met the senior minister in his study. She was wearing a pair of medium-sized gold earrings along with her clerical robe. Noticing the earrings, the minister asked her to remove them.

"I don't think he wanted to call attention to my being a woman," she said.

As she reported the event, my anger suddenly issued forth in a stream of fury. Feelings of outrage and insult. Pure, unblemished wrath. I wasn't responding to that one incident, I realized later, but to all of the injustice done to women. I'd given myself permission to get mad as hell.

"Sorry," she said. "I didn't mean to cause you to get so angry."

"Don't be sorry," I said. "It's about time we all got angry at this stuff!"

The violation of women is an outrage, and anger is a clear and justifiable response to it.

As I released my anger more often and more consciously, the cycle of depression ended. I began to express the anger when my friend Betty and I got together and talked (she is good about letting me rant without interrupting). I pounded pillows. I poured the anger into my journals. I let it come.

Yet anger needs not only to be recognized and allowed; like the grief, it eventually needs to be transformed into an energy that serves compassion. Maybe one reason I had avoided my anger was that like a lot of people I had thought there were only two responses to anger: to deny it or to strike out thoughtlessly. But other responses are possible. We can allow anger's enormous energy to lead us to acts of resistance against patriarchy. Anger can fuel our ability to challenge, to defy injustice. It can lead to creative projects, constructive behavior, acts that work toward inclusion. In such ways anger becomes a dynamism of love.

TRUSTING YOUR OWN FEMININE SOURCE

Going through the process of unnaming myself, forming a feminist critique, and questioning old certainties left me feeling unhinged. But it also created a space for my own feminine wisdom to break through.

Little by little, I began to contact a feminine source within that didn't come from patriarchy or need to be validated by it. The source was a deep, ancient-feeling place inside me, a place I hadn't known existed.

This surprised me because it made me realize that what I sought was not outside myself. It was within me, already there, waiting. Awakening was really the act of remembering myself, remembering this deep Feminine Source. Inside I carried the poem that says:

> oh woman
> > remember who you are woman
> woman
> it is the whole earth[57]

Signs of Exit

My remembering began that same autumn when an old woman came to me in a dream. In the dream I was standing in front of my Baptist church when suddenly she appeared at my side. I did not know it then, but this same figure would come to me often in dreams and meditations throughout my journey as a personification of feminine wisdom. And whenever she appeared, I learned to brace myself. Some grace and havoc were about to be set loose.

In dreams the wise old woman often symbolizes the Feminine Self or the voice of the feminine soul, and her coming can mark a turning point for women. This dream was my turning point:

The old woman has shining white hair and a face that hangs in folds and furrows down to her shoulders. Her lips are apple red, and she carries a walking stick with a snake wound around it. I notice strange flashes in the air about her as if someone is shaking out gold glitter.

She points to the church steeple. As she does, it changes from a steeple to a rocket ship aimed at the sky. The old woman shakes her head and says, "You think this will take you where you need to go. Think again."

Crazy dream, crazy old woman, I told myself when I woke. But there was no denying she was a numinous figure with enormous energy and power. She lingered in my thoughts for days.

Then one morning in late November, I sat by myself in the church balcony during Sunday service. My two children were sitting with friends. I don't recall why Sandy wasn't there.

The minister was preaching. He was holding up a Bible. It was open, perched atop his raised hand as if a blackbird had landed there. He was saying that the Bible was the sole and ultimate authority of the Christian's life. The *sole* and *ultimate* authority.

I remember a feeling rising up from a place about two inches below my navel. It was a passionate, determined feeling, and it spread out from the core of me like a current so that my skin vibrated with it. If feelings could be translated into English, this feeling would have roughly been the word *no!*

It was the purest inner knowing I had experienced, and it was shouting in me, *no, no, no!* The ultimate authority of my life is not the Bible; it is not confined between the covers of a book. It is not something written by men and frozen in time. It is not from a source outside myself. *My ultimate authority is the divine voice in my own soul.* Period.

I waited. Lightning did not strike. I looked around to see if people were staring. I was sure I must have said the word *no!* out loud, but everyone seemed properly engrossed in the sermon. One woman was nodding in agreement with the minister, nodding so profusely that I saw the depth of my heresy by comparison.

Later I would think of Ibsen's play *A Doll House,* how Nora had done the same thing. At the point when she decides to go away and discover her own life, her husband asks, "Have you no religion?"

Nora answers,

I am afraid, Torvald, I do not exactly know what religion is. . . . I know nothing but what the clergyman said. . . . He told us religion was this, and that, and the other. When I am away from all this, and am alone, I will look into that matter too. I will see if what the clergyman said is true, or at all events, if it is true for me.[58]

This is a stupendous moment for a woman—when she decides to live from her own inner guidance. It is, however, excruciatingly hard for a patriarchal daughter to accomplish. She may have to do it, as I did, in stages.

What is held over her head is condemnation, even damnation. We've been led to believe that leaving the circle of orthodoxy means leaving the realm of truth. Typically the church has considerable stake in our staying in the orthodox circle. It knows if we claim ultimate authority as something in ourselves, as some inchoate voice in our own souls, it has lost all power over us. We have rendered ourselves independent, outside its control. We have stepped out onto our own path. For some reason this scares people senseless.

It terrified me just pondering it.

Women grow afraid at this moment because it means giving up a world where everything is neat and safe. In that world we feel secure, taken care of; we know where we're going. Then we wake up and find the old way doesn't work, that it no longer fits our identity, that by clinging to it, we're cutting ourselves off from something profound. But we cling anyway because it's all we've got. We call our desire for security *loyalty.* We yearn for the something we've lost as women, but it's so unknown, so unbearably unknown. And then one day it all comes down to this: Can we trust ourselves, our inmost selves, our feminine wisdom?

That day sitting in church, I believed the voice in my belly. "[The female soul] resides in the guts, not in the head," wrote Clarissa Pinkola Estés.[59] I think that morning my female soul was shouting for her life.

I asked myself, How many times have I denied my innermost wisdom and silenced this voice? How many times can a woman betray her soul before it gives up and ceases calling to her at all?

My heart pounded throughout the rest of the sermon. When we stood for the closing hymn, I slipped out of the pew and descended the steps two at a time, holding onto the rail, trying to steady my impulse to bolt from the place. It was like that feeling of being underwater and scrambling for the surface, for air. Thirty-nine years in the fish tank had caught up with me.

I walked toward the exit sign, my eyes locked on it.

As I passed through the front door, light and wind hit my face along with the scent of pine and wood smoke. The sun was glinting off everything—trees, sidewalk, car windshields. For a few seconds I stood on the steps, taking in breaths of air like I was storing it up.

I waited in the car for the children. Sitting there, staring up at the church steeple, I remembered the dream I'd had—the old woman supported by her stick with the snake spiraling around it. I recognized her then as the image of my female wisdom. I also thought about Wisdom in the Bible, the feminine aspect of God who is personified as a woman. I knew practically nothing about her, but I resolved I would find out.

The voice in my belly was the voice of the wise old woman. It was my female soul talking. And it had challenged the assumption that the Baptist Church would get me where I needed to go. She was saying that by clinging to that steeple, I was somehow living against my female soul.

I eventually came to see that she was also challenging the androcentrism of the entire Christian Church, its singular aim toward a male God in the sky. She was challenging the way it took me away from earth, matter, and the feminine ground of my being, fueling a dualism that had split me in two.

"I'm not going back," I told my husband.

It was late Sunday afternoon. He was on the patio filling the dog's water bowl with the garden hose. He thought I meant I wasn't going back for the evening service.

"Fine," he said.

"No, I mean I'm never going back."

He didn't say anything. He just stared at me. The water ran over the sides of the bowl. I walked over and turned off the spigot.

"I can't explain it exactly," I said. "I just know I don't belong there. I have to leave. I've decided to join the Episcopal Church."

He was very uneasy, weighing everything he said. "If you think that's best. I guess you have to do what you think is best."

The Dam Breaks

The following March I was confirmed into the Episcopal Church. Of course, patriarchy was there, too. But leaving the Baptist Church was an important first step for me. It was an exercise in letting go, in trusting my Feminine Wisdom, trusting myself. I needed to do that, to *know* I could do that.

But looking back, I think some half-conscious part of me was also seeking a last-ditch way to make it all work. Moving into the Episcopal Church, I was looking for a more compatible circle of orthodoxy. I thought if I could be surrounded by the liturgies, rituals, and Eucharist—the things I had missed in an evangelical church, maybe that would fix everything. Maybe it would be enough.

So I plunged in. I went to the Episcopal Church regularly. I taught a class. I tried to focus on the ancient beauty within the Eucharist. I tried to connect with the sacredness of the liturgy. I knelt in the pew and crossed myself and tried very hard. I kept whispering to myself, Maybe I can find a way to live within patriarchal hierarchy and theology, take the good, ignore the rest. I won't think too much about what's not here. It will be okay, it really will.

And in the newness of it, in my determination, I drank up the beauty and sacredness of the experience.

Plus, there were the children to consider. They were, for me, the biggest concern of all. One evening that spring I paused in the doorway of the kitchen and watched them—Ann sitting on the floor doing homework, Bob busy with a video game. I'd explained my decision to them to attend a different church, and they'd been fine with it. In fact, the whole family had come with me at times. And in the years ahead, Sandy and the children would become confirmed in the Episcopal Church themselves. But what if I challenged that institution? Not setting the "proper and accepted" religious example for them conjured up images of the bad mother, the worst mother. Yet wouldn't the example of a mother being true to her journey, taking a stand against patriarchy, and questing for spiritual meaning and wholeness, even when it meant exiting circles of orthodoxy, be a worthwhile example?

As I looked at their faces, love filled me up. It was the wise and difficult love that reminds parents that all we can really do is be true to our own spiritual unfolding and trust that our examples will one day help them be true to theirs. For children have a guiding spiritual wisdom inside of them, too.

As summer came and went, I noticed my sense of betrayal had not diminished. Sitting in church listening to liturgies that excluded the feminine, feelings of restlessness, alienation, and anger began to well up again. I began to yearn for a sacred environment that could help me remember my deep feminine self.

One day, finding myself at a luncheon with a male Episcopal priest, I bravely (maybe even naïvely) explained my feelings about women and the church. He patted my hand. He said, "It's counterproductive to get hung up on side issues like that."

End of discussion.

Autumn came. I kept trying. But Sunday after Sunday I sat in church feeling a little like the Dutch boy with his finger plugging the dam. It seemed like I was holding back a reservoir of doubt, pain, and disillusionment.

One cold Sunday morning full of wind and flight, I went to church as usual. I sat on the last pew. I asked myself, Since when is women's spiritual well-being a "side issue"? Where is the feminine standpoint in this service? Where are the earth, nature, Mother? Where are the power and celebration of women?

The dam broke.

I knew right then and there that the patriarchal church was no longer working for me. The exclusive image of God as heavenly Father wasn't working, either. I needed a Power of Being that was also feminine. I needed a sacred space free of the stain of sexism with core imagery that embraced the feminine, a space that welcomed women to places of power, engaged them fully as equals, and helped to heal their wound and empower their lives.

Nearly one hundred years earlier Elizabeth Cady Stanton, one of the mothers of women's suffrage, wrote, "With faith and works [woman] is the chief support of the church and clergy; the very powers that make her emancipation impossible."[60]

I sat quietly on the pew. I knew that despite how unthinkable and forbidden it was, I needed to move beyond religion in a patriarchal institution. This may not be true for every woman. But for me it was crucial to my spiritual maturity and growth. At that moment I took sole responsibility for my spiritual life.

I went home with clarity about my feelings but frightened by them nevertheless.

Marriage and Spiritual Autonomy

My husband noticed my preoccupation. "Something on your mind?" he asked. When I finished telling him, I think he felt like the dam water had rolled over him, too.

He'd been seemingly open, if a little reluctant, about my awakening experience thus far, but now he objected with the finality of a slammed door.

"I just wish you'd stop all this," he said.

"What is *this*?" I asked him.

"You know, this whole feminist thing."

He felt threatened; I could recognize that even then. He didn't want anything in our comfortable world to change.

The next few weeks I struggled to stand my ground, the unfamiliar new soil of defiance. I was becoming more certain that I couldn't stay married in the same way. Not in a relationship built on patriarchal values. I was asking myself, What will happen to this marriage if I claim real autonomy? How can I blend my spiritual quest as a woman with my marriage?

During that time I was reading the journals of May Sarton. One day I came across this wise passage:

[Women] have to come to understand ourselves as central, not peripheral, before anything real can happen. We have to depend on ourselves. . . . This cannot be done *against* men, and that's the real problem. . . . It cannot be woman *against* man. It has to be woman finding her true self with or without man, but not against man.[61]

I adopted this as my guide, but it was difficult not to fall into adversarial confrontations. Over and over, out of his own fear, Sandy tried to talk me out of the powerful feelings erupting into my life. He would become logical, then angry, then frustrated. I think deep down he expected me to defer to his wishes.

In her poem "Cinderella," Anne Sexton suggests how far a woman will go for the prince. Drawing on Grimm's rather than Disney's version of the fairy tale, she records how Cinderella's sisters excitedly try on the glass slipper. When they find their feet too large, the eldest sister slices off her big toe in order to fit into it. The other sister chops off her heel.[62] I did not want to amputate the new growth happening inside me, yet wearing the prince's slipper seemed to demand it.

As a woman, I'd stuffed my foot into all kinds of slippers that assured me of winning patriarchy's love. When the cultural father told me I should be sweet, deferring, passive, silent, and secondary, I'd accepted those shoes and felt obliged to limp around in them for decades. When the church told me God was male only and relegated women to the peripheries, I'd sliced off a toe and put on that stance, too. When the priest told me not to get hung up on the side issue of women, I'd taken on that standpoint (for a brief while anyway). Now it seemed my husband wanted me to cut away one of the most vital awakenings in my life in order to go on being the good princess.

Years later a friend said to me, "When a conventional wife with a conventional husband experiences a feminist awakening, there is bound to be a marital explosion."

Now the explosion had come, and I kept telling him the matter was not man against woman or Sue against Sandy. Rather, it was change against stasis, freedom against control.

It was only at night when I lay in the darkness and thought about my marriage that I doubted myself. Beneath all my brave pronouncements, part of me could not imagine risking my marriage. There had to be a way through this.

But it wasn't only my marriage that held me back. I began to glimpse the chasm that lay between the inclinations of my soul and my ability to carry them out. I had had a clear, pure moment of knowing that compelled me to risk my religion and move beyond patriarchy at church and within my spiritual life, *but actually doing it?* Now that was something else altogether. And my career—could I actually risk that?

Yet, I was withering within these things. Internally I felt trapped.

Leaving the Jar

While entangled in these feelings, I happened to hear about an experiment in which flies were sealed in an aerated jar and left for an extended period of time. Finally the lid on the jar was removed, but—strange thing—the flies did not try to leave. Well conditioned by now, they no longer looked for the exit. They just kept circling the tight perimeters of the glass, going in their familiar patterns. Their reality had shrunk to that jar. It had become their entire world. It had become safe. Life beyond it had ceased to exist.

I'm in the jar, I thought.

I hadn't been able to leave the tight perimeters of the old, confining way of being a woman. It had been my entire world, and I questioned whether I could live beyond its safety. Unlike the flies, however, I knew the lid was off. I'd struggled, myself, to open it, but now that I had, I couldn't seem to muster the daring and insurgent energy I needed to fly. It's a peculiar thing, isn't it, that a woman can prefer the safety of cages to the hazards of freedom?

Throughout the previous two years, my awakening had shown me new truths about my religion, my life, and the lives of women. I had survived a landslide of awarenesses. But I didn't know if I could act on them.

When you can't go forward and you can't go backward and you can't stay where you are without killing off what is deep and vital in yourself, you are on the edge of creation. And so it was that I went that autumn afternoon to run my errands, walked into the drugstore, and found my daughter on her knees.

As I listened to the man say, "That's how I like to see a woman—on her knees," something broke within me. I felt there was nothing more of that old life worth holding onto. I saw that this was not only just about me. It was about my daughter. It was about all the daughters everywhere.

That day I took my leave of the jar. I made an unconditional relationship with the journey. The sound of dragging feet ceased, and the silence was deafening.

Later I would think of the poet's line:

Kabir says: The only woman awake is the woman who has heard the flute.[63]

I thought of it because in the silence that followed, I began to hear the first strands of a music that has pulled me unceasingly ever since.

I do not know what to name this music except to say it comes from a place of hope in the feminine soul. It awakens us even as we awaken it.

PART TWO

Initiation

Now here was I, new-awakened, with my hand stretching out and touching the unknown, the real unknown, the unknown unknown.

D. H. Lawrence

The familiar life horizon has been outgrown; the old concepts, ideals, and emotional patterns no longer fit; the time for the passing of a threshold is at hand.

Joseph Campbell

Death of the old form and new life or birth are fundamental to initiations.

Jean Shinoda Bolen

The days grew shorter and winter closed in. It seemed impossible that over two years had passed since the dream of birthing myself and the experience at the monastery that had started it all.

I often found myself mulling over the events that had followed—the painful acknowledgment of the feminine wound, my exasperating resistance to the journey, the night with the dancing women on the beach. I recalled the sketches I'd made, then burned, the Magritte painting, unraveling the cultural images of womanhood, unnaming myself as woman so I could begin to remember who I was. I relived the intense months of reading and reading, forming my critique, truth telling, anguish, and anger. Through all of this, I had conceived myself as woman. I had been reseeded.

I thought often, too, of the old woman with the snake-twined stick who'd come in my dreams, the struggle to disentangle myself from patriarchal institutions and their wounding power and to cast my lot, as theologian Carter Heyward writes, "with those who resist unjust power relations."[1] I thought of the struggle to make my husband understand, the tensions I'd felt inside—those stymied, trapped, aching, ambivalent feelings. And I was grateful for the catalytic day I walked into the drugstore and found my daughter on her knees, because it caused me to get off mine.

As I looked back, those events and images melded into my own unique landscape of awakening, into a craggy inner geography that I'd traveled but seemed now to be leaving for a different terrain. I had a vague sense of being perched on the lip of a new phase of experience, a whole new passage in my journey.

I would never have thought to call it initiation. Yet that's precisely what I was about to undergo. In the months ahead I would plunge into a series of initiatory events, making my transit toward a new spirituality, toward Sacred Feminine experience and a new way of being woman.

Initiation is a rite of passage, a crossing over, a movement between two worlds. For women on a journey such as this one, initiation is the Great Transition.

Making this transition into Sacred Feminine experience can be beautiful and deeply moving, even cataclysmic in its effect on our lives. But it also means a time of ordeal, descent, darkness, and pain. "In that experience of being formed anew, I may often feel torn asunder; old aspects of my self-conception must die in order for my new transformation into selfhood to take place," writes feminist professor Penelope Washbourn.[2]

If I had to reduce the meaning of initiation to just two words, they would be *death* and *rebirth*. Those are the essential tasks in any initiation, and especially they are the tasks of women who undergo initiation into feminist spiritual experience. The old forms, which grew small and confining as we woke, now crumble and give way as something new and large and mysterious rises up inside us. Attachment to the patriarchal world, which we've struggled to unname and unhinge, begins to dissolve and die away, and we are immersed in the feelings that go along with dyings.

Initiation is a sacred disintegration. Despite its pain, we carry the conviction (often only faintly) that even though we don't know where we'll end up, we're following a soul-path of immense richness, that we're *supposed* to be on this path, that it's required of us somehow. We move in a sense of rightness, of lure, of following a flute that pipes irresistible music.

Early that winter, approaching initiation, I carried the sense of belonging on this path, but I knew nothing of the intensity I was about to enter. I only knew I had waked and was entering a place where the old meanings, concepts, and values no longer fit. The vista of the Great Transition.

When landing in a place like this, usually the best thing to do is be still, be quiet, gather one's wits. Inside I felt queasy and alone, like I'd disembarked on some beautiful but unnamed island and was standing there, watching the last boat recede into the distance.

When a woman starts to disentangle herself from patriarchy, ultimately she is abandoned to her own self. She comes to an unknown place where she must let the old way of being woman die and the new way come forth. During initiation the new feminine potential—that rambunctious girl-child who was conceived and birthed inside during her awakening and who really had been there all along—starts to grow and develop into the woman she will be.

THE UNEXPLORED GORGE

It was New Year's Eve. Sandy and I sat together in the den reading. We did that some years, avoiding the parties and staying home by the fire. I was reading Adrienne Rich's poetry, beautiful lines about moving through an unexplored gorge. I laid the book down and closed my eyes, trying to take in the image.

Finally I walked outside onto the patio and stared at the sky, clear and speckled with stars. The evening was not cold by December standards, not even December in the South. Before me hung a sliver of new moon; behind me light slanted out from the windows of the house. As I looked back through the French doors, suddenly the arrangement seemed all too symbolic: me out here in the dark, looking back at a space both familiar and secure.

The thought of an unexplored gorge filled me with mystery and love, yet at the same time, fear. The unexplored gorge, I repeated. I had found a name for the new terrain I was entering.

But then I had another realization. Moving into a gorge implies descent.

Self-Captivity

Women's lives are made up of cycles of descent and ascent. At crucial times we must seek out periods of inner solitude, deep brooding and being, intervals of spiritual apartness where we move down into the depths of ourselves to mine the dark gorge and bring new treasure into the light.

Years back I'd visited the Cloisters in New York, a museum of medieval art and home of the famous unicorn tapestries, which had been woven around 1500. I was drawn to one tapestry in particular, *The Unicorn in Captivity.* It pictured the magical creature sitting alone inside a small circular fence beneath a tree, enclosed in a private space.

This image of captivity and containment returned to me that New Year's Eve as a picture of what I needed—to "capture" myself, to bring my inner process with all its tensions into a contained and private space.

According to Jungian analyst Karen Signell, the unicorn represents "a woman's deep feminine center." It is her "early feminine Self, free and solitary, yet also highly vulnerable."[3] This is the part of us that is newly developing, and at this stage it can be elusive, hidden, and difficult to contain. Like the unicorn, it can fade into the woods and be lost, writes Signell. It needs a safe inner sanctum and a time to dwell there in separateness.

I wanted to give myself this kind of space, to face what was happening, to let the small green shoot of my feminine soul have its hothouse. I needed an immediate retreat, but with writing deadlines piled on my desk, this was impossible. Flipping ahead in my calendar, I noticed a speaking engagement I had in California in late February. I decided to stay over for a while afterward. To let it become a place of self-captivity.

I told Sandy about my plans one evening as we sat across from each other in the den. I told him my world was unraveling. I asked him to try to understand, that I was tired of serving institutions designed to favor men while depriving women, that as a matter of fact, our marriage had in some ways been one of those institutions. I told him I needed time alone to sort through it. That I was going to take several days away.

He squeezed the little hump of flesh between his eyebrows. "Don't," he sighed.

He was talking about more than my going away. He was talking about the whole journey, and we both knew it.

I didn't say anything. He kept rubbing his thumb across his open palm. "I don't understand what you're doing," he said. "This journey you're on . . . I wish . . ." He shook his head. He wished I would cease and desist, that's what he wished.

I thought how scary it must be to have a wife of nearly twenty years wake up. About five thousand years of repressed feminine wisdom and strength are simmering in the cells of her body, and something way down inside him knows this, knows that if it ever gets loose, life as he knows it is over.

I was silent a long time. I loved him deeply, but how could I deny this journey? Women had made whole careers of self-abnegation and sacrifice because we've been told this was the noblest way, the "Christian way." But was it noble to cling to passivities and diminishments, to love ourselves so little we smothered any flame in our own souls? In my favorite May Sarton novel, *The Reckoning*, Ella writes to her friend Laura,

"Do you suppose growing up always means diluting [our] fierce purpose for the sake of others?"[4]

In some ways, spiritual development for women, perhaps unlike that for men, is not about surrendering self so much as coming to self.

"I have to do this," I told him softly. "I really have to."

His whole body went limp, reminding me of a glove when a hand has just been withdrawn. There seemed no fight left in him. He got up and walked away.

In a moment of sadness I wondered what would become of us. He didn't understand the extraordinary passion in my heart for this journey; he didn't know my fierce need to be unbridled, the ache for my feminine soul. I yearned for his support. I wished for a marriage where we could walk paths that allowed for the unconditional sharing of soul. Without it, marriage becomes very lonely.

Writing poignantly about the strain on her marriage that came from following her feminine journey, Jungian analyst Jean Shinoda Bolen wrote, "The need to share what we experience, to be listened to, to have what is going on *inside* us matter to the person we are married to, to engage in a two-way dialogue, is the cry of one soul yearning to meet another."[5]

It was my cry, but I couldn't seem to make it heard. And to be honest, I couldn't hear his cry very well, either.

In the weeks that followed, I canceled most of my social engagements, worked to clear off my desk, and stayed at home. I poured uncensored words into my journal, took walks in the cold, shed tears from old, forgotten reservoirs. I felt like I was dissolving. A dandelion going to seed.

I didn't have guidelines for what I was doing. I didn't really know if what I was attempting was possible. Was there really another story to be lived beside the one I was living? If so, no one had ever told it to me. I imagined there was another way of being a woman, but what was it?

At times near-panic swept over me. What am I doing, what am I doing? I would ask. What will become of my marriage? my religion? Are there other images of the Divine that do not obliterate the feminine? Is there another container to hold my spiritual journey? If so, what is it?

I had fond thoughts about regressing to the old way. I would stare at women in the grocery store, women who drove their carts about the aisles with seeming content, and I would think, I want to be like that again.

I wished for security, knowing it could not be had. In February I boarded an airplane for California.

Finding the Circle of Trees

It was night. I was sitting in an aisle seat on the plane. A beam of overhead light, thin and yellow as a pencil, drifted down to dilute the gathering dark. I turned off the light and tried to sleep but ended up nursing a sense of loss that seemed heavier than ever.

I ran down the list. I was losing my marriage (at least the marriage we'd had in the past). My spiritual life was crumbling (at least the way it had existed before). My career of inspirational writing might even follow. I was also losing my identity, the roles of daughterhood that had sustained me, and along with that, my way of receiving validation in the world. I was losing the values from my childhood, my orientation to life. I was on this plane flying through the darkness, and it was not lost on me that spiritually I was also flying blind. I had no real idea where I was headed.

Years after this plane ride, I traveled to Crete with fourteen other women, all of them on feminist spiritual journeys. While there, we descended into a cave called Skoteino, where thousands of years earlier women and men had come to worship the Goddess as Skoteini, Goddess of the Dark. We moved by candlelight, climbing down four levels, the air growing dark and cold, until finally we came to the cave floor. We sat, holding beeswax candles. On the count of three we blew them out. No one spoke, though I could hear our breathing loud as wind.

We stayed that way three, four, five minutes in the blackest black I've ever known. I began to lose my boundaries, even the sense of my own skin. I was floating in darkness.

And from the darkness, the one image that returned to me was that plane ride years earlier. Flying to California. I had the same sense in the cave that I had on the plane, of floating in darkness, having no markers by which to define my world, no path, no container, no place to be.

In the cave one of the women began to sing, "Skoteini." Others joined in, until an aria of women's voices sifted through the blackness, calling on the Goddess of the Dark. Finally someone struck a match, lit her candle, and offered her flame to the woman beside her. The light moved woman to woman around the cave, each woman's face flickering momentarily behind the flame. Watching the light grow, thinking back to the plane ride,

I realized that even back then something inside me was calling on the Goddess of the Dark, even though I didn't know her name. And I thought, too, how important it was at times like that to receive light from other women—to receive their permission to be where we are.

But on the flight to California I had no idea where to find light, and really it was too soon. Descent is not about finding light but about going into the darkness and befriending it. If we remain there long enough, it takes on its own luminosity. It will reveal everything to us.

A flight attendant swished along the aisle, paused, offered me a blanket. I tucked it around me, sliding over to the empty seat beside the window and staring through the small oval. The world outside was shiny black, glazed with the lights of the night. The moon hovered behind the wing. It was a pale crescent no bigger than my fingernail. I wondered if it was waxing or waning. I wondered what would happen when I got to California. Over the loudspeaker the captain said we would soon start our descent. Ha! I almost said out loud.

Restless, I raised the seat, turned on the light again, reached for a magazine in the seat pocket. I flipped the pages. Suddenly my hands rested on a picture. I was looking at a circle of trees in the woods. I cannot tell you now whether it was an aerial photograph or an artist's rendering. I only remember the circle of trees.

It was a near-perfect circle of oaks and evergreens in the middle of a forest. The sun was piercing its way through the limbs, striking the center, illuminating a golden ellipse of space—still, hidden, contained.

Once I'd read about a child who opened her favorite picture book on the floor and stepped onto the page, trying to get inside the world she loved. I felt like that now. I wanted to disappear into the magazine, into the circle of trees. The image seized me, as if it were some realm I had lost and suddenly found again.

I began to imagine the circle as a place where once, perhaps long ago, women had gathered, danced, dreamed, healed, grown wise and powerful together. A place where women were honored, loved, and supported, where they were invited, even encouraged, to become different sorts of women.

The circle of trees touched me like a memory and a promise both.

Later I came to realize that the circle of trees was for me an inner feminine sanctum of containment, support, and new life, the space of female soul that I needed to find and from which I needed to live.

A woman finds her way to this circle of trees in order to become fully woman, fully herself. But how do you find it? I wondered. Did I begin by creating a container—inner and outer circles of trees—that could hold and nurture me as I began the process of reconnecting to my feminine soul?

I closed my eyes. Yes, I thought. *Yes.*

Today, more than ever, I'm aware how much a woman needs a container like that. She needs an embracing, open-armed space where she can dissolve, go to seed, and regerminate. A place to be still and tend new roots. She needs a place away from every *man*-made thing where she can cry, even shout if she wants. In a place like that she can begin to heal what is wounded, recover what is lost. She can remember herself.

I ran my finger around the rim of the circle on the page and prayed my first prayer to a Divine Feminine presence. I said, "Mothergod, I have nothing to hold me. No place to be, inside or out. I need to find a container of support, a space where my journey can unfold."

When I landed I had a nebulous course of direction, a kind of bearing to live toward. What I did not know was that one day not so far away I would also find the circle of trees in the literal world.

A Solitude of Descent

After my speaking engagement, I settled into a small bed-and-breakfast in San Francisco for several days of solitude. I had hoped to stay at Mercy Center in Burlingame, a retreat house south of San Francisco that I'd wanted to visit for a long time, but at the last minute I couldn't arrange it. Not knowing of another, I decided on the inn because I'd been there before and remembered the rooms were cozy, that it had a fireplace downstairs with an overstuffed chair where a person could sit unperturbed and look out over Washington Square. Besides, I told myself, the place wasn't so important, it was self-containment that mattered.

Most of the time I spent in my room. The first day I was aware of noise on the street, but gradually it seemed to recede. I whiled away an hour following the pattern sunlight made on the carpet. I felt myself sinking into solitude. My sense of isolation was almost overpowering. I wished ten, twenty, thirty times that I hadn't come, but I made no attempt to leave. In the end the force in me to make the descent was stronger than the desire to flee it.

I had a book with me called *Womanchrist,* and I read passages from it now and then. One of them was this:

Whether we have taken the path of the fathers, educating ourselves in their institutions, learning their language, seeking their goals, energizing ourselves with success in their endeavors, or supported the fathers in their path, creating their homes, birthing and rearing their children, encouraging their dreams, healing their wounds, we have most often made beauty out of our work. We rejoice in our careers and in our children. We are proud of our spouses' achievements and our belief that helped to make those achievements happen. . . . Then one day everything is dry. Dust. Crumbled and blowing away on a stale wind. Being vice-president of the company no longer matters. Being a competent wife feels meaningless. . . . The time has come, not to reclaim what has been lost, but to descend. To find the ground of our own being we must descend.[6]

I closed the book. Wrapped in aloneness, with permission to feel my experience, I was suddenly overcome with an acute sense of loss. Loss of what had been, loss of identity. My experience was teaching me the truth of Nelle Morton's words that there is an "awful abyss that occurs after the shattering, and before the new reality appears."[7]

I also thought about Adrienne Rich's poem "Diving into the Wreck," in which she writes of the experience of "unmeaning," which a woman encounters when she dives into the wreck of patriarchal culture and, seeing what it is, begins at last to swim beyond it on her own.

For a time we feel stripped of ourselves, which is only natural since so much of our meaning has come from our identity in patriarchy. "Patriarchy has created us in its image," writes Starhawk, writer, teacher, and activist. "Once we see that image, however, it no longer possesses us unaware. We can reshape it, create something new."[8] But first, before the reshaping, the re-creation, there is the blank, stunned space of feeling stripped and peeled. We are not who we used to be and not who we will become. We are in the terrain of "unmeaning." And we are alone in it.

I do not think in words so much as in pictures, and the image that often came to me as I was cloistered away in that small inn was a wind sock, hanging still and empty on some lonely stretch of land. I could see myself as the wind sock. The prevailing wind, the identity and meaning that had filled me like a gale-blown force, had died away. Unable now to point the direction, I felt emptied of my meaning, unable to know the shape of myself.

I wept at the possibility of losing my marriage, my career, at the vulnerability of shedding my daughterhood, the loss of religious alignment.

My perception of the Divine had proved rigid, inadequate. Western Christian patriarchal boxes could not hold it. The Divine was more of an unmapped mystery than I'd fathomed. Yet as expansive as that might sound, I did not lose the accustomed symbols of my religion without grief. Also, the thought of forfeiting my dependence on masculine validation and giving up salvation through male saviors left me feeling alone and denuded, thrown back completely on myself.

I'd struggled to come to terms with my feminine woundedness. I was aware of my lost feminine standpoint and the severed connection to my feminine soul. I sensed how my *exclusive* identification with a Father in heaven had encouraged my estrangement from my female self, from earth, nature, Mother, and the wisdom and validation of these things. Patriarchy had created a world where spirit is split from body, humans from nature, and natural from divine, and I could feel those splits in myself.

I mourned those gaping holes. During those isolated days I sometimes stood before the mirror, inwardly saying the first of many goodbyes to the woman I had been.

In crossing the unexplored gorge (an act that cannot be accomplished in several days, to be sure, but can take months and years), our task is to surrender to the experience and make the descent consciously, with intention and awareness. We will need to let the old forms break, giving up our identity as spiritual daughters of patriarchy and learning to say good-bye.

In the trek across the gorge, we often scan about for shortcuts. During that period, I often wished some wise woman who'd been there before me would appear and tell me how to zip through it. If she had, though, she probably would have admonished me to give up seeking a shortcut and just be where I was.

There is deep wisdom in giving up the fight to make it go away. When we instead come home to our path, we come home to *what is*. You are where you are. So be there. Stop trying to protect yourself from the harshness of right now, fleeing into a long fabrication about how it's going to be one day. That's a way of avoiding the here-and-now truth of our lives.

Women who want to be grown-up women will have to come to a blatant self-acceptance. I think the wise woman, if she had appeared, would have said, "Don't try to leap over yourself. Just accept what is and be with it, really be with it, because when you do that you are being in the moment, in the truth. You are being present as you live your life." In the end, is there anything else?

In an old Sumerian myth, the Goddess Inanna, making a descent to the underworld, moves through seven gates. At each gate she must strip a piece of her clothing away until at last she is naked, arriving without any of her former trappings. At the depth of her descent she is turned into a piece of meat and hung on a meat hook for several days before being resurrected as a woman.

I've often wondered if that's where we get the idea of wanting to be "let off the hook." Those days at the inn were my meat hook (one of many), and a lot of the time I wanted someone to come and get me off it. But I also began in bits and pieces to be present while I lived my life, to stay on the hook despite the sense of loss and unmeaning I felt.

Holding onto the circle of trees helped me stay there.

Even when my sense of losing everything, of disappearing into nothing, was at its most vivid, the image of the circle of trees appeared and reappeared. Once when I fell asleep in the middle of the afternoon I dreamed of it. On waking, I drew the first of many circles of trees in my journal, strengthening the hope that I could create a sacred and vital space in which to be free as a woman and unfold my feminine journey.

My last morning at the inn I rose early and went downstairs for breakfast. I gazed through the window across the square, where dozens and dozens of Chinese Americans moved in slow motion under the trees. They were doing tai chi, a form of exercise as exquisite as ballet. Compelled, I walked across the street and sat beneath a tree to watch.

Jean Shinoda Bolen has written that when we're at significant junctures of transition, outer events and meetings are often filled with messages that should be heeded. That was the case as I fixed my eyes on a lone Chinese woman among a sea of men. A striking elderly woman, she had deeply wrinkled skin and long graying hair that had slipped partially from its coil.

The group was copying the movements of a leader out front, following them with rigid exactness. But with bold improvisations all her own, the old woman ignored the rest and moved spontaneously to a soundless music inside herself. Wildly out of sync, she danced her own dance and no one else's. This woman has heard the flute, I thought. And for the first time during that interval of pain, I smiled.

I watched until the class had finished and she had gone. What was it about her? I realized suddenly that she reminded me of the old woman in my dreams, the one who'd come with the snake-twined walking stick, bidding me to follow my own feminine path instead of a male-defined way.

I remained sitting there a long while. For days my thoughts and feelings had been like shards of glass flying in all directions, but now they came together, forming something solid and singular, an unimpeachable knowing: What I was experiencing was okay; I was okay feeling it; and moving to the soundless music inside, even when that music became a symphony of pain, was necessary and beautiful.

An energy rose in me from down under, the kind of energy that sends flowers and grass through cracks in the driveway. I told myself this: Whatever time it takes for the old patterns to die and the birth of a new feminine consciousness, I would allow it. I would not, could not forfeit my journey for my marriage or for the sake of religious acceptance or success as a "Christian writer." I would keep moving in my own way to the strains of feminine music that sifted up inside me, not just moving but embracing the dance. I knew that by being here in my solitary descent I had already begun to create a circle of trees and that I would go on creating it.

My descent didn't abruptly end here, though I found the sense of loss and fear lessening for a while. Descent would continue for many months as I traveled new places in the gorge.

It is worth noting that rarely is any awareness or process on this journey a one-time event. We seem to return to it over and over, each time integrating it a bit more fully, owning it a little more deeply. I may be laying out the general contours of the feminine spiritual process, but there are no neat, clear-cut lines where one phase precisely ends and the next begins. Each woman has her own timing and her own way. The passages she takes will overlap and spiral around, only to be experienced again.

OPENING TO THE FEMININE DIVINE

The afternoon after encountering the Chinese woman, I made my way to Mercy Center in Burlingame for a quick visit before returning home. As I came into the entryway—a shadowed, still room deserted of people—I found myself gazing at a large picture, one I'd never seen before. It was a replica of Leonardo da Vinci's *Cartoon of St. Anne*.

I felt a quickening sensation in my body, a soft current that spread from my belly up through my breasts and down my arms. Jean Shinoda Bolen calls the sensation "a sensory intuition" or "tuning fork phenomenon." It may occur when something deep inside us responds with an instinctual awareness to sacred moments and events. Feminine knowing often registers in the body even before the mind.

The picture portrayed a great, flashing-eyed woman whose immense lap held both Mary and Christ. I felt I was looking at an image of the Divine Feminine, the Great Mother, for the woman in the picture seemed to birth, contain, and encompass everything, even the male savior.[9]

Standing there, I felt a deep, magnetic awareness of her.

When we truly grasp for the first time that the symbol of woman can be a vessel of the sacred, that it too can be an image of the Divine, our lives will begin to pivot.

Today a lot of women are seeking feminine imagery of the Divine. More women than we can imagine have embarked on the quest, enough women to set in motion a whole shift in our religious paradigm. I've met countless numbers of these women—married, divorced, and single, some of them Christian theologians and ministers but also insurance agents, real estate agents, nurses, students, psychologists, travel agents, schoolteachers, mothers who stay home and work, artists, writers, accountants, to only name a few—all of whom are talking passionately about the return of Mother God or Sophia or Goddess. I've been struck by how these women's lives are anchored in the "real" world, how bright and unique yet ordinary they are. The Divine Feminine is returning to collective consciousness, all right. She's coming, and it will happen whether we're ready or not.

That day at Mercy Center, I studied the picture a long time. The lap dominated the image. It seemed to me like a sacred space, another circle of trees, a place of loving containment and feminine embrace where a woman could be reborn.

I carried that image with me on the plane home. The whole way I had that feeling you get inside when you stop swimming salmon-backward against yourself and yield to your own internal flow. But I knew it didn't necessarily mean everything around me would coincide. I kept thinking of my husband.

Sandy met me at the airport and he held me tightly for a very long time. Then on the forty-minute drive home, he asked about my trip. I did not hold back. I told him how I'd felt at the inn, about the Chinese woman, the painting at Mercy Center.

The car filled with silence, but I could see in his face that he was struggling to get something out. "While you were gone, I was thinking," he said. "I realized I've been so invested in maintaining everything exactly as it is, I couldn't allow your experience."

My eyes widened.

He didn't say much else, and I knew that he didn't really understand what I was doing and maybe would never be at peace with this journey of mine. And although neither of us knew whether things would work out in the end, because there are never guarantees, I knew that right now he wanted to try. And for me it was enough.

Sometimes you get very unexpected gifts.

I think of the dictum that when one person in a relationship starts to become conscious, the other is compelled to become conscious, too. Awakening precipitates awakening, and sometimes a woman's dogged groping for enlightenment and wholeness will ignite the process in her mate (or vice versa). But it's not always so. There has to be enough wick present—enough willingness, openness, pliability, and grace—to receive the flame.

Women should not be naïve: wicks, wind, and fire are uncertain business. Sometimes rigidity and resistance are too encrusted and the relationship cannot survive the changes going on in a woman. No matter the patience, love, and consciousness brought to bear, it may happen that the relationship simply cannot break through to a new place. I've met women who in such circumstances have stayed and others who've left. Such choices are achingly difficult, and I've learned to respect whatever a woman feels she must do.

Sandy's transformation began with that tiny pivot of consciousness he described that day in the car. Over the next few years, I watched a slow but dramatic evolution unfold in him. I watched with stupefaction and awe. I will not say much about it because it is his story, not mine, to tell, but as time went by he, too, was thrust into soul-searching. He began to look at the roots from which his own life sprang. He came to see, and I did, too, that patriarchy wounds men also, that men have their own journeys to make in order to heal and differentiate themselves from it.

He began a spiritual and psychological journey of his own. He began to open up in new ways, to read new books, to ask new questions, to change and grow. After a lot of struggle, he came to support an egalitarian and feminist vision, not in name only, but in the way he lived and related. And he came to support me.

Feminist writer Naomi Wolf sums up what is happening as men make this choice:

The world of men is dividing into egalitarians and patriarchalists—those men who are trying to learn the language and customs of the newly emerging world, and those who are determined to keep that new order from taking root. The former group welcomes these changes, seeing that though they are painful in the short term, over the long term they provide the only route to intimacy and peace. But the latter group sees only loss. . . . The patriarchalists' world view, shared by women as well as men, is battling the emerging egalitarian world view, which is also shared by people of both sexes.[10]

After nearly fifteen years as a teacher and chaplain on a college campus, my husband returned to school and obtained his credentials as a licensed psychotherapist. Today, in a private counseling practice, he has a particular sensitivity to helping couples face the changes that are inevitable in the life of souls and relationships.

That's how it turned out in the end, but in the first months after my return from California, we experienced doubt and tension. I woke every day to uncertainty about my marriage. We found ourselves standing at the site of a leveled relationship, one we ourselves had purposely collapsed from top to bottom like those old buildings that explosive experts bring down in a cloud of dust and applause in order to make way for new construction.

A marriage or any relationship between partners is meant to be created and then re-created. It is an edifice a couple builds until the day the edifice can no longer hold them and they must bring it down and start again from scratch. And without any of the old assumptions. It's exactly like Carolyn Heilbrun says, all good marriages are remarriages.[11]

Psychologist Jean Baker Miller, who has done extensive research on women's development, has written about "a growth-fostering relationship" as having five characteristics. She says that in the relationship:

1. Each person feels a greater sense of zest (vitality, energy).
2. Each person feels more able to act and does act.
3. Each person has a more accurate picture of herself or himself and the other person.
4. Each person feels a greater sense of worth.
5. Each person feels more connected to the other person and a greater motivation for connections with other people beyond those in the specific relationship.[12]

Though it was slow, hazardous, and often exasperating work, Sandy and I worked to undo the old marriage and create a new one stripped of the old dependencies and patriarchal set-up, a growth-inducing relationship that offered each of us freedom to choose and be, that not only allowed for but enhanced the soul in each of us.

A Ritual of Intention

The April following my trip to California, I went on an overnight speaking trip and invited my friend Betty to come along. I was eager for time to talk. We spent a lot of the trip sharing stories and mulling over the growing feminist consciousness we were both experiencing, wondering how to create a spiritual path that would allow for it.

As we were driving home, the top down on Betty's convertible and the two of us full of excitement about our discussions, we approached a lake and she suddenly pulled the car off the road. The sun was about to set, and a sheet of burned light stretched across its surface. "We've talked for two days. It's time to *do* something about all this," she said.

We decided we would create an impromptu ritual. Right there, on the spot. Two long-stemmed red roses lay on the seat between us, a gift from someone who'd come to hear me speak, and in Betty's purse we found a vial of perfume. They were the only ritual objects we could come up with. We carried them down a slope of trees to the edge of the lake.

Standing there in our heels and dress-up clothes, without any particular idea about how it would unfold, we spoke of our need and desire to know and relate to a Power of Being that was feminine in essence, to graft back what had been excised and absent from our spiritual lives. We asked the Feminine Divine to welcome us as her own. To guide us. To bless our launching.

We sprinkled the perfume on the water and tossed the roses onto the lake. We did this in silence, then watched the roses float across the water, moving farther than we would have imagined. In that act, we ritualized our intention to cast ourselves upon a new life, to cross to a new shore.

As we returned to the car and drove on, I felt almost buoyant. I remember thinking that I would ever after mark that event along with the one at Mercy Center as the advent of Her into my life.

It was my first creation of ritual. And now, after so many other creations, I still cannot understand how they are able to alter my consciousness in such remarkable ways. I don't really try. I am glad to let certain mysteries be mysteries. I simply know that rituals performed consciously can be powerful catalysts of change. They can be moments of integration, making something suddenly clear, making us stronger inside, opening up unknown places within us and imbuing new meaning.

CROSSING THE THRESHOLD

A couple weeks later Betty and I were driving together once again, this time through the low country of South Carolina, when we happened upon a sign that said "Springbank Retreat Center." I was on my way to another speaking engagement but had some extra time, so we turned off the main road and wound back into solitary woodlands, a land of gnarled oaks draped with floating moss. We stopped before a two-story white columned house.

I looked at Betty. She looked at me. Our eyes said, "What have we found?"

A Catholic sister met us at the door, introduced herself as Kathleen, and happily showed us around. Once a plantation during the Civil War, the place was now a center for spiritual retreat run by a small group of sisters. They had created an open, safe space that embraced the creation spirituality of theologian Matthew Fox and honored feminine and Native American spiritualities, ecology, and contemplation.

Already I had the inscrutable sense that something purposeful had guided us here. Then Kathleen led us into the chapel. There in a soulful moment I came face to face with the identical picture I'd encountered in California, the *Cartoon of St. Anne*.

I gazed at it with the same electric hum running through my body that I'd felt before, the same magnetic pull. I was filled with awe at happening upon a synchronicity such as this. Synchronicities, those times when an outer event resonates mysteriously and powerfully with what's happening inside, are more numerous during great shifts and upheavals. If we pay attention, if we approach them as symbolic and revelatory, they will often illumine a way for us.

Coming upon the *Cartoon of St. Anne* a second time suggested many things to me, not the least of which was that this place would become deeply significant to me. Perhaps here I would begin to find my way into the space of the Great Lap.

And so it happened.

Three months later, in July, Betty and I returned to Springbank for a weekend stay. On Saturday morning, despite a muggy heat, we followed a trail through Springbank's fifty-eight acres of woods.

After twenty minutes or so, we entered a clearing. It did not take but a second to realize that we were standing in a circle of trees.

Another synchronicity, but one that startled me far more than the picture. Here was the symbolic circle I'd happened upon on the airplane, the circle I'd sketched, imagined, dreamed about, and looked to as a guiding image of the feminine ground.

The circle was formed by pine, dogwood, magnolia, small oaks, and scrubs, the clearing inside thirty or so yards in diameter with a small fire pit dug in the center.

I walked around the circle, touching the tree trunks as the circle and the Great Lap became one and the same. Far from churches, prayer books, sermons, and theological propositions, I felt intimately embraced by nature.

The circle touched Betty in an equally strong way, and we sat within it on the ground. There were only two seeming blemishes in the entire clearing, two small unsightly stumps. They need to go, we agreed, and before we had really thought about it, we were on our way back for tools.

Much of the afternoon we spent digging up the stumps. It turned out to be harder than we had anticipated. The roots went deep. As I worked, I became aware of anger, the anger at patriarchy that wants to come like a purifying blaze. I felt it with every swing of the ax and jab of the shovel.

It wasn't until we'd finally wrestled the stumps out of the ground, refilled the holes, and sat down to rest that we fully realized the symbolism of what we'd done. We'd ritualized digging up the dead, stunted tree—the old way, the old model, the patriarchal stump. We were getting rid of it, releasing anger, transforming it into something creative. We were reclaiming the feminine ground.

The space began to feel like ours somehow. We looked around, glad to be rid of the stumps, but something seemed to be missing.

We found a large white stone, rolled it through the woods, and placed it at one edge of the circle. We dug up soft emerald moss and planted it around the stone. Then we stood back and looked at it. We had built an altar.

Dancing by Night

That night we entered the woods again, following the trail by flashlight. At night the woods was a ceremony of sounds; crickets, tree frogs, and night birds all joined in a chorus of song, outrageously loud. I had never done anything like this in my life, and I kept thinking how strange it would appear—two grown and proper women picking their way through the woods at night in search of—what? But at the same time I was compelled, almost as if some ancient homing instinct inside had been activated and was pulling me along.

We found the circle of trees easily enough, having marked the trail earlier that afternoon. After building a fire, we sat and watched the light leap around the trees. I looked up at the ring of sky, at the moon, full and bulging, and I felt an exuberant, cage-rattling energy rise inside, something feminine, primal, free.

Like the women on the beach two years earlier, we began to dance. I moved slowly around the circle of trees, around the fire, past the altar of stone and moss, then faster until my bare feet were pounding the ground. *Thump, thump, thump.* The sound landed in the silence with an untamed energy that was new to me but also recognizable and right, like feet staking out their ground, announcing their existence, stomping out of exile and coming home.

Later I would be surprised at our lack of inhibition, but then it seemed the most natural, the most necessary thing in the world, this dancing. We didn't stop to analyze what we were doing, and when an owl lifted from a low branch, beating her wings over our heads, it seemed to us like some sort of blessing.

We danced, danced, danced, while the fire sank to embers, until we were nearly breathless and I had wrung open all the cages inside and set myself free.

Is there a feeling more gleeful than opening a cage and setting something captured free? I was reminded of the time I stayed at a bed-and-breakfast owned by a retired couple. One morning as I strolled in the backyard gardens, I saw the man checking wire cages the size of shoe boxes, which were tucked discreetly among the shrubs. Most of them, I noticed, were filled with squirrels. I watched, horrified, as he carried the cages to the backyard pool, lowered them one by one into the water, and left them there until the squirrels' frantic little bodies stopped scrambling and they drowned. Then he disposed of the bodies and reset the traps.

That evening when the man had left to go to church (that's right, church!), I went all about the yard throwing open the cages and feeling the most delicious sense of glee as the squirrels shot out and up the trees, making riotous leaps through the branches.

I believe most women have inside us one of those figures who goes around laying discreet traps, trying to cage, restrict, and drown the spirited, natural parts of us, the parts that go leaping through life. And it is a good thing, a holy thing even, to circle around by stealth, if necessary, and set them free again.

That night in the woods I felt a little like those squirrels must have felt as they reveled among the trees with their freedom. Something lost and caged was returning to me—the unrestrained and essential woman I'd lost by becoming a daughter of patriarchy. I realized this free and dancing woman was the one I'd been asked to birth that day at the monastery when I sat on the nest of yellow leaves. Now here she was emerging.

A mist of rain began, but we danced on. Finally we plopped down laughing, satiated, prodding the fire, which was now sodden. I could never remember feeling so vibrant and alive.

That night in my dreams I was once again back in the circle of trees. Two red snakes crawled to my feet. I wanted to run at first, but I stood still, sensing they had a beneficent, sacred quality. They stared into my eyes and almost seemed to smile. I felt my heart grow warm beneath my breast, and reaching down I picked them up, one in each hand, and lifted them over my head.

When I woke, my thought was that I was finally being reunited with the snake in myself—that lost and defiled symbol of feminine instinct. (Weeks later, however, I would come upon an even deeper layer of meaning in the dream.)

Before leaving Springbank, Betty and I walked back to the circle in the woods. Standing there in the clear light of morning, I knew I'd crossed a threshold.

A woman's initiation includes many moments of crossing a threshold. This threshold is the bridge to our feminine soul, and crossing over is the beginning of becoming. By crossing it we are moving into a new landscape of feminine consciousness, one in which we feel regenerated or expanded as women.

There are many ways to cross the threshold. One woman I know made a pilgrimage to the ruins of a prepatriarchal culture. Another met with a group of women who came together and told the truth about their lives as women. One woman told me she crossed a threshold when another woman embraced her as she wept. "It was," she explained to me, "like I was being held by Mother Goddess herself. I have not been the same since."

And that is really the telling thing. When a woman crosses a threshold, she knows that something inside her has shifted, if only slightly. She knows that she is on a different trajectory.

A GUIDING FEMININE MYTH

My experiences over the year—the trip to California, moments of descent, loss, grief, fear, the struggle to blend marriage and journey, the magnetic pull to the Divine Feminine, crossing the threshold in the woods—all left me with a strong desire to find a space where my journey could unfold in the midst of a wise, guiding presence. In September I crossed another threshold when I entered Jungian analysis with a woman analyst. It ushered me into another circle of trees.

I had just started analysis when a compelling cache of images turned up in my dreams. Large spiraling labyrinths and a bare-breasted woman with snakes wound up her arms. Being in analysis is occasionally like sleuth work; not only did I spend time amplifying the personal meaning of dream images, but I also sometimes ended up in libraries researching their deeper, more archetypal meanings.

One day at a university library, while researching labyrinths, I found myself at a little desk in the stacks surrounded by books on Minoan Crete.

Until then I'd known practically nothing about Minoan Crete. That day I discovered it was a highly evolved culture that existed in Greece up until around 1450 B.C.E., a culture in which the supreme deity was female and women and feminine values enjoyed high cultural valuing. Scholar Riane Eisler suggests Minoan Crete was the last surviving example of a prepatriarchal society.[13]

The labyrinth was a dominant symbol of Minoan culture, appearing repeatedly and centrally in its art, architecture, stories, and religion. The word *labyrinth* even originated in that culture. I also discovered a picture of two ancient statues of the bare-breasted, flounced-skirted Minoan Goddess, which now reside in the Heraklion museum in Crete. One statue pictures her holding a red snake in each hand, lifting them over her head. The other pictures her with a snake wound up each arm.

I sat a long while marveling, remembering my dreams of labyrinths, the dream of the woman with the snakes wound up her arms, but especially the dream I'd had after dancing in the circle of trees—picking up the two red snakes and lifting them over my head. How had these images gotten into *my* dreams?

My question was answered in Jungian analysis. As Jung showed, our dreams sometimes spring from the collective unconscious, the place that holds collective human history. The images in my dreams were coming from a place inside me that predated patriarchy. With time I would see that the dreams were suggesting that I needed to dig beneath the patriarchal layers within myself and find an earlier ground, a realm of feminine valuing.

A few days after visiting the library, I listened to an audiotape someone had given me that related several Greek myths. One was the myth of Ariadne, who, the storyteller said, was a princess from Minoan Crete. I'd come upon a myth, a sacred narrative set in the Minoan culture.

I once heard author Gertrude Nelson repeat the definition of a myth that her young son had come up with. He said, "A myth is something that is true on the inside but not true on the outside." Like a dream, a myth can paint a true picture of a person's psyche. Myths, however, also reveal a lot about the contents and dynamics of the group mind.

As I began to study the myth of Ariadne, I felt I was discovering a drama that gave symbolic expression to the process going on inside of me and of women in general.

But when we use a myth this way, we need to hear author Charlene Spretnak's caution to delineate between those myths that were created within patriarchy and those that predate it.[14] Myths born in patriarchy offer a limited source of data on women. What they usually tell is how women *react* under patriarchy.

The myth of Ariadne that exists today was created within patriarchy during the seventh century B.C.E., many hundreds of years after the Minoan culture had disintegrated. As such, it reflects how women respond within patriarchy. From my perspective, the story tells how women revolt against patriarchy, and it illumines a process we go through as we make our exit from it. But to fully grasp the significance of this later story, we need to understand the story's earlier layers.

An earlier myth of Ariadne, which predated patriarchy, no doubt flourished during the time of the Minoan culture. We no longer have direct access to this layer of the myth, but we can surmise what the earlier Ariadne looked like. For instance, the original Ariadne was not a mortal princess, as in the later story, but the Goddess herself. The name *Ariadne* means "Most Holy," and she was no doubt revered as the supreme power, the Great Mother whose totem companion was the snake.

She was also known as the Lady of the Labyrinth. As the Great Mother, Ariadne was the source of all that is, and her womb was envisioned as a labyrinth that humans threaded on their journey through life, death, and rebirth. Her role was that of sacred guide, the one who aided persons through the dark, difficult passages.

The Ariadne of the later story is the figure that emerged after patriarchal Greece got through with her. She was demoted, downsized from Goddess to a daughter-princess in her father's kingdom. She went from Ariadne, Holy One, to Ariadne, Daddy's princess.

But even this discrepancy between the two myths has much to teach us. For the same sort of thing has happened to and within women. We have gone through our own demotion in power and status, stripped of the image of the Divine as feminine in our own souls. Growing up in patriarchy, many of us went from embodying feminine wholeness to being good princesses of the cultural father.

My work with the myth, which would continue for a long time, focused mostly on the later story set in patriarchy. I have come to interpret it as a woman's struggle to win her freedom from patriarchy, though I also draw on ideas from the earlier version. As I worked with the myth through that long winter, it gradually became a lens through which I viewed my experience, a "containing" story that not only elaborated and clarified my journey, but also showed me the possibilities in it.

Ariadne and the Old King

We know from the myth that Ariadne was a princess in her father's kingdom. That doesn't seem like a lot of information, but symbolically it tells us all we need to know. It tells us that psychologically and spiritually Ariadne was a good daughter of patriarchy, a "little princess."

In myths the "old king" usually symbolizes the old patriarchal consciousness. As a daughter of the old king, Ariadne is presented as being identified with her roles in patriarchy, as trying to be what it wants and needs her to be. We could say that as a woman Ariadne is asleep.

It was easy to see myself in her—all those sleeping years I'd identified with patriarchy. The myth forced me to go back and consider the ways I'd been a good little princess. It caused me to finally deal with the faces of daughterhood I'd identified in myself, to probe where and how I had lived them out, to understand what had motivated them, and to begin to break their patterns, not just by giving some intellectual assent in my head, but by living out the struggle each day.

The myth does not tell us explicitly what evoked Ariadne's awakening. Perhaps she began to feel the confines of living in her father's palace or to wonder if there was some reality beyond the realm of her father. But most certainly something inside her started to rouse and stir, for soon she would seize her moment and make a dramatic exit.

During this time in her journey a woman begins to receive wake-up calls. She begins to peel away the illusions and come to see and feel her entrapment in patriarchy.

For me the disenchantment had started with the strange slip of tongue when I had introduced myself as Father Sue, which led to uncovering my feminine wound. There was the moment I'd stood to sing "Faith of our Fathers" in church and could not open my mouth, the tears and devastating feeling of betrayal that fell over me. And later a thousand small bombs had gone off in my chest as I read and studied, forming my feminist critique. There had been all these things and so many others.

Theseus Comes

Whatever sets off Ariadne's disenchantment is uncertain, but at her moment of ripening, a new figure appears in the story. The myth says a daring young hero from Athens arrived on the shores of Crete.

"Every myth is *psychologically* symbolic," wrote Joseph Campbell. "Its narratives and images are to be read, therefore, not literally, but as metaphors."[15]

If Ariadne's father, the old king, is the consciousness of patriarchy operating inside her, then Theseus, who comes from a distant land across the water, suggests new ideas and attitudes. He represents Ariadne's freeing energy or the way out of her sleep.

In the story Theseus is a daring adventurer and hero who has come to Crete to liberate Athens from the curse of the old king, King Minos. Theseus's mission is to slay the Minotaur, a half-man, half-bull monster that lives in a labyrinth beneath the palace. Because of an old debt, every seven years King Minos requires Athens to send seven youths to Crete, where they are placed in the labyrinth to feed the Minotaur. By killing the monster, Theseus will defy the old king and liberate Athens from the curse. When Ariadne sees Theseus, she falls in love and devises a way to convince him to take her away with him when he leaves Crete.

Theseus, or the liberating energy in my own life, emerged in part the day I entered the drugstore and saw Ann on her knees before the laughing men. The scene tapped my defiance. That day my intention was consolidated. Theseus also came when I mustered the will to free myself from supporting patriarchy within the church and began to align myself with liberation theologies and ideals. Theseus came when I sat in the den and explained to Sandy that our marriage would have to be undone and redone, that I would be going away. Wherever there is deliverance and release in a woman's life from the oppression of patriarchal consciousness, there is Theseus.

Often, like Ariadne, a woman cannot recognize or contact the heroic, freeing energy in herself. Instead she projects it outward, usually onto a man. Theseus may be a figure she literally falls in love with, someone who can shatter her identification with the old consciousness and help deliver her from it. For some women, especially younger women, Theseus may be a husband, the man who rescued her from the patriarchal father. For other women Theseus may be projected onto some other man—a mentor, lover, counselor, father, someone who rescues her at some level from a patriarchal husband. Or Theseus may come when a woman takes a different job or adopts a dissident cause, or he may be projected onto a new group or a new place—anything that carries an aura of insurgence, opportunity, even destiny, that brings new thoughts and attitudes and undermines her loyalty to the "old king." The projection—as precarious and havoc wreaking as it may sometimes be—becomes a force that acts to free her.

When a woman projects her liberating energy outward, she is acting unconsciously. If she projects it onto a man, she may be unable to initiate real independent action apart from him. She will be dependent on Theseus, not on herself. She cannot see that Theseus embodies her own unconscious potential and desire for freedom and wholeness. The hard moment will come when she needs to withdraw the projection, break the spell it has over her, and own up to what she is doing. She will have to claim the qualities she saw in these external figures as possibilities in herself. She will need to take up her own autonomous life.

The Feminine Labyrinth

During the first few weeks of looking at my life through the lens of this myth, I was trying to determine where, if at all, I presently was in the story. I'd already discovered my Ariadne, Little Princess, self. Theseus had already appeared. Now as I explored the next portion of the story, I knew I'd found the experience I was beginning to undergo. The labyrinth.

Underground, beneath the palace of King Minos, is the labyrinth Theseus must enter in order to kill the Minotaur. Besides the danger of being devoured by the Minotaur, the labyrinth is so dark, vast, and complex that no one who wanders into it can find a way back out.

Ariadne offers to help Theseus return from the maze if he promises to marry her and take her with him when he leaves her father's kingdom. When Theseus agrees, she gives him a ball of thread and tells him to unwind it as he enters the labyrinth and then to follow it back out. In this way Theseus is able to kill the Minotaur and return successfully.

The labyrinth is a centerpiece in Ariadne's story, as it was in the actual Minoan culture. In that ancient time the labyrinth was not the complicated prison of a monster, as it later became in patriarchy, but a symbol of the divine womb. In the earlier, prepatriarchal form of the myth, Ariadne herself is the Goddess whose womb is being threaded. Entering it and returning from it were not a hero's ordeal but a ritual of rebirth.

I discovered that initiation rites in that time often involved threading the spirals of a ritual labyrinth. The initiates moved to the sacred center, where they surrendered to a symbolic death, and then returned through the passage to symbolize their rebirth.

For women on this journey, the movement through the labyrinth means threading the Great Womb of death and rebirth. As a woman moves *into* the labyrinth, she undergoes what Carolyn Heilbrun calls "the marvelous dismantling."[16] She sheds and lets go of the old. She goes through a "dying."

What she is dismantling is the woman who was once asleep in her relationships, her religion, her career, and her inner life, the woman who never questioned any of it but blindly followed prevailing ideas and dictates. She is the woman dependent on the masculine, whose life is composed of adaptable femininity. She is the woman severed from her own true instinct and creativity. She is the woman in collusion with patriarchy. When we enter the labyrinth, these parts of ourselves die little by little.

The solitude and descent I'd experienced at the inn in California had meant moving into the labyrinth, an initial step toward letting the dying take place. But like most initiations, mine would be a slow dying, a long succession of one small death after another as the old identity gradually sloughed off and I let go of the values and attitudes that no longer sustained me within.

Eventually we come to what Jean Shinoda Bolen calls the "core or center of meaning in ourselves, which is the center of the labyrinth."[17] At the *center* of the divine womb we begin to connect again with our feminine soul.

We go to the core many times, in many ways. I had my first taste of the labyrinth's core when I found the circle of trees in the woods and felt myself reclaiming and celebrating feminine ground, discovering for the first time the woman I was (and would be) at soul level.

The movement *back out* symbolizes the process of rebirth. We are taking on a new life, bringing a new consciousness back into the world, bringing more and more of the new woman into being. This was the work that stretched in front of me.

But before I would thread my way back out of the labyrinth, I would go even deeper into its slow, spiraling passages.

Another New Year's Eve came, and I had what could be called a dismantling experience concerning my career. My family and I were staying at a friend's house in the North Carolina mountains. A light snow was falling, dusting the cedars outside the windows. As the new year turned, I settled down before the fireplace, intending to look reflectively over the past year. The year had begun with the poem about the unexplored gorge and had ended with finding myself ensconced in the drama of an inner myth. It had been a year of initiation.

But instead of reflecting on the past year, my thoughts floated over and over to the contract I'd just signed with the inspirational magazine I wrote for. I was feeling uneasy about it.

Lately I'd been feeling a lot more tension between my writing and where my journey was taking me, a growing incongruity between my public image and my inner truth. I poked the fire and watched a swirl of sparks slip up the flue, and I felt suddenly afraid. I was a writer deeply compelled to write out the story of my soul. But when that story collided with religious boundaries, then what? I mean, if I were to write about the demise of patriarchal religion in my life, the anger and feelings of betrayal, my dissidence, my mutiny, the tug to the Feminine Divine, where would I find an audience? There seemed little, if any, room for such writings within the boundaries of existing religion.

In truth, it was far too early to be thinking about writing any of it. Internally I hadn't completely dissolved the old or begun to heal the wounds. I didn't have enough experience, enough cohesion inside, enough of anything. But still the portending tension was there, a small seismic vibration of things to come.

I wondered, Would I have to start over with my writing career? And if I did, what would I do? Because I'd worked at "Christian" and inspirational writing for so long with nice success, it was hard to envision any other writing taking its place.

A terrible voice inside was telling me that I couldn't do any but the old kind of writing. That I'd spent more than a decade building this particular career and public persona and that only an idiot would walk away. It urged me to stay in line and please the powers that be, or I would I drop off the face of the writing world.

I tried to tell myself that I must trust the process I was in: If I lost my career, well, I lost it. But inside, the thought was frightening. That night I dreamed:

I come upon a group of people gathered around a coffin. I wonder who's died. I creep closer, close enough to see that the person in the coffin is me. I am holding an issue of the inspirational magazine with which I'd just signed the contract. And not just any issue, either. I am holding the one with me on the cover.

The dream signaled a small dying inside my labyrinth. I couldn't admit it then, but my career with the magazine, indeed, a career doing the kind of writing I'd been doing in the past, ended right there, though it would be nearly two more years before I would be able to make it official.

This marvelous (and often not-so-marvelous) dismantling actually goes on at two levels—inner and outer. On the outer level it means confronting patriarchal patterns externally within marriage, religion, culture, and career. On the inner level it means confronting the voices of patriarchy you've internalized. Those voices are your own personal Minotaur.

The Minotaur

In the myth the Minotaur, half-man, half-bull, lurks in the underground labyrinth beneath King Minos's palace. In the old religious ceremonies of Crete, the Minotaur represented the spirit of King Minos himself. One of the titles for the king was actually Moon Bull, and it was believed he was personified in the Minotaur.[18]

In the female psyche the Minotaur represents negative, uncivilized (beastly), masculine power—that part of the old king driven underground. In other words, the Minotaur is the bullish, bullying, bulldozing force of patriarchy internalized in the cellar of a woman's psyche. It is a presence that works invisibly, hampering, limiting, driving, even destroying a woman's inner and outer life.

"It is not surprising in a patriarchal society, to find a monster like the Minotaur there at the center of the maze," writes artist Buffie Johnson.[19] I recognized the presence of the Minotaur in my life in the belittling, driving, judging inner voice that could throw me into self-doubt or cause me to retreat. It was the voice inside that said, "You can't do that," the voice that told me I wasn't good enough, pretty enough, smart enough, capable enough. Most recently I'd encountered it as the voice that said if I wasn't doing "Christian writing" I couldn't write at all. It was the voice that censored, silenced, devalued, and criticized, sometimes driving me to higher, impossible standards.

Jungians describe this inner voice in a woman's psyche as the negative animus, the inner masculine that has turned against her. But whether it is called negative animus, internalized patriarchy, or the Minotaur within, women know its power.

Sylvia Plath's diary describes graphic battles with the Minotaur whom she described as an "inner voice," "a demon of negation." He would seize her, saying, "Oh, you can't teach, can't do anything. Can't write. Can't think." He robbed her of confidence, froze her into a "quivering jelly," pressured her to run away from tasks where she would be fallible and flawed. Finally she described how she mobilized herself to battle him:

I cannot ignore this murderous self: it is there. I smell it and feel it. . . . When it says: you shall not sleep, you cannot teach, I shall go on anyway, knocking its nose in. Its biggest weapon is and has been the image of myself as a perfect success: in writing, teaching and living. . . . My demon of negation will tempt me day by day, and I'll fight it, as something other than my essential self, which I am fighting to save.[20]

In the myth Ariadne forms a bond and a plot with Theseus to kill the Minotaur. Likewise, our task is to discover and mobilize the energy inside that will battle and slay the internal Minotaur. It is an essential work of the labyrinth—destroying the brutal power of patriarchy within.

A first step for me was acknowledging that the forces I was up against weren't just "out there." They were also "in me." Women, too, have the impulse toward dominance, aggression, and control, and we use it not just against ourselves, but also in our families and the world at large. Etty Hillesum wrote from a Nazi concentration camp, "Each of us must turn inward and destroy in himself all that he thinks he ought to destroy in others."[21]

Starhawk says the voices from patriarchy, which attack our inherent worth, become internalized as the self-hater. It is the old king, she says, with five faces: the Conqueror, who treats the self and those around us as enemies to be feared and destroyed; the Orderer, who inflicts a rigid control; the Master of Servants, who demands that we deny our own needs and desires to serve others' ends; the Censor, who keeps us silent; and the Judge, who offers to restore value to us in exchange for obedience.[22]

Just let a woman start through the spirals of the labyrinth with a design on ridding herself of the Minotaur, and the self-hating voices will become a cacophony. Threatened, they rise up even stronger in the hope of holding on. They may appear with more frequency or intensity in her dreams, and their voices may harangue her in her conscious thoughts.

I began to have regular visits from a patriarchal figure I called the Bishop, because he often appeared in my dreams in bishop's garb. I know, of course, that most bishops aren't like the figure in my dreams. In fact, one of my friends, a retired Episcopal bishop, is pretty much the opposite of my inner bishop, and I feel a little like apologizing to him and bishops everywhere that my Minotaur took this form. But then dreams have a mind of their own.

The Bishop represented the authoritarian, oppressive, patriarchal voice, a part of myself that thwarted the new woman who wanted to come into being. His message was: Get back in line. And be quiet. In one dream he destroyed some of my writings about my feminist experience—echoes of the bishop of Constantinople, who in 350 C.E. ordered the writings of the poet Sappho burned wherever found, condemning her voice throughout the world.

The Bishop also appeared in various other forms to remind me that *real* authority, divinity, and power were rooted in men, that I was, after all, "just a woman." Understand, this wasn't my *conscious* attitude. Dreams are symbolic expressions of the hidden and half-glimpsed truths that operate in the dark, in our blind spots. They reveal what's unconscious to us but what nevertheless affects our thoughts, feelings, and motives.

It's important to recognize when we are caught by the Bishop's power, when we give in to self-doubt, the impulse to pull back, the scramble to get back in line, to please, to go silent, or to berate ourselves. ("You can't do it. Why try? You aren't capable enough. Stupid woman.") Or, conversely, the bullish need to prove ourselves may rise up so that we drive ourselves. (Strive, work. Harder, harder. Get it perfect, perfect, perfect. Keep fooling 'em.)

Whenever the Bishop came, I tried to bring him to consciousness, where I could challenge his authority and begin to depotentiate his power. I reminded myself that his opinion was not who I was but only an aspect of me—my own negative masculine.

Nevertheless, this kind of work is never quick and easy. After many months, I had a dream that affected me very deeply:

I am shut up in the Bishop's house and feeling terribly ill. I have a desperate need to vomit, and I beg the Bishop for a trash can so I can throw up. He adamantly refuses. I feel that if I don't vomit I will die, and I keep pleading with him, but he is determined to keep me from vomiting.

I woke nauseated, depressed. I came to realize that my urgent necessity to vomit symbolized my need to expel the whole patriarchal ideology that I'd swallowed and that was now making me sick. I had the inexplicable feeling that my feminine soul was somehow at stake, but spiritually, psychologically I could not "throw up." I became full of doubt that I would ever get out of the Bishop's house. I grew discouraged.

My analyst suggested I reenter the dream where it left off, using Jungian active imagination. I was to close my eyes and let the images come without directing them, without conscious choreography.

Once again, I found myself begging for a trash can so I could throw up. But this time as the images played on the screen in my head, I was startled to see myself growing a massive pair of antlers. Of all things, antlers.

I lowered my head and tossed the Bishop across the room, then rammed through the wall of the house. Outside in a nearby woods, while the Bishop's house collapsed on his head, I finally threw up. I relieved myself of all the stuff that had poisoned my insides.

Throwing up while wearing antlers. It was such an odd, ludicrous image, I began to laugh. My depression and doubts left almost immediately. At home, I pulled books off my shelf to see what I could find out about the deer as a symbol. Somehow I was not surprised to find the deer was an animal associated with Artemis, the Greek Goddess of independent women. After this, the Bishop presence became much weaker, his appearances fewer and fewer, until he rarely if ever appeared at all.

I told Sandy about the Bishop and the antlers, and soon after, he presented me with an actual pair of deer antlers that a friend of his had found in the woods. Besides being a wonderful gift, it was a strong sign of his growing support for my journey. I hung the antlers on my wall, a reminder that as women we must sprout the strength to break the power of patriarchy in our inner lives. I wanted to create a ritual to support the work of dismantling patriarchy. When I mentioned the idea to my friend Betty, we decided we would carry out a ritual funeral for patriarchy. We would enact externally what we were trying to do internally.

At Springbank on a winter weekend, we placed a number of objects symbolizing patriarchy in our lives inside a shoe box (coffin) and carried the box to the woods. We dug a small hole and squeezed the box inside, spoke the words we needed to say to lay it to rest, covered the coffin with the dirt, and marked the spot with a stone. Then we had our wake.

The ritual didn't magically end the power of patriarchy in my life, but it did create an intention, a feat for my soul to replicate. Like most rituals, it was an act of leavening that would go on working in me for months, probably even years.

"If we leave our father's house, we have to make ourselves self-reliant," writes Marian Woodman. "Otherwise, we just fall into another father's house."[23] If we don't keep up the work of burying patriarchy, we may climb out of one oppressive situation only to land in another. We may get rid of one facet of the Bishop only to have him show up in another guise, sometimes a far subtler one. He may turn up as a benevolent, kind-faced dictator who gets you back in line, not through bullying, but by his "caring": "Father knows best." But benevolent patriarchy is still patriarchy.

For a woman, slaying the Minotaur is a spiritual work, not only because it brings her redemption and new life, but because in freeing ourselves we help to free the world. Writer Cynthia Eller reminds us, "We need to concentrate upon changing our internal reality, knowing that as the foundations of oppression inside us crumble, external patriarchal reality must give way."[24] Or as Charlene Spretnak writes, "We are building a revolution of the psyche as well as of society."[25]

Following the Inner Thread

On another cold weekend visit to Springbank, I wandered into the woods to plant a handful of spring bulbs in the circle of trees that, even at its winter-barest, was still a mirror of the feminine ground within.

Confronting the Bishop, confronting patriarchal voices that held me hostage to old patterns, had been painful. I was feeling, really feeling, how wounded my feminine life was, how wounded the feminine was.

And feeling, too, the betrayal, the anger, the sense of being a woman homesick for her female soul—homesick at home. I had been struggling with the changes that were sweeping through my life, trying to re-create my marriage, responding to people who wanted to know why I wasn't at church, worrying, feeling torn. Things were a mess.

When you're in the midst of initiation, when your "old" womanhood is dying away, you may think you'll be stuck in the dying place forever. You cannot see beyond it. It is hard to keep moving, to put one foot in front of the other, because they are always landing on some new and unfamiliar plot of ground, and half the time that place is a swamp. For weeks I'd been walking in swamps, feeling lost. I didn't know which way to go next.

So here I was back at the circle of trees with a bag of daffodil bulbs. Hardly anything affirms rebirth to me like daffodil bulbs. Put those seemingly dead, brown lumps in the ground, and they will defy rock, storm, and pestilence to emerge and unfurl themselves.

I dug the holes and placed the bulbs in the ground. Patting the earth over them, I thought about the invisible force inside the bulb, which moves it toward life. And it occurred to me, The thing in the daffodil bulb is in me, too. I knew then the only thing to do was reconnect with the thread that had been tugging me along on this journey and hang on for dear life.

I thought about the thread in the Ariadne story, of Joseph Campbell's words: "That's all you need—an Ariadne thread."[26]

In the myth Ariadne gives Theseus a saving thread to follow into the labyrinth and back out. For a woman, the thread symbolizes the umbilical cord of the Goddess, the life-cord that sustains you as you move through the spirals of the Great Womb. Your Ariadne thread is the thread of your feminine soul, your wisdom and intuition, the voice of your feminine Self. I imagine it spinning out from my solar plexus, ready to guide me.

Thread is closely associated with the idea of destiny or fate. In mythology, one's life thread was spun, measured, and cut by the three Fates.

We each have an inner destiny, one imprinted in the soul. This destiny is contained in us the way a daffodil is contained inside a daffodil bulb. Each of us also possesses a very goal-directed energy that seeks to bring the seed of ourselves to fruition. It pulses inside us, trying to complete who we are uniquely meant to be.

There's even a name for this energy in science: *entelechy.*[27] That, however, is a mouthful, so I simply call it Big Wisdom. This energy is really the wise force that spins the Ariadne thread, wanting to take us toward our fulfillment as women.

Unfortunately, most of us either ignore Big Wisdom or thwart it. The day I planted the bulbs in the circle of trees, I became aware that whenever I'd trusted my truth as a woman and was loyal to it, it had become like a thread in my fingers, unwinding, guiding, taking me where I needed to go. When I denied it and refused to trust, refused to pick up the thread, I became lost, afraid, off-center. Like now.

The way to find your thread again is to be still and remember who you are, to listen to your heart, your inner wisdom, as deeply as you can and then give yourself permission to follow it. If you can't give yourself this permission, then find someone who can. Everybody should have at least one permission giver in her life.

Betty and I have been daring one another into being for years now. Once when we were letting our playful selves come out, we climbed a tree beside a river. One of its huge limbs arched out over the water, and after prodding and encouraging one other, we climbed out onto it and sat there together, watching the river rush beneath us. After a while she looked at me and started laughing. She said, "What we're doing right now captures one of the best parts of our friendship—the way we keep going out on limbs together."

The best female friendships are about encouraging full personhood, giving the other permission to follow her Big Wisdom, even when it means going out on a limb, even when it means her thread takes her away from safe conventionalities.

When I left the circle of trees that day, I had picked my thread back up. I could feel my own thread leading me onto a path all my own, and I knew I would need all the permission I could get in order to follow.

Soon after this, Betty and I decided to ritualize threading the labyrinth. Returning to Springbank on a spring day when the woods were fragrant with wisteria, we unwound several hundred yards of textile thread from a huge spool, laying the thread along the narrow trails in a spiraling fashion so that it eventually led into the circle of trees at the center.

That night we intended to move singly through the woods without flashlights, holding the thread and following it through the darkness.

Navigating a dark, unknown space by thread alone is a lesson in trusting the thread of your own soul. I didn't appreciate what that meant until I stepped alone into the blackness of the woods, reached down, and lifted up the white string, barely perceptible except as a faint trace of silver extending a few feet in front of me.

When we'd first planned the ritual, it had seemed like a good idea, but as I began to feel my way along the path, I kept thinking, How did I get here, doing *this?* It was one of those moments common in feminist spiritual journeys when part of you steps out of the experience and watches it like a shocked observer, the way your mother might watch it, and you wonder how in the name of good sense you got there. But the deeper, knowing part of me was still immersed in the moment, was still thrusting beyond the borders of my known world. I kept walking.

I held on and moved one step at a time, turning when the string turned, knowing that if I abandoned it I would be quite lost. It took nearly an hour of inching my way along the trail before I finally moved into the circle of trees. There the moon poured down and lit the clearing. I moved to the center of it with a sense of coming to the center of myself. Coming to the core.

Betty had already arrived in the circle, having set out some time before me. Together we sat, contemplating what we'd just done.

Across the circle the daffodils were blooming bright.

Rebirth

As I struggled to cling to my thread and go where it took me, inevitable moments of rebirth began to happen.

One took place that same spring as I sat in the blue wing chair in my analyst's solarium, a place I'd been coming to sit for a long while now. That day I told her, "I suppose this new part of me that's coming into being can't go on writing forever in the same way, but it's where my success is, my income. So many people expect this of me. I don't see how I can possibly leave it."

As I said the words, I felt suddenly on the verge of tears. I couldn't imagine turning this way of writing loose, even though I knew deep down my thread was spinning in another direction. I was like a scared, belligerent child on the first day of school, holding onto anything I could to prevent being dragged to my destiny.

She gave me a long, deliberate look. "If you write to please others or write for success or stardom or money, you're writing out of your ego. *When are you going to write out of your Self?*"

I could not answer her. I had never even considered the issue in this light. For a second I almost resented her showing it to me—this clear, true choice.

"You're outgrowing the old way," she said. "You're being asked to create from your feminine soul."

What flickered unbidden through my mind was a desire I'd harbored from the inception of my writing life, the desire to write fiction, something that had always seemed a remote and implausible prospect.

I would have to start over. I would lose so much—speaking engagements, money, safety, security. I felt like Jo in *Little Women* when she realizes that what she is writing is no longer from the purity of her soul and she mutters, "I almost wish I hadn't any conscience, it's so inconvenient!"[28]

Besides, there were no guarantees that if I gave all that up, I could succeed with fiction or any other sort of writing. I was starting to realize that in some ways my career as it was had become my identity, and as such it seemed impossible to shed. "I don't know if I can do it," I told her.

Then, for the first time, I heard a sharp edge enter her voice. She looked at me solemnly, sternly and asked, "Do you have anything to say to your generation of women or not?"

Inside me something gave way and let go. Her words became tiny keys unlocking the place inside where I'd been trapped. It still amazes me how this process works—the key words from the enabling person, coming at the height of our readiness, after we've tried so long to pick the lock ourselves, enter the lock with a resounding click!

Late that same afternoon I took my journal to the patio and wrote:

Why didn't I see this before? That my creative life is my deepest prayer. That I must pray it from my heart, from my soul. Not from my head or my need for security or approval or to gain some sort of repute.

What did she say to me? I must write from the Self. The deep and true place. Not from the ego.

And now, oddly, there is something inside me, something thick, full, and chaotic like water just before it boils. Write your personal story, it tells me. Write your female experience, but go deeper, further. Write unbarred, untethered. Say what you want and need to say. Forget selling the words or pleasing. *Just do it.*

Just do it. The words sound so wise, so simple, even if they are from a Nike ad. But I remember that long before Nike was a shoe company, there was Nike, Goddess of Victory.

There is this other clamoring in me, too. The desire I've carried around but never dared. The thing I thought I could never do. Now here it is. The urge to create characters and stories. The ones that are mine to tell. Fiction, the passion tells me. Fiction.

So my thread is spinning new courses. And my thread, like my dreams, never lies, never leads me astray. Still I cannot stop thinking how brave I will have to be to follow it.

Rebirth was happening slowly in other ways, too.

The Many-Breasted Mother was starting to decay in earnest. I remember an utterly simple moment when I felt her going and something new rising to fill her place.

I was standing in my son's room, putting a stack of clean clothes on top of his dresser. I looked at his high school picture wedged between the old soccer trophies, and I thought—no, I didn't think, I knew: *Their lives are theirs to live. My life is mine to live.*

That's all, just this thought that swept through me and changed my mental landscape. I felt as if I'd been released. I sat on my son's bed just taking it in.

When I stood up, I no longer had that bittersweet need inside that mothers know so well, the one driven by love and nurture gone overboard, that need to bend, spindle, and spread ourselves over the lives of our children as if we are the St. Louis Gateway Arch. I felt it go—the need to oversee and manage all the aspects of their lives. The need to work constantly, relentlessly to make them into happy people and their world into a perfect place. As if they had little steering wheels protruding from their backs and it was my job to drive their lives around, never taking my hands off the wheel for fear they would bump into something, get lost, rear-end things, run a caution light, show up late, miss the destination.

Ultimately I was not responsible for the living of their lives. They were at the helm of their own lives, and I was suddenly willing to let that be— to let them pilot their courses, make their mistakes, learn their lessons, choose their roads, and take on for themselves the job of being human.

Somehow I think this deep release needs to take place before a Many-Breasted Mother can take up her own life fully. Released of the need to oversee, overnurture, and overmanage, a woman's life becomes newly her own.

The demise of my Secondary Partner had been going on for some time now as Sandy and I renovated our marriage. There were many renewals, but I particularly remember one small event that took place that same spring. Betty and I decided to travel to Santa Fe for a week. Just two female friends leaving husbands at home and taking off on vacation. "Spontaneous adventure," we called it.

At an earlier time in our marriage such a trip would not have been considered. Today it seems like such a small thing, but at the time making that choice and carrying it out was an initiation in itself. In a symbolic way it marked the end of an old way of being married and signaled the beginning of a new autonomy. In New Mexico Betty and I hiked mountains, explored gorges, and tramped around in the desert. Left to ourselves, we became downright plucky. In town we bought audacious straw hats, stuck big feathers in them, and wore them everywhere, laughing at our reflections in store windows. I noticed we walked differently in those hats; we went just where we wanted to go, and we went with our chins flung back. We had caught the spirit of belonging to ourselves. And when we got off the plane back home, still wearing those hats, our husbands, who'd come to meet us, looked at us then at each other. "I see you had fun," Sandy said, smiling.

Rather than dilute our relationship, the freedom I was claiming helped solidify it. For in the long run, when a woman breaks out of boxes that have limited her, when she sets her plucky self free and begins to nourish and enrich herself, her relationships are nourished and enriched as well. In fact, Sandy seemed to *like* the woman who climbed mountains and wore the audacious hat.

With that experience more than any other, I felt the crumbling of the old patriarchal foundation our marriage had rested upon in such hidden and subtle ways. Though both of us would always need to compromise, there was no more sacrificing myself, no more revolving around him, no more looking to him for validation, trying to be what I thought he needed me to be. My life, my time, my decisions became newly my own.

The Silent Woman inside began to slowly unmuzzle herself. I first recognized her rebirth when I spoke at a conference for church women.

I planned to give a speech I'd delivered several times before, and the evening before, hunched over a little desk in my guest room, I pulled out my notes and read over them.

This isn't my real voice, I thought. This voice belongs to a woman speaking the father tongue, a woman stifling her deeper truths, a woman interested in being safe and approved of. The real stuff was silenced.

I went to the window and gazed at the grounds of the conference center sloping down to the banks of a river. I was groping around for courage.

I went back to the desk, took a red pen in my hand, and struck out sentences. I wrote furiously between the lines, up the margins, on the back of the paper, writing things that came from my soul, truths I'd never dared, words about women in search of their souls, about the Feminine Divine.

To show you what a grand humor the dream-voice can have, that night I dreamed I was staring at a picture of Nefertiti, the Egyptian queen who was known for her unusually long and beautiful neck. The picture accentuated the elongation of her neck, and I was struck by how unique and magnificent it was. I stretched out my own neck and was startled as it, too, lengthened.

I woke laughing at the image, thinking, Yeah, I'm about to stick my neck out, all right. But it's okay, even beautiful. I broke my silence before five hundred women. Not all of them were happy about that. In fact, a few were so distressed they organized a letter-writing campaign to me and to one of the magazines I wrote for, expressing their anger. Dozens of letters poured in. One suggested that I was a "dangerous woman." *A dangerous woman.* I smile every time I think of it. The writer did not mean it as a compliment, but I took it that way. I remembered the old woman who told me that one day we may all owe our survival to subversive women. Dangerous ones, too, I thought.

I fell into a soup of controversy. I had to swim my way out or sink. At first I felt overwhelmed, lamenting the loss of support and approval. But as the blow wore off, I experienced the freedom and enlargement that comes from unsilencing the feminine soul, from being true to myself.

But perhaps the most vibrant rebirth going on inside me was the transformation of the Church Handmaid. My thread had already lead me away from the religious collective, away from its projections about what a Favored Daughter of the Church ought to do and be. And I was fretting less over what friends and family would think.

I was also beginning to name my own spiritual meaning. Already I had named a myth that could hold a feminine spiritual process, claiming the thing most denied to Church Handmaids—the creation of spiritual myth, symbol, and meaning. But mostly I sensed rebirth as my heart opened wider toward the Divine Feminine presence.

Landing on Naxos

In June Sandy and I flew to London to spend a week. As we were wandering through the National Gallery, we came unexpectedly upon Titian's gargantuan painting of Ariadne on the island of Naxos. The painting portrays the final part of Ariadne's myth, and I played it back in my mind as I gazed at the picture.

Before Theseus had entered the labyrinth, he had promised to take Ariadne with him when he escaped, a promise she'd extracted in exchange for the ball of thread. When the Minotaur has been slain, they flee the realm of King Minos together. Ariadne, defying her father, leaves her old life forever.

They sail to the island of Naxos, where they stop for the night. The next morning, however, when Ariadne wakes she discovers that Theseus has sailed on without her. She is alone in a strange place.

But something dramatic is about to happen, and the painting captures it perfectly. It shows Ariadne standing desolate on the shore, watching Theseus's ship disappear on the horizon. Her hand is reaching out toward the ship, but her head is turned back toward the island as she is startled in midgesture by the sudden arrival of the Greek god Dionysus.

He is leaping from his chariot to console and love her. Ariadne's face registers surprise, her lips parted as if saying, "Oh my! What's this?" It's obvious that the ship receding into the distance is her past and that in turning to meet the gaze of Dionysus, she is meeting her future.

The myth tells us that the two marry and create a deep and lasting love, that Dionysus gives her a crown as a sign of his devotion. She goes on to become leader of the annual sacred dance performed by the maenads, the dancing women who honor Dionysus. Along with him, she becomes enshrined in the Villa of Mysteries at Pompeii as the overseer of women's mysteries, to be known as the wise mentor who initiates women into the feminine journey.

But what did all of this signify in the life and journey of a woman like me? I'd focused mainly on the stages of the myth that lead a woman out of the father-world and through the labyrinth, meditating little on Ariadne's arrival in Naxos. But now, confronted unexpectedly with that part of the story, I went and sat on a nearby bench and tried to sort out the meaning.

I recalled that one of the dangers in leaving the realm of the old king is that in our desperation and pain we will create a savior "out there" because we cannot recognize our own strength, daring, creativity, and power. So if, like Ariadne, we find some external Theseus on whom to project the savior role, we will eventually face a moment of truth.

Theseus's leaving suggested to me that the last of a woman's dependence on male deliverers must be stripped away. She needs to see that the external Theseus is really an extension of the patriarchal father—another male figure upon whom she's dependent.

Theseus's departure forces a woman back completely upon herself. She learns that to become fully reconnected with her feminine soul, the projection must be withdrawn. Now she must set about the business of discovering *within herself* the daring, hero strength she saw in Theseus. In doing this, she renders herself independent of patriarchal values and judgments.

So here is Ariadne on Naxos—abandoned to herself, abandoned to new possibility.

But whatever could the arrival of Dionysus imply for a woman? I got up from the bench and wandered back to the book shop in the National Gallery, where I picked up a book on mythology. I leafed through the index for Dionysus. I was not surprised to find that he was the god of women, a god close to and inclusive of the feminine. One of the animals he was associated with was the snake—often a symbol of the Divine Feminine. Jean Shinoda Bolen indicates that as Dionysus traveled through Greece in his mythological travels, he called women away from their household hearths and looms, liberating them from conventional, narrow roles.[29] He was also the god of dance, joy, creativity, spirit, and wine, the god of ecstasy.

I walked back to the painting. As I looked at the figure of Dionysus, it hit me that, unlike Theseus, who was a mortal man in the myth, Dionysus was an immortal god. In other words, he symbolized an inner figure. He represented something Ariadne must find *within*. As Jungian analyst Nancy Qualls-Corbett points out, at this point in a woman's life, she can begin to appreciate the strength of the god within, who emerges at this crucial point without threatening her budding connection to her feminine nature.[30]

With the arrival of Dionysus, we meet a positive masculine force, one that supports women and the feminine from within, one that helps a woman manifest her new vision and voice in the world. Dionysus, I realized, is the opposite of the Minotaur.[31] When a woman works consciously and diligently to slay her Minotaur, she makes a way for Dionysus to come.

I began to pace around in front of the painting, feeling excited. I realized that the arrival of Dionysus is a momentous time in a woman's life. It is when she knows that she is beginning to find completion and wholeness in herself. And I couldn't help feeling I was on the verge of this step myself.

I remembered that in the myth Ariadne and Dionysus are wed, symbolizing an inner marriage of the positive masculine and the conscious feminine. When these two aspects of ourselves come together within, we arrive at new wholeness, new completion. As C. G. Jung taught, "Wholeness . . . is not achieved by cutting off a portion of one's being, but by integration of the contraries."[32] A woman who finds this integration can assume her own authority as a woman. She becomes a woman with a true feminine center and an inner masculine partner who is supportive and helpful. And no telling what sort of new, creative "children" could be born from such a union, I thought.

My husband had long since wandered off to see the rest of the paintings, and I found him now in a little sea of people in the next room, his head cocked in a funny way as he looked at a picture I couldn't see. Looking at him, I realized that a woman who finds wholeness does not *have* to have an external man in order to be complete. She can choose this, but she is not *dependent* on it for her wholeness. But in the same moment, still staring at him, I also knew that I chose him with all my heart. He was a human man and I was a human woman, and here we were, both of us with all our faults, struggling along, moving on our parallel journeys. I knew I didn't need him to be a Theseus or a Dionysus. He could be what he was.

That day in the museum, it seemed to me that I had at last landed on Naxos. Like Ariadne, I had left the father world and crossed over to a new place. Like her, I had watched the last ship sail, then turned, knowing that it was time to look within. So now what? I wondered if I could begin to find my own positive inner masculine while at the same time forging a connection with my feminine soul and allowing myself to be led by that connection. Could I bring together the deep splits inside, find healing, and tap new creativity? Could I begin the process of assuming my own authority as a woman? What, I wondered, would I discover on *my* Naxos?

Sandy was crossing the room, coming toward me. "The gallery is about to close and you've hardly seen anything," he said.

I smiled.

PART THREE

Grounding

As I go into her, she pierces my
heart. When I have reached her
center, I am weeping openly.
I have known her all my life,
yet she reveals stories to me,
and these stories are revelations
and I am transformed.

Susan Griffin

Until women can visualize
the sacred female they
cannot be whole and
society cannot be whole.

Elinor Gadon

As I left the museum and walked out onto Trafalgar Square, I had the sense that a new season of my journey was beginning. After a year and a half of initiation—moving with the tumultuous rhythms of dying and rebirth—it was time to ground myself in a new feminine place.

You know how you feel when you get off a boat that has been pitching around on the sea and the ground still seems to be moving under your feet? Inwardly I felt like that. I'd traversed a body of experience, riding the roils and swells of change, and while much change still remained, I'd moved through enough initiation that I could begin to anchor myself in the new place where I'd arrived.

I leaned against the massive lion statue in front of the museum while Sandy snapped a picture. Things around us swirled—people hurrying, London traffic jostling around the square, flurries of pigeons taking to the sky. It only heightened my sense of need to become grounded and moored. To meet that need, I knew I needed to sink my roots deep into Sacred Feminine experience, to deepen and fortify my budding relationship with my new female self and the Divine Feminine.

ENCOUNTERING GODDESS

We were driving, Sandy and I, on the "wrong" side of the road through English countryside, which undulated like a quilt of overwashed colors—heather greens, faded blues, browns paling into tan and chalk.

We were on our way from Oxford to Glastonbury when unexpectedly we found ourselves in the village of Avebury, gazing through car windows at a monumental stone circle spread through a sheep field. A circle like Stonehenge, only far larger. "What's this?" I asked, amazed that these megalithic structures had appeared seemingly in the middle of nowhere.

"I have no idea," said Sandy. "Wanna stop?"

I was already pulling on my coat, reaching for the tourist book to see if I could identify the place.

"Listen to this," I said as we pulled into a small parking lot set aside for visitors to the stone circle. "Avebury was a religious center dating back to the third millennium B.C.E. It says here that the arrangement of the stones may have represented the shape of the body of the Goddess."

"Goddess?" asked Sandy. His eyebrows went up. Very high.

"Yes," I said, smiling at the look on his face. "Goddess."

The word no longer caused disquiet for me. My earlier anxiety had derived from the way the word had unfairly been associated with things base and sordid, from the long historical repression and despising of the Divine Feminine, and from the taboos against women seizing the power to name sacred experience from their own perspective. When I understood this and unloaded all that baggage off the word, I was left with a mere word, which pointed to a female Power of Being. But I sensed Sandy's discomfort, so I tried to unpack the word for him, too.

I told him about some of the things I'd been reading for the last six months or so—the work of UCLA archeologist Marija Gimbutas, who'd studied and written about the Goddess-worshiping, earth-centered cultures of prehistory,[1] as well as other books I'd read by female scholars, anthropologists, art historians, and thealogians who were recovering the rich history of Goddess, a history that had been lost or suppressed. And as I talked, I felt again the amazement that first washed over me as I began to discover that for many thousands of years before the rise of the Hebrew religion, in virtually every culture of the world, people worshiped the Supreme Being in the form of a female deity—the Great Goddess.

He seemed open and interested, and so as we walked toward the field with the circle of stones, I told him some particular things I'd learned about her. That she was known as the creator and sustainer of the universe who ruled over the rhythms and forces of nature. That she was all-wise, all-knowing, all-powerful, bringing both birth and death, light and dark. I explained that she was immanent, compassionate, ever-nourishing, associated with earth, fertility, and sexuality, but also a transcendent being who bestowed order, justice, and truth.

"But weren't there a lot of Goddesses?" he asked.

"She certainly had lots of forms and names," I said, and my mind returned to the Minoan Snake Goddess of Crete, represented by a woman holding a snake in each hand—the image I'd discovered through my dreams.

"So what happened to her?" Sandy wanted to know.

We had reached the field and began to walk now along an avenue of wide-spaced stones. I felt very moved inside, being in this place. I thought about his question, about the global phenomenon that had taken place probably beginning in the third millennium B.C.E., some kind of patriarchal revolution that spanned around 2500 years, during which there was a massive shift from female Goddess to male God.

"She disappeared," I said. "In some cases she was conquered, sometimes violently by cultures worshiping a male sky God. Basically she went through a series of demotions, as the male God ascended, until finally she got demoted out of sight. Not only that, but her memory was maligned, distorted, and suppressed. She was hardly mentioned in history books."[2]

We walked on in silence. I was thinking how her passage into oblivion had happened not only historically, but also deep within the psyches and consciousness of human beings. With her disappearance came a sweeping demotion in women's status. Concepts of female inferiority and subordination began to develop in earnest.

Over the last few months, this untaught history had become a lump in my throat, a forgotten piece of my female heart that had begun to beat again. Now here in the stone circle I felt it even more, like a sad, sad sweetness, like a sorrow and a hope melded into one.

The light was soft and dimly fogged as it can be only in England, so that looking at the stones was like gazing through a steamed window. I walked through the field with a weight of longing and love lodged in my chest, like a cumulus cloud ready to burst into rain and thunder after a long drought.

I moved from one stone to another placing my hand flat against their surfaces, the same way I had moved around the circle of trees placing my hand flat against the trunks. One stone had a hollow place with a white votive candle sitting inside it. The candle had been lighted recently, for the wax was still warm.

As Sandy scouted for high ground in order to take a picture, I fished in my purse for the hotel matches I'd picked up as a souvenir, struck one, and lit the candle. A few minutes later, from somewhere a flute began to play. Clear, pure Celtic notes floated in the air behind me. I looked around to see a woman on a knoll about forty yards away, her head weaving as she piped the music.

Other tourists turned and stared. No one seemed to have any idea who she was or why she was there playing the flute, but I knew somehow that she was a woman like myself, a woman with the Sacred Feminine full to bursting in her chest, and that *she* was the one who'd lit the candle earlier.

In the haze-blown light with the notes of the woman's music in the air, the fullness inside me broke. Divine Feminine love came, wiping out all my puny ideas about love in one driving sweep.

Today I remember that event for the radiant mystery it was, how I felt myself embraced by Goddess, how I felt myself in touch with the deepest thing I am. It was the moment when, as playwright and poet Ntozake Shange put it, "i found god in myself / and i loved her / i loved her fiercely."[3]

I could not have distinguished then the difference between discovering the ancient Goddess and discovering Goddess within myself. It was too soon. I knew only that in some deep way I had encountered her.

Sandy walked over, looked at the burning candle, at my eyes full of tears, then at the woman still playing her flute. Later that moment would remind me of a line in the play *Julian,* about the Christian mystic Julian of Norwich: "Though many thought she had lost her wits, I knew that she had found her soul."[4]

WHY A FEMININE FORM FOR THE FORMLESS?

One hot day in July not long after returning from England, I was sitting in my study reading when I came upon this statement by Vanderbilt theologian Sallie McFague: "God is she, he and neither."[5] As I pondered it, the statement brought back what I had always known as true—the genderless, formless nature of the Divine.

I was aware that Jewish and Christian theologians point out that God is genderless. The ultimate ground of being, the Divine One, is neither male nor female. Anne E. Carr says, "No image or symbol is an adequate 'picture' of God."[6] In the Bible God names God, saying, "I am that I am." The Absolute Being simply is. It participates in the form or symbol; it is in or behind the picture, but it always transcends them.

The question then occurred to me: Well, if that's so, if the Divine is ultimately formless and genderless, what's the big deal? Why all this bother?

The bother is because we have no other way of speaking about the Absolute. We *need* forms and images. Without them we have no way of relating to the Divine. Symbol and image create a universal spiritual language. It's the language the soul understands.

And yet—and here was the crux—the images that have pervaded our speech, thought, and feeling about the Divine have told us the Divine is exclusively male. They have told us there is only one form and that form is masculine. Indeed, the image, language, and metaphor of God as male has been used so exclusively, for so long (about five thousand years) that most people seem to believe God really is male.

McFague points out that when only one image is allowed to serve as the grid for speaking about God, it becomes idolatrous. It comes to be viewed not as symbol, but as fact, as an actual description.

I'd read Paul Tillich's work years before and accepted his view that the transcendent always transcends every symbol used to describe it, that a symbol may point to God or participate in the reality of God, but that God cannot be identified as that. Tillich pointed out the tendency of religions to substitute symbols for the divine itself, which he referred to as a tendency toward idolatry.[7]

My friend and mentor Dr. Beatrice Bruteau once described it to me like this: The Absolute Reality, the I Am, can be likened to a dancer. And the forms that the Absolute takes can be likened to the dances. The Absolute, she said, dances many dances, in a variety of movements that are constantly giving way into others. When we see the dance, the dancer takes on expression, shape, immediacy, presence, and meaning for us. We can observe the relationship of the dance to the dancer, and we understand that the choreography is infinite. We cannot look at just one movement or one dance and say, that is the dancer.

That day with these weighty thoughts spinning in my head, I reaffirmed to myself the deep, formless, indescribable nature of the Divine. But I also affirmed the human need for forms, for dances or images that express the Divine. And I realized that if we were going to meet that need without being idolatrous, and do it in an egalitarian and just way, we must recover a Divine Feminine.

So, why a feminine form for the formless?

I sat at my desk, took out my journal, and scrawled that question across the page. Then I tried to unravel, solidify, understand all the tangled reasons why I was doing what I was doing, why it was important to recover the Divine Feminine—not just for me, but for my daughter, my mother, all the women out there.

What reasons were there for recovering her besides the mystery and love she ignited in the female heart, besides all those unsayable reasons that lived in a woman's soul?

I tried to get pragmatic.

First I noted that the lack of a divine female image supported an imbalance in our consciousness that diminished our wholeness as persons. The feminine goes underground in our psyches just as it does in our God. When this happens we exclude, overlook, and undervalue the feminine within ourselves and in the world around us.

Not only that, but as long as we have a divine Father who is able to create without a divine Mother, women's creative acts are viewed as superfluous or secondary. And as long as the feminine is missing in the Divine, men would continue to experience entitlement and women would be prey to self-doubt and disempowerment. It was that simple.

Internalizing the Divine Feminine provides women with the healing affirmation that they are persons in their own right, that they can make choices, that they are worthy and entitled and do not need permission. The internalization of the Sacred Feminine tells us our gender is a valuable and marvelous thing to be. It suggests the "goodness of female sexuality and the equal authority of the experience of women."[8]

As I spilled these thoughts across the pages in my journal, I recalled a story a woman had told about her six-year-old daughter. The child, freshly home from Sunday school, was reporting to her mother what she'd learned that day about God. Over and over she referred to God as "he." Her mother asked, "Why do you say 'he,' Ashley?"

"Because God is a man, Mommy."

"But why is God a man?"

Ashley thought a moment. "I guess because God thought that was the best thing to be."

There's something infinitely sad about little girls who grow up understanding (usually unconsciously) that if God is male, it's because male is the most valuable thing to be. This belief resonates in a thousand hidden ways in their lives. It slowly cripples girl children, and it cripples female adults.

In one of her essays, Nelle Morton wrote, "The Goddess shattered the image of myself as a dependent person and cleared my brain, so I could come into the power that was me all along."[9]

The second thing I wrote down that day was that exclusive male imagery of the Divine not only instilled an imbalance within human consciousness, it legitimized patriarchal power in the culture at large. Here alone is enough reason to recover the Divine Feminine, for there is a real and undeniable connection between the repression of the feminine in our deity and the repression of women. Mary Daly's famous statement had never seemed more true to me: "If God is male, then male is God."[10]

As I pondered other reasons for recovering female images of the Divine, I remembered the biblical claim that humans were made in the image of God. Now since human meant *both* male and female, didn't that mean both male and female should be used when referring to the Divine? It seemed so logical, so simple, so obvious, that it made one wonder, as McFague put it, "what all the fuss is about."

She suggests that the fuss is because Western theology has been infected by a fear of female sexuality. She points out that while sexuality is cloaked in the male metaphor for God, it seems blatant in a female metaphor. We are so familiar with male metaphors and their sexuality has been so masked that when female metaphors appear, they seem overtly sexual by comparison.[11] They register in us as taboo.

The fear of and resistance to feminine images goes deep. I knew that from my own experience with those feelings. I'd spoken to women who could not say the word *Goddess* without whispering, laughing nervously, or looking over their shoulders for the lightning bolt that a jealous Father-God was bound to aim at them for daring such a thing. I'd seen people stomp out of a worship service when prayers were said to Mother-Father God. The fear and resistance were evident, too, in those who refused to consider her at all.

I remembered the time I discussed this fear and resistance with a minister who was genuinely interested in creating inclusiveness in his church. He thought we should forgo recovering Divine Feminine images and move directly toward abstract, androgynous images; we should neuter the language and symbol of the Divine. He said we should use only the word *God,* not *Father* or *he* or *his.*

"But the word *God* does not register in us as neuter," I said. "Technically it may not imply any particular gender, but what registers and functions in the mind is male."

As McFague says, androgynous terms only "conceal androcentric and male assumptions behind the abstraction."[12] How many times had I heard someone say, "God is not male. *He* is spirit"?

The minister looked at me. "Then where does that leave us?"

"I think it leaves us in the position of finding ways to speak of the Divine equally in female as well as male terms," I said.

He looked at me with alarm and dismay as his own ambivalence about the feminine surfaced. "Oh dear," he said.

The "oh dear" reaction is common. It's the uh-oh-what-will-they-think? how-can-it-be-done? questions that surface inside.

But that day in my study, I came to a new sense of the urgency and importance behind it. I felt in my bones how crucial it was, "oh dear" response or not.

When I closed my journal, it seemed as if a gate that had been open only a few inches had suddenly been flung wide. I made a decision. I would not limit my quest. I would go through the gate with what Zen Buddhists call "beginner's mind," the attitude of approaching something with a mind empty and free, ready for anything, open to everything. I wouldn't tell myself things like, "don't think that, don't approach that, don't explore that." I would be Eve opening her eyes on creation for the first time. I would give myself permission to go wherever my quest took me.

And it took me to some pretty surprising places.

THE COMING OF HERSELF

One night soon after this, I had a dream. In it the Goddess was born. Her messengers came like angels of annunciation and told me her name. It was: "Herself."

I woke up thinking, The Goddess, Herself.

It sounds a little odd, I suppose, but that became my name for the Divine Feminine.

Relating to Herself is like having your own personal big bang. She comes with an eruption of consciousness that is like a new universe being born, one that is forever expanding outward. The thing we need to realize, of course, is that the place of expansion is always on the border. On the edge. If we're going to turn from restrictive God-talk and images that confine the Divine to one gender, if we're going to become whole, we have to go to the edge.

Now for the paradox. When we get there, we find it's not the edge at all. No, the edge is still further in the distance. The thing is, you can never overtake the Divine.

For me, Herself was and is primarily an *inner* experience—not "out there," not "back there," but ultimately "in here." I agree with Nelle Morton when she wrote:

When I speak of Goddess I am in no way referring to an entity "out there," who appears miraculously as a fairy godmother and turns the pumpkin into a carriage. I am in no way referring to a Goddess "back there" as if I participate in resurrecting an ancient religion. In the sense that I am woman I see the Goddess in myself.[13]

To embrace Goddess is simply to discover the Divine in yourself as powerfully and vividly feminine. Since the day in the stone circle at Avebury, the Divine Feminine was becoming a presence, an experience, a knowing born deep inside. She was becoming more than a concept in my head—something abstract and separate—or a figure out of the ancient past.

Sogyal Rinpoche, a Tibetan spiritual teacher, says, "We often assume that simply because we understand something intellectually . . . we have actually realized it. This is a great delusion."[14] Women need to understand the Sacred Feminine in our heads, but most of all we need to "realize" her in our souls.

And the moment does come. When we set out to find the integrity of our feminine souls, when we defy and dare and venture beyond prefabricated identities and little cages and patriarchy's dogma into the circle of deep feminine ground, the moment of realizing Goddess Within comes.

Carol P. Christ tells of a moment like that when she heard a still small voice saying, "In God is a woman like yourself," and embracing this truth became the beginning of claiming her female being.[15]

The first time Nelle Morton embraced the female aspect of divinity was in 1972 at the second annual conference on women exploring theology. At that time she had already conceptualized the Feminine Divine, but it was confined mostly to the region of intellect.

She writes about that pivotal day when sixty-five women gathered for worship in the oratory. They sat on cushions on the floor, facing one another. The leader rose and read the passage from Corinthians that says, "If anyone is in Christ, now he is a new creation." But the reader read it this way: "If anyone is in Christ, now *she* is a new creation."

This is what happened to Nelle Morton, in her own words:

I felt hit in the pit of my stomach. It was as if the reader had said, "You are now coming into your full humanity. That which has been programmed out is authentically yours—essentially you." It was as if intimate, infinite, and transcending power had enfolded me, as if great wings had spread themselves around the seated women. . . .

Suddenly I came to, my hand on my stomach, my mouth open. . . . When I looked about me, it seemed many other women were responding as I had. The leader paused. Then one of the women lifted her fist in the air and shouted, "Yeah! Yeah!" All the women followed as the oratory rang with "Yeah! YEAH! YEAH!"

This was the first time I *experienced* a female deity. I had conceptualized one before, but I had not experienced one directly.[16]

Her experience, like mine, suggests that Herself is found not so much in the conceptualization of feminine imagery (though that's very important) as in the act of embracing the one contained within it, in the experience of being relational with her.

After Avebury, I realized that a big part of grounding the inner experience involves recovering external images and symbols that have carried and pointed toward her presence. I wanted to know the ways Herself had been experienced by humans throughout history, to allow those images and symbols to sink in, resonate, enliven, evoke, fortify, and expand the deeps of my female life. So began a passionate work of recovery. I started to repossess the Divine Feminine presence within the Christian tradition as well as in the lost history of the ancient Goddess.

Herself as Ancient Goddess

Several years after this period of discovery, during my trip to Crete, the other women and I walked among the ruins of an ancient Minoan town known today as Gournia. Crete was one of the last places on earth where the Great Goddess flourished, and we wandered up the hill, seeking the remains of a religious sanctuary where once women had come to worship her. They'd come bringing offerings of fruit and grain, leaving them on a special altar called a *kernos* stone. Now, thirty-five hundred years later, we were planning to do the same thing.

We found the courtyard leading to the ancient sanctuary, and with our hands overflowing with grapes, pears, lemons, seeds, nuts, and beans, we began a procession across it to the kernos stone. According to our guidebook, the stone was supposed to be just west of the courtyard, beside some steps. It would be easily distinguishable by the thirty-two time-worn receptacles carved around the edge of the stone to receive offerings. We came to the steps and gathered around an impressive stone located in the spot the map indicated. Only it was not the kernos stone.

We spread out, inspecting stones, searching for the lost altar. Ten minutes passed, fifteen, twenty. Still no altar. Finally another woman and I found it—a small, unlikely looking rock surrounded by weeds but bearing the thirty-two receptacles.

As we gathered around it, I couldn't help but think how metaphoric the episode had been. There we were, fifteen women searching for an altar to the Goddess lost among the ruins of history and neglect. And it struck me: I'd had to find my inner connection to the Sacred Feminine the same way. I'd had to put orthodox guidebooks aside and set out on my own. I'd had to reclaim those lost, ancient altars in order to find my way.

Standing in a circle around the lost altar stone, we brushed away the dust, then adorned it with our offerings, pouring wine, milk, and honey into its crevices. By participating, I seemed to be reclaiming more than that one altar; I was retrieving a consciousness that had been lost, one in which women had the right to define for ourselves what is sacred, one that connected me to my deepest self, other women, the earth, and the Sacred Feminine embodied within them all.[17]

This retrieval, though, had really begun for me the summer I dreamed of Herself and began to search for her within ancient Goddess history.

That July Betty and I traveled to New Mexico, where we visited friend and artist Meinrad Craighead, who painted magnificent images of the Divine Mother. We sat one afternoon in her studio talking and looking at her new paintings. One painting, portraying a woman in a red-hooded cloak positioned between two owls, caught my eye. I studied the woman's face, the labyrinth in her belly, feeling drawn to the image in the same way I was drawn to the *Cartoon of St. Anne.* The painting was called *Hagia Sophia.*

Meinrad's studio had seven altars, which seemed to me like tiny windows into her soul, a soul deeply grounded in the Divine Feminine. As I looked from altar to altar, I felt the desire to create my own sacred space.

Back home, I hung a shelf on a wall of my study. It stayed empty while I waited, not sure what to place on it. I figured I would know when the time came.

I came to know a few months later, once again traveling, this time in San Francisco. In the area to speak at a writer's conference, I took time out to visit the Archives for Research in Archetypal Symbolism at the Jung Institute.

The assistant curator casually told me about the tens of thousands of slides they had on file—mythological and symbolic images from around the world and every epoch of history. He gestured toward a wall of file drawers, then opened one at random. He pulled out a slide and dropped it into a small viewing screen. I was looking at the Minoan Snake Goddess of Crete. Out of thirty thousand or so slides. Here she was again, the figure I'd dreamed about and later discovered as I researched the myth of Ariadne, the figure I'd come across often as I read Goddess history.

Herself, I thought.

Merlin Stone's provocative line, "At the very dawn of religion, God was a woman. Do you remember?"[18] flickered through my mind and sent an electric shudder through me. As I stared at the image, down deep some part of me did remember. I felt the same connection and love I'd felt at Avebury. Only now I understood that what I was experiencing was the recognition and presence of Goddess Within.

When fall came, I stumbled upon a museum catalog that offered lovely replicas of the Minoan Goddess and ordered one.

Over the next few months I went on remembering her. I explored many of her ancient images, but I wasn't interested in worshiping neolithic figures. I was, however, immensely interested in relating to them as transmitters of possibility.

I grew compelled by the consciousness *behind* these ancient Goddess images, a consciousness in which the Divine was imaged in feminine form, in which women were honored as equals, and in which earth and nature were sacred. Indeed, the more I reached back into Goddess history, the more a portal opened through which I could retrieve it.

It's not that I felt we should go backward in history to a bygone time and live out the old matriarchal consciousness as it was then. The ancient Goddess cultures were probably not utopia, but still they appear to have been remarkably egalitarian and nonviolent. The feminine was honored, sexuality was sacred, and the cultures apparently supported no splits between nature and spirit.

The images of Goddess reflect this consciousness. They reveal to us what we've excised from our lives today. I didn't want to toss aside the evolutionary progress we'd achieved or the masculine symbols of God. Rather, I wanted to wed them with lost feminine dimensions, whose origins and promise lay unclaimed in antiquity.

Reclaiming the ancient feminine consciousness as a model of what's possible, integrating it into the world as it is now evolving, and balancing it with masculine symbol, image, and power together allow us to go forward and create an utterly new consciousness, one large enough and strong enough to carry us into the future.

Perhaps one of the most important things I learned as I explored the ancient Goddess and retrieved this consciousness was that these Divine Female images reflected the *wholeness* of divinity. This was a new and explosive realization—that the fullness of deity can rest in a single female form.

Theologian Elizabeth A. Johnson clarifies this immensely important point. She presents three distinct approaches frequently taken as we seek to recover the Sacred Feminine:

One seeks to give "feminine" qualities to God who is still nevertheless imagined predominantly as a male person. Another purports to uncover a "feminine" dimension in God, often finding this realized in the third person of the Trinity, the Holy Spirit. A third seeks speech about God in which the fullness of female humanity as well as of male humanity and cosmic reality may serve as divine symbol, in equivalent ways.[19]

My approach became the third way. My aim wasn't helping Yahweh get in touch with his "feminine side." I wasn't interested in merely identifying one aspect of the Trinity as feminine. When we stop there, inevitably the feminine aspect ends up secondary and subordinate, acting in the same "limited roles in which females are allowed to act in the patriarchal social order."[20]

I was interested in a balance, which meant envisioning female image, form, and symbol that could contain the *fullness of divinity,* just as there were male image, form, and symbol that contained the fullness of divinity.

As I recovered ancient Goddess images, I saw that Herself encompassed *all* divine activities, not just ones typically stereotyped as feminine. In other words, she should not just be relegated passive and nur-turing qualities, but active and powerful ones. She would not only be associated with earth and sexuality, but with order and justice as well.

The replica of the Minoan Goddess, which I'd ordered, arrived a few days before Christmas, having come all the way from Greece. I opened the box, dug through the straw, and found an exquisite statue cast in plaster and hand-painted in delicate earth tones. Twelve inches tall, she wore a flounced skirt, the bodice open in the ancient Cretan style, ex-posing her life-giving breasts. On her head sat a cat, and in her upraised hands she held two red snakes, all symbols of the feminine.

With Christmas near I placed her on my altar. Her coming was a dif-ferent kind of nativity.

Herself as Sophia

As I had explored the ancient Goddess that autumn, I had also begun a quest for the Sacred Feminine within the Christian tradition. I was aware of feminine allusions to God in the Bible, so I began there, exploring an array of lost and suppressed feminine references.

I was especially intrigued with the phrase *El Shaddai,* an interesting name for God that occurs forty-eight times in the Bible. It has been traditionally translated as "the almighty" or, more exactly, "God of the mountain." But *shad* is also a Hebrew word for breast. The ending *ai* is an old feminine ending, therefore a probable ancient meaning of El Shaddai was "the breasted one." God, the breasted one.

There were also uncounted references to God's compassionate, merci-ful, tender qualities. Rosemary Radford Ruether reminds us, "The root word for the idea of compassion or mercy in Hebrew is *rechem,* or womb. In ascribing these qualities to Yahweh, Hebrew thought suggested that God has maternal or 'womblike' qualities."[21]

We've lost the idea of God having a womb, yet now with deep rifts exploding between cultures and races and in other groups, the recogni-tion that all of us originate from a common womb brings forth a new vision of kinship. Suddenly we are, every one of us, close relatives.

I spent many evenings that fall recording numerous feminine refer-ences in the Bible, struck by how many of them incorporated bird imagery: God as a mother bird, caring for her young, or a mother eagle watching over her nest. Even Jesus refers to himself as a mother bird in Matthew, and later in Christianity Christ appeared in images as a mother pelican tearing at her breast in order to feed her young.

Yet it was interesting how a lot of the female imagery—and there really was a lot of it buried and camouflaged in the language—became obscured in translation. For example, in Deuteronomy 32:18 the Revised Standard Version reads, "You forgot the God who gave you birth." But actually the words in the verse about giving birth are the Hebrew words for "writhing in labor," which makes "giving birth" a remarkably subdued translation. Even more interesting, the Jerusalem Bible translates the verse "You forgot the God who fathered you."

I began to wish for a thawing of the divine symbol so it could take on new life and connotations. So many of the symbols within Christianity became frozen at some point, after which they no longer allowed users to participate in the Divine in new ways.

By unfreezing the symbols, we could, for instance, draw on women's experience and think of baptismal waters as uterine waters or approach the Eucharist through the imagery of breastfeeding to emphasize the intimacy and nurture between the Divine and her children. We could take the unique, secret-sharing, heart-to-heart epoxy bond of soul-sisters to explore the covenant of attachment between humans and Divine. The possibilities go on and on.

All in all, I found the feminine references in scripture interesting and hopeful, but I wanted to know: Is there a primary Female Ground of Being within the Jewish and Christian traditions, a Divine Feminine in whom rests the fullness of divinity? And if so, what happened to her?

This is a hard question. But as women we have a right to ask the hard questions. The only way I have ever understood, broken free, emerged, healed, forgiven, flourished, and grown powerful is by asking the hardest questions and then living into the answers through opening up to my own terror and transmuting it into creativity. I have gotten nowhere by retreating into hand-me-down sureties or resisting the tensions that truth ignited.

I knew that if I asked this hard question of Jewish and Christian traditions, I might find a complete absence of her. And if I did find there had been a Feminine Divine presence, I would still have to live with the reality that she wasn't there now.

My search went on until the spring, days and evenings of study and questions and probing. Here's an abbreviated and simplified account of what I found over those months.

Starting with the Hebrew tradition and the Old Testament, I found that the term for the spirit of God or Holy Spirit is a feminine term. It is the word *ruah,* and it occurs 378 times. Many times *ruah* is used to refer to the life of God or the essence through which the Divine acts. It is this transcendent spirit of God that eventually came to be known as Wisdom, referred to in Old Testament scripture by the feminine term, *hokhmah.* But the fascinating thing is that *hokhmah* or Wisdom is not merely a concept but is personified as a woman.

Over and over in the Bible and in Jewish wisdom literature, Wisdom is spoken of in Godlike ways. She's portrayed as an entity, persona, or manifestation of God, one who was brought forth from God before creation. Preexistent with God, she participated in creating the world. She is said to order all things as well as to permeate or inspirit all things. She is referred to as a teacher, a lover, at one with trees and plants. She is the one who mediates God's love and work in the world. She guides and reveals God's will. For example, she is the one who guided Noah through the flood and led the children of Israel through the Red Sea.

She is said to knock inwardly at the door of the human soul or "hover outwardly" in the beauty of the natural world, awaiting acceptance. She is referred to as a tree of life and her fruit as that which satisfies. Other references to her are as the breath of the power of God, a reflection of eternal light, and one who renews all things. In Luke 7:35 Jesus implies that he and John the Baptist are Wisdom's children.[22]

In the Old Testament, Wisdom says of herself:

> The Lord created me at the beginning of his work,
> the first of his acts of old,
> Ages ago I was set up,
> at the first, before the beginning of the earth.
> When he established the heavens, I was there.
> When he marked out the foundations of the earth,
> then I was beside him, like a master workman;
> and I was daily his delight.[23]

Her importance is obvious. Theologian Elisabeth Schüssler Fiorenza has suggested that Wisdom is the God of Israel expressed in language and imagery of Goddess. C. G. Jung referred to her as "God's self-reflection."[24] Indeed, if you highlighted all the references to her acts in the Bible, they would far exceed references to the Old Testament giants we are so familiar with—Abraham, Isaac, Jacob, Moses, Isaiah.

Yet we have scarcely heard of her.

When Christianity came along, Wisdom was not completely lost, though specific references to her in the New Testament are far less frequent. There she's referred to by the Greek word *Sophia*.

In 1 Corinthians 1:23–24, 30, and 2:6–8, the Greek rendering of Paul's words spells out something so remarkable it astonishes me that we've not recognized it more fully. The text says boldly that Sophia became the Christ. Intimations of this idea are also sprinkled elsewhere throughout the New Testament.

John's description of Jesus as the Word or *Logos* corresponds in dramatic and pointed ways with descriptions of Sophia or Wisdom in the Old Testament. Biblical scholars recognize that while John 1:1–4 and other descriptive passages may not be using the name *Sophia*, they do seem to be referring to her. For some reason the writer substitutes the male term *Logos* for *Sophia*. But by comparing the texts, one can see that the figure being described is indeed Wisdom from Hebrew scriptures.

Logos and Sophia were perceived as interchangeable because they played the same role; both are portrayed as coexistent with God before creation, as reconciling of humanity to God, as revealing the will of God, and as God's immanent presence in the world.

It was by now January, and the little altar in my study was becoming a sturdy presence, a place to go and remember the Divine as feminine and myself as woman, a place to encounter sacred depths and have the breath blown into my feminine sails. Herself was represented there as the Minoan Goddess; now I wanted her there as Sophia, too. I thought of a simple brass figure of Christ that I'd bought years before at a monastery gift shop. I found the Christ-figure, the Jesus-Sophia, and placed it on my altar.

Each time I gazed at it, I wondered why Sophia had been nearly deleted from the Christian tradition. Why the substitution of *Logos* for *Sophia?* Many Christian feminists believe it is because of the Gnostic controversy that was going on in the early churches during the time the Christian scriptures were being written.

The Gnostics were a formidable faction of Christianity that flourished the first couple of centuries after Jesus but were eventually surmounted by what came to be the orthodox Christian tradition. The Gnostics didn't fully acknowledge Jesus' humanity and death. They believed it was the *knowledge* or *gnosis* of Jesus' message that saved humanity, not the crucifixion. To them he was a divine redeemer, not one who came to suffer and die.

The opposing group, the form of Christianity that came to be canonized into the New Testament, embraced Jesus' humanity and believed it was his death that was saving. By the second century, a severe fissure had developed between the two groups.

The deletion of Sophia from Christian tradition arose because Gnostics recognized and proclaimed Jesus as Sophia. "In this historical situation proclaiming Jesus as Sophia was tantamount to accepting the Gnostic stance against Jesus' humanity and crucifixion."[25] So naturally, the churches who came to be represented in the New Testament, not wanting to appear to align themselves with Gnosticism, referred to Sophia only in the most muted ways. It must have been an odd dilemma for them. The churches wanted and needed to recognize how important Sophia was in developing their understanding of Jesus. For as many have pointed out, it's unlikely they could have taken the Jewish messianic figure and developed their Christology without her.[26] But the churches were also forced to steer clear of Sophia directly for fear of colluding with the Gnostics.

And, too, it may be that Sophia was sidestepped for plain old patriarchal reasons, as a way of shoring up male power. Whatever it was, her absence was sealed.

Sometimes in the evenings as I sat curled up in my chair with my books, my children would ask, "What are you reading about?" and I would tell them about the feminine references to God. Their eyes would widen a little, especially Ann's. She grew eager to hear about the things I was discovering.

One night when she asked, "What are you reading about tonight?" I told her about Sophia.

"Really?" she said.

"Really," I told her.

She came and sat cross-legged on the floor by my chair and said, "Tell me everything about her." And I could almost see in her face the way it affected her sense of her female self. The fears and concerns I'd had earlier about how my journey would affect my children were long gone.

I was learning that when it came to the children, I simply needed to pursue my journey in an open, quiet way. When the moment arose naturally, I mentioned my new awareness about things, but I tried never to push it onto them, to struggle to get their approval, or to insist they embrace my views. And most important, I realized I must not contaminate them with my own anger. I let them know that patriarchy and the suppression of the feminine caused me angry feelings, but I tried not to spew that emotion around or say things that would color their own religious experience. More and more I was learning that they were on spiritual journeys of their own, and I could trust them to pursue those journeys in their own ways.

Sophia, however, was not the only reference to a Sacred Feminine presence within early Christianity. Other female imagery for the divine existed, but unfortunately it, too, was located within the Gnostic Christian communities. We might never have known about it if it hadn't been for a group of ancient manuscripts—gospels written in the fourth century—that were discovered in an earthen jar in 1945 at the base of some cliffs in Egypt. A stunning discovery, the manuscripts contained forty previously unknown works from the Christian Gnostic tradition. The texts, which had circulated as early scripture, gradually came to be attacked as early as 150 C.E. and were not accepted into the canon, or the orthodox Bible.

It wasn't until the late sixties and early seventies that copies of the Gnostic writings became available to the West. Elaine Pagels at Princeton, one of the scholars who translated them into English, says that the main thing distinguishing the Gnostic gospels from the orthodox gospels is their abundance of powerful feminine imagery of the Divine.[27]

They reveal that many early Christians described and worshiped God as dyad, a being consisting of both masculine and feminine elements. They prayed to both the divine Father and the divine Mother—to Mother-Father. One of their prayers, still intact, begins, "From thee, Father, and through Thee, Mother, the two immortal names, Parents of the divine being."[28]

The Gnostic gospels also referred to the Holy Spirit as female. The *Secret Book of John,* for example (one of the gospels that was rejected from the list of books that were to comprise the New Testament), describes a vision John had after the crucifixion:

As I was grieving . . . a unity in three forms appeared to me, and I marvelled: how can a unity have three forms? . . . It said to me, "John, why do you doubt . . . ? I am the One who is with you always: I am the Father; I am the Mother; I am the Son."[29]

In other Gnostic books, the Gospel to the Hebrews and the Gospel of Thomas, which also were not included in the New Testament, Jesus himself speaks of "my Mother, the Spirit" and compares his earthly father, Joseph, to his divine Father of Truth and his earthly mother, Mary, to his divine Mother, the Holy Spirit.[30]

Later a number of Christian mystics, like Julian of Norwich, Jacob Boehme, and others, drew on the Gnostic tradition in their development of God as Divine Mother. Boehme particularly recovered the idea of Sophia as the female aspect who existed with the masculine God before creation.

All of this material suggested to me that in the scriptures, in the Gnostic roots of Christianity, there really did exist a concept of the Feminine Divine. But it was also true, as Rosemary Radford Ruether pointed out, that while the Goddess was behind the image of Sophia or Wisdom, in Hebrew thought she never became a fully autonomous, divine female manifestation but rather remained a dependent expression or attribute of God.[31]

Still, it heartened me that something of her was there in the early fabric of Christianity, even if most of her threads had been obscured or torn away. Recovering the Sacred Feminine is not completely foreign to and outside of Christianity but is in some way a fulfillment of its original potential and intent.

The summer before, while visiting Meinrad Craighead in New Mexico, she'd shown us some of the paintings that were going to be included in a new book of her art. I recalled the one portraying Wisdom—the woman in a red-hooded cloak flanked by two owls—entitled *Hagia Sophia*. At her belly was the divine womb, pictured as a labyrinth.

The image had lingered in me. Now as winter deepened and I continued my study of Sophia, I had a dream:

I am walking into the basilica of an old church where it seems I've been many times before. But looking up, I am awed to find it now holds the vast image of Sophia painted across the ceiling in brilliant colors, the same image that had been in Meinrad's painting *Hagia Sophia*.

I knew then a remarkable thing was happening in me. Brightly hued feminine images were emerging; they were being painted across the old "church spaces" inside.

THE SYMBOL FUNCTIONS

As I grounded myself in Divine Feminine imagery, it had an unforeseen, yeastlike impact on my consciousness. Elizabeth A. Johnson expresses the dynamic succinctly: "The symbol of God functions." By this she means that the symbol gives rise to ways of thought and patterns of behavior. The core symbols we use for God represent what we take to be the highest good. They become "the ultimate point of reference for understanding experience, life and the world."[32] These symbols or images shape our worldview, our ethical system, and our social practice—how we live and relate to one another.

For instance, Johnson suggests that if a religion speaks about God as warrior, using militaristic language such as how "he crushes his enemies" and summoning people to become soldiers in God's army, then the people tend to become militaristic and aggressive.

Likewise, if the *key* symbol of God is that of a male king (without any balancing feminine imagery), we become a culture that values and enthrones men and masculinity.

I had spent nine months immersed in Divine Feminine symbols. As spring approached I was riveted by a question: What will Divine Feminine symbols create among us when integrated into the symbology we now have? What new ways of thinking, living, and acting will emerge?

THE DAWN OF FEMININE SPIRITUAL CONSCIOUSNESS

March, month of sweeping wind and spring's slow coming. One day I worked in the backyard garden, planting three young cedar trees. I dug three holes in the earth, tucked the cedars inside, and patted the dirt around them. Along with the oaks, pines, tea olive, and azalea already growing, the cedars helped form an irregular circle. A circle of trees.

I dragged the hose over, watered the new trees, then sat down to rest. Coins of light moved under the branches where a few late crocuses protruded. Earlier I'd placed a white stone the size of a pumpkin in the middle of the trees and hung wind chimes from the limbs. Now that the "circle of trees" was taking shape here in my backyard, I felt I was bringing the journey home to the ordinary dimensions of my life, rooting it in the place I lived every day.

I lay back on the earth and looked up through the branches of an oak, feeling suddenly like the sun was my own heart pulsing up there with light. Wind swirled, and it seemed to me it was my own breath billowing through the branches. The crocus bulbs were buried in my tissue, the cedars growing from my body. The birds flew inside me. Stones sat along my bones.

It was a jubilant, stunning loss of boundary, a deeper sense of oneness than I'd ever felt. I knew myself not separate from anything. I *knew* that I was part of one vast, universal quilt, as one writer says, "a kind of invisible quilt that has creation stitched into it."[33] I knew that this quilt was itself, the Holy Thing, the manifestation of the Divine One. And I loved this universal quilt, every stitch, color, and fiber, with a heartbreaking love.

It was one clear moment in time. Like going to the Deep Ground that underlies all things and seeing, really seeing, what is and being pierced by the unbounded nature of it.

The experience I had in my backyard revealed to me a new feminine consciousness that grows out of feminist spiritual awakenings, initiations, and groundings.

It is first of all a consciousness of *we,* in which relationship with all that is is held in primacy. It is a consciousness of mystical oneness and interconnection. Second (and growing out of the first), it is a consciousness of resacralized nature, one in which the earth is alive and divine. And third, it is a consciousness of liberation, thrusting a woman into the struggle for value, dignity, and power for every human.

What gives rise to these three layers of overlapping consciousness?

Herself, of course.

We-Consciousness

We-consciousness is knowing and feeling oneself intimately connected with and part of everything that is, and coming to act and relate out of that awareness. It is experiencing oneself not as I, but as We. To carry this consciousness is to come to the bare mystery of it all, that we are all one in the universe.

Beatrice Bruteau writes, "The question is: How big is your 'we'?"[34] Who knows, our future on this planet may hang on how we come to answer that question.

For a long time we've lived under an illusion of separateness. We've lived as detached egos, unaware that we're part of a vast fabric of being, a divine and communitarian oneness. Now we're learning from the new sciences that the universe has actually been constructed as a We. Everything in creation—oceans, whales, mountains, humans, eagles, roses, giraffes, and viruses—is a dance of subatomic particles. Fields of energy flow and mingle together. They are all stitched into the cosmic quilt, which underlies and gives rise to everything.

When we relate to Herself, we're inviting a new force to bring us into relationship with this whole. Goddess is that which unites, connects, and affirms the interrelatedness of all life, all people. Being related is at the core of Divine Feminine Being. She is the dance of relation, the mystery of the Divine communing with Herself in all things.

Connectedness is intrinsic in female life, and certainly when we envision the Divine as female we release a new and unique emphasis on relationship.

Her love is primarily envisioned as Mother love, a love that, as Sallie McFague argues, is unifying and reuniting, nonhierarchal and inclusive.[35] Despite loving descriptions of Father God in the scriptures, our perception of Father love has sometimes retained a kind of distance about it. This distance emanates from the classical approach to theology that dominated until modern times. Called *theism,* it shaped many of our ideas about how God relates to the world. Theism held that God was basically unrelated to the earth and should not be identified with the world. "He" was beyond it, over it. In theism God is distant, at the top of a heavenly hierarchy—the ruling king high in heaven. We're all familiar with the image of God as the white-bearded man on a throne in the sky. Theism emphasized God's transcendence, "his" untouchability, dominance, power, kingship, and judgeship.

This view has broken down considerably in present-day theologies, but nevertheless, Father love has often retained a faint theistic tone.

The world has not really tried divine love as Mother love. But when it does, divine love may break upon us with fresh and unexpected intimacy, shattering these theistic traces in a dramatic way.

I know of nothing needed more in the world just now than an image of Divine presence that affirms the importance of relationship—a Divine Mother, perhaps, who draws all humanity into her lap and makes us into a global family. Many have suggested that having only parental models of the Divine works to idealize and overemphasize our role as children, fostering dependent and infantile patterns rather than full, responsible personhood. Considering that, we could also image a Female Friend, whose model of relating is symbolized by a web of interconnection. We could also consider the Divine as Sister, seeing her in the mutual dance of love that is ideally reflected between sisters.

I remember the aftermath of the fights I had with my brothers when I was a girl, the way my mother would draw us together and say, as if introducing us to one another, "This is your brother. And this is your sister. No matter how angry you get, there's nothing as important as that."

She would make us stand there without speaking and gaze into each other's faces for a whole two minutes without looking away, and it would become impossible not to take him in, not to grin at him and understand that he was my brother. And what mattered next to that?

This is what feminine love does. It reunites us with each other, with nature, with the whole. It causes us to look deep into the face of whatever is before us and understand that it is our very sister we are gazing upon. And more than that, it is our very selves.

The fact is, we all come from the same womb and are related in ways we haven't yet allowed ourselves to experience. Through the body parable of pregnancy we learn how our lives indwell one another. As one spiritual feminist wrote, "Certainly the distinction between me and not me becomes a little blurry, to say the least, when one is inhabited as a mother."[36] We-consciousness means carrying that pregnant sense of being spiritually inhabited.

I had a memorable experience of we-consciousness breaking through one rainy afternoon in my study. Spring had almost gone, and I was primed with nearly a year of grounding myself in Divine Feminine imagery. I was reading an interview with philosopher Jean Houston. She referred to her work with dolphins, pointing out that they have evolved millions of years more than humans, that they don't have wars or attack each other, and that they don't experience the levels of anxiety we do. She said dolphins do real work, use language, play using a high degree of whimsicality, and even seem to reflect on death, exhibiting high concern when one of their members dies. All this was quite interesting, but then Houston said something that totally captivated me. She said there seems to be evidence dolphins are beaching themselves out of despair when caught in polluted water.

Suddenly I was engulfed by an image—dolphins despairing, weeping over what humans are doing to their waters. I sat still, gazing through the window, my heart starting to burn in a strange way. I tried to imagine what it was like to be a dolphin. I took myself out of the skin-encapsulated ego I often walked around in and placed myself in the sleek body of a dolphin. I imagined swimming waters laced with drift gill netting, poisoned with billions of tons of toxic waste, oil, and sewage.

Some weeks later I read Susan Griffin's lines about a red-winged blackbird: "I fly with her, enter her with my mind, leave myself, die for an instant, live in the body of this bird whom I cannot live without . . . because I know I am made from this earth as my mother's hands were made from this earth."[37]

I had entered that same elusive place inside where consciousness overlaps and boundaries dissolve. Grief boiled up. Tears curved under my chin. I felt a deep and holy connection with dolphins that startled me with its intensity. I had, as the mystic Mechthild of Magdeburg put it, lay down in fire.

I began to wonder why I'd ignored the earth, the despoiling of oceans, and the plight of dolphins so long. Was it because I'd become so locked in a narrow ego-consciousness that I failed to understand that dolphins and I came from the same stuff of life and were linked more deeply than my wildest imaginings? Had I existed so long in a culture of hierarchies, which fostered a sense of estrangement from the earth, that I'd lost the ability to feel and identify with the rest of the planet? Had my own Western Christian roots, with their deeply embedded separations of spirit and matter, created a rift between myself and the natural world? Probably it was all these things.

One day not long after this experience, in one of those odd, synchronistic moments that can only be acknowledged, not explained, I walked into the den and saw my daughter, Ann, watching television with tears in her eyes. On the screen was a fishing boat carrying a garbage heap of dead dolphins that had been trapped in drift gill netting for tuna. The dead dolphins were being tossed overboard, while the dolphins who had escaped the nets bobbed beside the boat, watching and making an eerie, wailing sound almost like crying. And there it was: an actual image of weeping dolphins.

You know the feeling you get when you stumble on a moment like that, like some great mystery has brushed your shoulder? I stood there and watched Ann crying with the dolphins, discovering her own primal connection to the earth. I sat beside her and touched my finger to her tears. I was trying to say, "I understand. The suffering aches in my heart, also." She nodded at me. She understood.[38]

More and more I found my illusions of separateness crumbling. I was feeling my connection to the earth, my compassion for it, sometimes like a raging empathy. I find such fierceness in the poet Susan Griffin, especially in this, my most beloved passage of hers:

This earth is my sister; I love her daily grace, her silent daring, and how loved I am how we admire this strength in each other, all that we have lost, all that we have suffered, all that we know: we are stunned by this beauty, and I do not forget: what she is to me, what I am to her.[39]

As the symbol of Goddess begins to function, we will wake to the knowledge that we are connected with everything in a deeper way than we've imagined. It will free a new valuing of the force that moves us into relationship with everything else.

I have a carving that I bought in 1974 while in East Africa. It's called an *ujamaa,* which in Swahili means "family" or "community." The *ujamaa* carvings are native sculptures done in totem style, sometimes representing a particular tribe or family group.

One day in the village of Limuru, Kenya, I came upon an old African woman completing an *ujamaa* out of rich, black ebony. The color of the wood and her skin were nearly identical shades, and the totem was the same circumference as her forearm. When she held the carving in her hand, it almost looked as if she was carving an extension of her own arm. I asked her, "Is that your family group you're carving?"

"No," she said. "This one is the family of *Mungu.*"

Mungu is Swahili for "the Divine." I looked at her with surprise, but she only smiled through very old eyes. Perhaps you would like to know what the Divine's family looks like. Picture a fifteen-inch totem. Squatting at the base are five pregnant women in a cluster. On top of them are four more pregnant women and on top of them four more.

I bought the carving, thinking it would make an interesting conversation piece. When I returned to the United States, the *ujamaa* sat on a shelf and people asked about it. Eventually, though, I packed it away.

Then during the summer when we-consciousness was erupting and breaking down the old partitions in my life, I opened a box in the back of a storage closet and found the carving again. I turned it around and around, seeing for the first time what the old woman meant about it being *Mungu's* family. I saw how inextricably linked all these figures were, how they grew out of one another—their heads joined, their faces blending, this one's foot flowing from that one's hand, and all their arms wrapped around one another like vines circling a great tree.

In her art the African woman introduced a new origin myth for me, one that shifted my inward reference point further from me to we. Holding the *ujamaa,* I thought: Maybe the Divine One is like an old

African woman, carving creation out of one vast, beautiful piece of Herself. She is making a universal totem spanning fifteen billion years, an extension of her life and being, an evolutionary carving of sacred art containing humans, animals, plants, indeed, everything that is. And all of it is joined, blended, and connected, its destiny intertwined.[40]

Resacralizing Earth and Body

After the dolphin experience, I had begun to spend more time in the natural world. I started placing things on my altar that I found outside or during trips to the woods, mountains, and beaches of the Carolinas. Rocks, shells, feathers, driftwood, seedpods, a snake skin, a turtle shell, pieces of bark.

As summer gave way to autumn, Ann wandered into my study. She pointed to the Minoan Goddess who stood on my altar next to the brass Jesus-Sophia. "Who's she?"

So I told her she was a symbol, an image in which to glimpse the Divine Feminine.

"And what about these rocks and things?"

"Same with them," I said. "They show me the Divine, too."

As we interact with Divine Feminine symbols, as we relate to the world with a new sense of connection, we often experience a second wave of feminine spiritual consciousness. We come to recognize the innate holiness of the earth, the sacred dwelling in nature, matter, and body. We understand these things are not only creations of the Divine but manifestations of the Divine. We see that nature is a dance and Divine Reality is the dancer.

In other words, the Divine *coinheres* all that is. *Coinhere* is a fancy word but is closest to capturing the meaning I intend. To coinhere means to exist together, to be included in the same thing or substance.

As the months went by, I began to embrace a vision in which the fullness of the Divine penetrates the whole universe. But I also saw the Divine as more than the universe, distinct and unexhausted by it. To see the Divine as encompassed by the universe is pantheism; to see the Divine as expressed by but also larger than the universe is pan*en*theism, a middle ground between pure pantheism and pure theism. The feminine offers us this middle ground.

As I indicated earlier, the feminine carries an old and deeply entwined connection with nature, body, and earth. Women's experience has been largely invested in these things as we go through menstruation, pregnancy, childbirth, and nursing. We've also traditionally been the ones involved in the earthy matters of caring for children, cleaning up bodily excrements, and nursing the sick and dying. If, then, we envision the Divine as female—a symbol that incorporates nature, body, and matter—then as a people we will come to honor the feminine, nature, body, and earth. A Divine Feminine symbol renders obsolete the old idea that these things are outside the realm of divinity. It begins to shift thousands of years of dualistic thinking, setting up a new mandate for the divinity of the earth and the holiness of the body.

That fall I noticed the phrase *divine immanence* started turning up a lot in my journal. Patriarchy has majored in divine transcendence, which means separateness from the material universe—being above, beyond, or apart from it. Divine immanence, on the other hand, is divinity here, near and now, inherent in the material stuff of life.

It occurred to me that patriarchy's emphasis on transcendence grew out of a flight from death. It sought to transcend death by transcending body and nature, which inevitably die and decay. "To be in a body is to hear the heartbeat of death at every moment," says scholar Andrew Harvey.[41] Is it any wonder, then, that patriarchy fears and negates the feminine?

Restoring the feminine symbol of Deity means that divinity will no longer be *only* heavenly, other, out there, up there, beyond time and space, beyond body and death. It will also be right here, right now, in me, in the earth, in this river and this rock, in excrement and roses alike. Divinity will be in the body, in the cycles of life and death, in the moment of decay and the moment of lovemaking.

I love this statement by Andrew Harvey:

Everyone has known something in lovemaking of the great lovemaking of the universe. Everyone who has ever had one tender orgasm with someone else has known something of the divine. The divine is in everything foaming around everywhere. We're all in connection with it, but we've not been given permission. . . . We've not been taught how to understand our glimpses and how to follow them.[42]

The symbol of Goddess gives us permission. She teaches us to embrace the holiness of every natural, ordinary, sensual, dying moment. Patriarchy may try to negate body and flee earth with its constant heartbeat of death, but Goddess forces us back to embrace them, to take our human life in our arms and clasp it for the divine life it is—the nice, sanitary, harmonious moments as well as the painful, dark, splintered ones.

If such a consciousness truly is set loose in the world, nothing will be the same. It will free us to be in a sacred body, on a sacred planet, in sacred communion with all of it. It will infect the universe with holiness. We will discover the Divine deep within the earth and the cells of our bodies, and we will love her there with all our hearts and all our souls and all our minds.

I remember a moment when that happened to me. We were in Crete on the far, southern side of the island, gathered on a remote stretch of beach. We'd had a long hike up a mountain, and now, tired and hot, with the sun setting and our feet aching, a few of the women began to peel off their clothes for a swim.

The beach was strewn with a billion rocks of all sizes, and I was combing through them at the water's edge when I happened to look up. A number of the women, most over fifty, moved toward the sea, picking their way together over the rocks, holding hands to help steady one another. Their bodies were nude, sculpted by long years of life and love. Full breasts, prolapsed breasts, Venus of Willendorf thighs, dimpled thighs, skinny thighs, gray hair, brown hair, puckering veins, silver scars, taut bellies, bellies stretched out from bearing children. They moved together, laughing, and I was touched by how beautiful they were. It was like a transubstantiation on the beach, the "real presence" coming into their flesh.

As I grounded myself in feminine spiritual experience, that fall I was initiated into my body in a deeper way. I came to know myself as an embodiment of Goddess. This awareness, so crucial to women's development, has been shut away from us. In Christianity God came in a male body. Within the history and traditions of patriarchy, women's bodies did not belong to themselves but to their husbands. We learned to hate our bodies if they didn't conform to an ideal, to despise the cycles of menstruation—"the curse," it was called. Our experience of our body has been immersed in shame.

Waking to the sacredness of the female body will cause a woman to "enter into" her body in a new way, be at home in it, honor it, nurture it, listen to it, delight in its sensual music. She will experience her female flesh as beautiful and holy, as a vessel of the sacred. She will live from her gut and feet and hands and instincts and not entirely in her head. Such a woman conveys a formidable presence because power resides *in* her body. The bodies of such women, instead of being groomed to some external standard, are penetrated with soul, quickened from the inside.

For this we need Herself. "For the body to be considered holy once again, the Goddess (the female aspect of the deity) must return, for it is only through a Goddess consciousness that matter can be perceived as having a sacred dimension," writes Jean Bolen.[43]

The same is true of nature. We also need Goddess consciousness to reveal earth's holiness. Divine feminine imagery opens up the notion that the earth is the body of the Divine, and when that happens, the Divine cannot be contained solely in a book, church, dogma, liturgy, theological system, or transcendent spirituality. The earth is no longer a mere backdrop until we get to heaven, something secondary and expendable. Matter becomes inspirited; it breathes divinity. Earth becomes alive and sacred. And we find ourselves alive in the midst of her and forever altered.

How are we altered? For one thing, if we discover Herself in the earth, we will not be so inclined to rape her forests, pave over her jungles, poison her rivers, dump fifty million tons of toxic waste into her oceans each year, or wipe out whole species of her creatures. Sin becomes defined as refusing to befriend and love the earth, for in doing so, we refuse to befriend and love the Divine.

This new feminine spiritual consciousness will help us recognize that humans, having special abilities, are responsible to the rest of the earth, not superior to it. We will realize that everything here has a purpose all its own, that its value lies in its own "beingness," not in its usefulness or how well it benefits humankind. This means something dramatically new—that the rest of creation is here to be related to, not dominated.

In many ways Goddess is a symbol of ecological wisdom, and as we face a massive ecological crisis, this particular symbol becomes timely and important. Passionist priest and geologian Thomas Berry says that when it comes to saving the planet, the return of the feminine is the most important thing happening. Many are saying that we may have no habitable future without her. Berry maintains that to survive we must "reinvent the human." We must reverse our severe alienation from the natural world, which lies at the root of its devastation. Christians have gotten so committed to the Bible, he says, we've lost our capacity to deal with a primary revelation of the divine in the natural world.[44]

As Christmas came that year and I thought about the incarnation, I finally took it to its ultimate conclusion. For the first time I discovered a new and radical incarnation in which the Divine comes not only through human form (which the doctrine of Christ revealed), but through the earth as well. Here, as Teilhard de Chardin pointed out, is the "second coming" of Christ, the birth of the Divine within earth and matter.

Mystical awakening in all the great religious traditions, including Christianity, involves arriving at an experience of unity or nondualism. In Zen it's known as *samadhi,* the experience of the mind no longer divided against itself. When our nature is no longer divided against itself, the inner splits are healed and we see earth and spirit as one. Transcendence and immanence are not separate. The Divine is one. The dancer and all the dances are one.

The Christian mystic Hildegard of Bingen reflected this when she wrote about the Divine as a Spirit-Sophia filling the cosmos:

I, the highest and fiery power, have kindled every living spark and I have breathed out nothing that can die. . . . I flame above the beauty of the fields; I shine in the waters, in the sun, the moon and the stars. I burn. And by means of the airy wind, I stir everything into quickness with a certain invisible life which sustains all. . . . I, the fiery power, lie hidden in these things and they blaze from me.[45]

And Mechthild of Magdeburg, another Christian mystic, confessed, "The day of my awakening was the day I saw and knew I saw all things in God, and God in all things."[46]

For those who go deep into spiritual practice, at some moment the veil slips away and you see what *is,* and everything that is has a spiritual essence.

Goddess offers us the holiness of everything.

And Still I Rise

The previous spring I'd planted cedars in my backyard and begun a yearlong process of realizing a new feminine spiritual consciousness. It had been a remarkable year of waking up to my relationship to all things, discovering the Divine within the earth. But in this year I'd also been discovering another aspect of this consciousness.

One evening I gathered with Betty and our friend Ramona beside the lake in Betty's woodland garden to participate in a ritual. Standing among cedars, river birch, and arbor vita, beneath a moon two days past full, we symbolically tied each other's wrists together with yarn then asked the question "What binds you?"

As Ramona asked me the question, two things came instantly to mind: fear and silence.

We wandered to private places to contemplate our answers to the question. Sitting beside the water, I thought of the fear that was never far, the deadening inclination toward silence. The yarn was cutting a little into my skin. It was somehow appropriate.

Fear and silence. As I pondered the powerful ways those two things cut off a woman's journey, I thought about the book I was currently reading, the autobiography of New Zealand writer Janet Frame. Much of it was her personal struggle to break free from silencing structures and a life that confined her true female self. I remembered her description of the day she realized she was trapped:

"You're so thoughtful," Mrs. T. said. "I'm lucky to have such a quiet student. You wouldn't even know you were in the house, you're so quiet!"

(A lovely girl, no trouble at all!)

I had woven so carefully, with such close texture, my visible layer of "no trouble at all, a quiet student, always ready with a smile (if the decayed teeth could be hidden), always happy," that even I could not break the thread.[47]

Lovely, quiet girl, no trouble, no trouble at all. You wouldn't even know she was in the house. That is often the yarn twisted around women's wrists.

I thought about all the yarn on all the women, how it constricted and stopped our journeys, and I began to feel an energy rise up inside me. I didn't know what to call it, but it made me want to tear the yarn not only off my wrists, but off the wrists of Betty and Ramona and all the other women, too.

Finally the three of us came together and, holding hands, broke the yarn. Then we stretched out on the ground atop the scratch of an old army blanket. Overhead a shooting star blazed across the sky beneath the Big Dipper. And once again I couldn't help thinking it seemed appropriate.

The yarn ritual symbolically captures the sort of consciousness I'm speaking about, the forceful, emphatic energy ascending from a woman's gut, wanting to join hands with other women and together break every yarn on every wrist.

Women suffer. Sometimes they suffer because they're human and it's part of the human condition to suffer. Other times, lots of times, they suffer because they're women. Women have suffered everywhere in the world and throughout history.

In her book *Texts of Terror,* theologian Phyllis Trible documents little-known biblical accounts of women who endured unspeakable abuse and suffering because they were women and no help came, neither from humans nor from God. For me, the most despicable and heartrending story is that of the concubine from Bethlehem.

The Old Testament tells what happened when a gang of ruffians threatened to defile a man staying overnight as a guest in the home of an old man. The old man admonishes the ruffians not to act wickedly, and he offers them his own virgin daughter or the guest's concubine. Ravish either of them, he says, do with them what seems good to you, but don't harm the man.

The men outside do not listen, so the guest throws his concubine out to them. They rape and abuse her all night long. The Bible says the next morning the man finds her lying at the door. "Get up," he told her. "Let's be going." But there was no answer. And when they got home, he took a knife, cut her murdered body into twelve pieces, and scattered her body to the twelve tribes as evidence of what had been done.[48]

When I found this story I wondered: Why is *this* story not told and re-told as a narrative of suffering and injustice? Why have most of us never heard of the nameless, raped, tortured, murdered, mutilated woman who was betrayed and sacrificed so easily because she was female?

Trible wrote, "Her body has been broken and given to many. Lesser power has no woman than this, that her life is laid down by a man."[49]

One day I saw a painting of a crucified woman hanging on the cross and thought of all the suffering, violated women throughout history. Thousands of women murdered in the name of God during witch burnings; little girls sexually abused; women beaten by husbands, harassed by "superiors," abandoned to poverty, genitally mutilated in Africa, forced into brothels by the Japanese military, tortured in Nicaragua, raped in

Sarajevo. I thought of women cut off from equality, passed over at work, silenced at home, marginalized at church—women suffering in all kinds of ways from the pathology of exclusion. And once again I embraced their struggle as my own.

The Divine Feminine symbol creates a feminist spiritual consciousness, which includes a passionate struggle for women's dignity, value, and power. These lines from Maya Angelou's poem "And Still I Rise" capture the transformation of consciousness that happens inside a woman on this journey:

> Did you want to see me broken?
> Bowed head and lowered eyes?
> Shoulders falling down like teardrops,
> Weakened by my soulful cries?
> . . . .
> You may shoot me with your words,
> You may cut me with your eyes,
> You may kill me with your hatefulness,
> But still, like air, I'll rise.[50]

It's important that women on feminist spiritual journeys birth that cry from within. *No matter what has been done to women, no matter how long we've been on our knees inside, no matter, we will rise. We . . . will . . . rise.* We will break this yarn. The words may begin private and small, a whimper of a sound, growing until they are a roaring inside, a roaring not only for oneself but for every woman. After it comes, a woman cannot be tamed back into silence.

Poet Susan Griffin writes about the encounter of a female lion and several men who are trying to put her to sleep. They wonder what she will do if they enclose her in the room with them. One of them shuts the door. She backs her way toward the closed doorway and then roars. "Be still," the men say. She continues to roar. "Why does she roar?" they ask. The roaring must be inside her, they conclude. They decide they must see the roaring inside her. They approach her. . . . They are trying to put her to sleep. . . . She has no soul, they conclude, she does not know right from wrong. "Be still!" they shout at her. "Be humble, trust us," they demand. "We have souls," they proclaim, "we know right from wrong." They approach her with their medicine. . . . She devours them.[51]

Goddess becomes the roaring inside us, the force that refuses to be subdued, tamed, stifled, silenced, mollified, or put to sleep. It becomes that which challenges and "eats away" at structures that cage and oppress, that deny justice and inclusion.

I am talking about a consciousness of liberating action in which we work to change the patriarchal structures that deny women dignity, value, and power. Feminist theologian Carter Heyward suggests we consider the analogy of a house. If there's a structural problem, we don't fix it by changing the wallpaper. She says we must dig deeply into the foundation, discover the problem, and reconstruct the house. In other words, we must transform the house from the ground up.

It is through our roaring and rising that we become architects and builders of a new house, one that holds everybody in mutuality.

Along the way, a crossing over occurs in which we move from the private struggle for dignity, value, and power to a larger, more universal struggle. The cry "still I rise" is no longer merely personal and univocal but a choir of voices inside us. We begin to identify not only with other women, but with all disenfranchised or oppressed people because we know we are not separate from anyone who has been denied power because of gender, race, nationality, or economic class.

Like Latin American and black liberation theologies, feminist spiritual consciousness focuses on the Divine as the liberating one who seeks to end suffering and bring justice. It takes to heart (generally in ways more fervent and radical than the church) the acts and teachings of Jesus when he placed love and justice above traditional law. I suspect nothing today would be more heartbreaking to Jesus than seeing an institution that bears his name exclude, devalue, and marginalize women in order to enforce and protect traditional laws.

Elizabeth A. Johnson explains that including divine female symbols and images not only challenges the dominance of male images but also calls into question the structure of patriarchy itself. "It gives rise to a different vision of community," she writes, "one in which the last shall be first, the excluded shall be included, the mighty put down from their thrones and the humble exalted—the words of Mary of Nazareth."[52]

A Divine Feminine symbol acts to deconstruct patriarchy, which is one of the reasons there's so much resistance, even hysteria, surrounding the idea of Goddess. The idea of Goddess is so powerfully "other," so vividly female, it comes like a crowbar shattering the lock patriarchy holds on divine imagery. Nelle Morton often pointed out that the word *Goddess* is important because it bursts the exclusivity of the old symbol and opens the way to reimage deity.

Now whenever I used the word it caused reverberations in me, setting off the "still I rise" voice. Goddess became both the force that ignited the voice and the voice itself. Believe me, there is no way *this* word, this symbol, can be used to hush women up or get them back in line.

One of my favorite short stories comes from the pen of Tillie Olsen. In "I Stand Here Ironing," a mother stands at the ironing board aching for her daughter to have the life she never did. She thinks: "Only help her to know—help make it so there is cause for her to know—that she is more than this dress on the ironing board, helpless before the iron."[53]

As women we are, none of us, dresses, helpless before the iron, and we can help make it so there is cause for every woman to know.

HEALING THE FEMININE WOUND

During this grounding time, healing was also taking place.

I've discussed things that make up the feminine wound within women, church, and culture: the devaluation and negation of the feminine, the disconnection of women from their feminine soul, the silencing of the *real* voices of women, the loss of feminine feet, hands, mouths, and hearts. All this becomes a ravaged geography in the souls of women, a wounded Eden. Most of us have lived there in varying degrees of settling down and have normalized it as the lay of the land.

But just as a wounded Eden has been created in women's lives, we can also create a deep refuge, a space of healing.

In her book *Pilgrim at Tinker Creek,* Annie Dillard wrote that she could not cause light, but she *could* put herself in its path.[54] The same may be true of healing. Maybe in the end we cannot make healing happen; perhaps it is, after all, a grace. But we can put ourselves in its path. We can create a healing refuge for ourselves.

The word *refuge* comes from a French word that means "retreat." My dictionary says a refuge is a place of safe retreat, a shelter, a stronghold that protects by its strength or a sanctuary that offers a place of healing because of its sacredness.

Some time ago I watched an episode of the television show *Northern Exposure* set in the fictional town of Cicely, Alaska. It portrayed a showdown between two of the town's characters, Maurice and Ruth Ann. Maurice, a rich, powerful, conservative, ultracapitalist former astronaut, situated at the top of Cicely's social hierarchy, represents a tough masculine figure who sees feeling as weakness. He often acts in arrogant and insensitive ways, other times in kind ways, but almost always in patriarchal ways. In the show Maurice is planning a fox hunt.

Ruth Ann becomes involved when the fox that Maurice has ordered arrives at her general store. Cast as the wise old woman of the show, something of the town crone, Ruth Ann is the opposite of Maurice in many ways. Embracing a simple, no-frills lifestyle, she is liberal-minded, down to earth, sensitive, and compassionate with the fierceness to back it up.

Now enters the fox. It stares at Ruth Ann from its small cage, gnawing desperately at the latch as if it senses its fate. So she does what any self-respecting old crone would do. She kidnaps the fox and gives it refuge in her house.

When the fox turns up missing, Maurice has his hounds track it to Ruth Ann's house. There Maurice meets Ruth Ann in the garden and demands she turn the fox over or he's going inside after it. Ruth Ann picks up a shovel. Over my dead body, she tells him. I've given the fox sanctuary, she says, and you aren't coming anywhere near it.

Maurice looks at the determination on her face and, knowing he's licked, leaves and doesn't challenge her again.

I was intrigued with the symbolism in the story. If we look at it as a modern myth, we see that the characters exist inside us. We carry around our own Maurice—a figure of internalized patriarchy—who represents the wounding voice inside that identifies with power and hierarchies, denies feeling, and denigrates feminine values.

We also have a part inside represented by the sad fox in the cage, the part of us that's been victim to patriarchal power and imprisoned in our wounds. And best of all, we have a Ruth Ann, a wise, fiercely compassionate presence who creates refuge.

Of these three aspects of ourselves—the wounder, the wounded, and the healer—we've recognized the first two. We need now to get in touch with the third, the internal Ruth Ann who wants to make a healing sanctuary, who will, if need be, pick up a shovel to defend it.

Feminine Pietá

That spring, after I ritually broke the yarn on my wrists, I began to create a refuge of healing. I had a dream:

I am wandering through a dusty old museum looking at statues of the divine. All of them are male. I wander a long time until I come to one of those hidden rooms that often turn up in dreams. Inside is a huge-lapped, marble statue of a seated woman. A Goddess. She looks very much like Mary in the *Pietá* who held the grown, crucified Christ in her lap, but *this* lap is empty. So I climb up into it, and to my astonishment the marble turns to warm, soft flesh. The Goddess comes to life and holds me, kissing my wounded places.

The dream suggested I seek a Great Lap, a place of feminine refuge where I could have my feminine stigmata healed. It informed me that I would find this healing space not by keeping my distance from sacred feminine experience, but by climbing right into the lap of it.

In the following months I began to climb more often into the lap of Sacred Feminine experience, to ground myself deeper and deeper within the healing "circle of trees."

The Communal Basket, Female Solidarity

By now my friend Betty and I had found other women with whom we gathered from time to time to talk, listen, create rituals, and support one another. On a hot day in September five of us sat within the circle of trees at Springbank. Earlier we'd walked through the wood's trails cutting long coils of wisteria vine with the intention of making a basket. Now we began to weave it.

Betty had woven baskets before and provided the instruction we needed, but much of it came naturally as we fell into a rhythm of passing the vine around the circle, each woman taking her turn braiding it in and out, over and under, then handing it on to the next woman. We talked about our lives as women, our fears, struggles, and hopes, offering our stories, receiving stories, and always weaving.

Weaving a basket is a lot like weaving solidarity; it's similar to the way women braid their lives and stories and experiences together, making something solid, real, and beautiful—a woman-made container that holds you. I remember thinking, even commenting to the others, that the vines are like women's arms, that linked together they can hold anything.

One of the most profound ways to engender energy for healing is through this kind of communal weaving. We wove our solidarity all afternoon until the sun dropped behind the trees. Somehow our basket turned out huge. I mean, huge. We laughed at the immensity of it. It could have held a large watermelon easily. The bigger the better, we said.

We beamed over our basket, basked in its presence. Then someone asked, "So what will we do with it?"

Do with it? Until now that hadn't entered anyone's mind. It must be true that when we are left to our natural selves, women are more engaged by the process than the destination or the end product.

We pondered. "We can pass it among us," someone said. "It should go to the one who needs the most holding."

So that's what we did. To this day the basket moves back and forth among us. When one of us is struggling, she phones around. "So who has the basket right now? . . . Well, do you think she's ready to send it my way?"

And the funny thing is, it works. The basket conjures up the solidarity and support we wove that day. It reminds us who we are and that we are not alone. The basket offers its "arms."

As Mary Daly has acknowledged, "A minority of one has little chance of survival. The 'bonding' phenomenon among women, expressed by the word 'sisterhood,' is therefore essential. . . . Only women hearing each other can create a counterworld to the prevailing reality."[55]

My earliest experience of solidarity goes back to an earthy childhood event with Sweet, the African American woman who was housekeeper for my mother and nanny to me. Growing up in the South before the Civil Rights movement, I saw caravans of black maids driven to and from work in the back seats of white women's cars and "White Only" signs over restroom doors. But I really saw none of it. On Saturday afternoons I watched the matinee in the town's only theater, only vaguely aware that above in the dark reaches of the balcony were people who were not allowed on the main floor because of their color. At eleven years old I was living inside the story of segregation without any consciousness of it.

Then one day as Sweet traveled in the car with my family, we stopped alongside the road for her to urinate, since she was not allowed in the gas station restrooms. As she took toilet paper from her purse and walked toward a privy of trees in the distance, I was struck as much as an eleven year old could be by the degradation and inhumanity of what was happening. I wanted suddenly to be with her in the worst way, not to wait for the next gas station to relieve myself but to do it now with her. I bolted out of the car after her.

We squatted behind the trees, side by side on the slope of a hill watching our urine cut two golden paths through the dirt. It wound down until the streams converged like two tributaries coming together to form a river. Sweet said absent-mindedly, like she was commenting on a peculiarity of the weather, "Look how our waters run together."

Even then I felt the hot rush of kinship with her, the unbreakable love, the way my life flowed into hers and hers into mine. I felt something of the pain of her life, had my first flicker of awareness that despite the differences between us, most of them forged by injustice, our lives ran together.

That is female solidarity—the squatting on a hill in mutuality, gazing down a common slope and seeing the way our lives make rivers together.

It is a telling postscript to that story that as I grounded myself in female community, I dreamed many dreams about Sweet. The one I most treasure is Sweet coming to me with a gold and silver box. "Here," she said, "this is to keep your snake in." She was speaking about my symbolic snake, the symbol of feminine wisdom, instinct, and female divinity, and I thought how appropriate it was that other women should offer us containers of value for this wounded aspect.

Like the communal basket, the image of squatting together on a Georgia hill is a metaphor of female solidarity. Both reminded me that coming together as women is both healing and transforming. It allows us, as Nelle Morton put it, to "hear one another into speech."

The truth is, in order to heal we need to tell our stories and have them witnessed. "All sorrows can be borne if we put them in a story or tell a story about them," said Isak Dinesen, a writer who had plenty of sorrow and told stories to bear it.[56] The story itself becomes a vessel that holds us up, that sustains, that allows us to order our jumbled experiences into meaning.

As I told my stories of fear, awakening, struggle, and transformation and had them received, heard, and validated by other women, I found healing.

I also needed to hear other women's stories in order to see and embrace my own. Sometimes another woman's story becomes a mirror that shows me a self I haven't seen before. When I listen to her tell it, her experience quickens and clarifies my own. Her questions rouse mine. Her conflicts illumine my conflicts. Her resolutions call forth my hope. Her strengths summon my strengths. All of this can happen even when our stories and our lives are very different.

Solidarity is identifying with one another without feeling like you have to agree on every issue. It's unity, not uniformity. It's listening without rushing in to fix the problem. It's going deeper than typical ways of talking and sharing—going down to the place where souls meet and love comes, where separateness drops away and you know these women because you *are* these women.

I began to meet often with groups of women, at Springbank when we stood in a circle and fed each other little crescent slices of apple, saying, "The fruit of the earth is good and you are good," or outside beside Betty's lake as two or three of us gathered to talk. Over and over these women caused me to see that the circumference of my life was much larger than I had imagined. They listened to me as I struggled to expand my world. They heard me into speech and loved me into healing.

On the Bridge

When winter came, Sandy and I went to a Jungian conference in the mountains of North Carolina. One morning we walked through the woods around the lake. A snow had fallen overnight, and everything was molded white. As we walked, we talked about lots of things—feminism, dream symbols, his new course of study. The air stung with cold, but we hardly seemed to notice.

After a while we came to a little footbridge that arched over a stream, and we stood in the middle of it, leaning on the rail. I was telling him something about the importance of the Divine Feminine in my life, how important it was for women to internalize her. He was nodding. He was nodding in such a way that I was struck suddenly by the depth of his support for me and for what I was doing.

"The culture needs feminine spiritual consciousness," he was saying. He went on, but all I could think was, Would you look at us! Who would have ever thought we would be standing here talking like this? More and more we'd been sharing a new intimacy. I thought of the evenings we had talked about the Ariadne myth and what it meant. Evenings when we had talked just as we were talking now. I realized how much he had tried to understand me and what all this meant to me. And wasn't he the one who lately, whenever the children said "he" and "his" when talking about God, reminded them that the Divine could also be a she? And wasn't he the one who'd given me the deer antlers and not so long ago brought home a candle for my altar?

But it wasn't until that moment on the bridge that I stood back and took it all in. Amazing, I thought. And I felt somehow that something had been healed between us.

Silence came as we leaned over the rail and watched the water trickle by. It seemed exactly right that we were on a bridge, and when we walked on, I felt like the two of us were in a whole new place.

Deep Being

We are also healed through experiences of Deep Being or what might be called "being at the core of oneself." When we exist at the core of ourselves, we're departing from how we normally exist. We're bringing the heart, mind, body, and soul into focus and being present with them in a particular way: doing it on purpose, doing it with unconditional acceptance, and doing it with deep attentiveness.

Deep Being is a kind of meditation for the female soul, for such experiences provide a woman with the time and space she needs to create a new relationship with her inner Feminine Self and mend the fragmented places inside.

How do you practice Deep Being? How do you go to the core of yourself and be? There are as many ways as there are women.

Each woman must create her own ways, but it can be helpful to discover the kinds of things other women do in order to heal, for they show us what is possible and direct us back into the passion of creating our own healing sanctuaries.

JUNGIAN WORK My first experiences of Deep Being had begun with Jungian analysis. Week after week, month after month, I sat in the little solarium in my analyst's house trying to gather my soul into focus and be with it, trying to enter the deep of myself. Many times I felt like a child at the edge of the sea, sticking in one toe and then running for the dune before gaining courage to wade on in.

The sessions with my analyst were like talking meditation, for the dialogues seemed to be holy discourse created for the purpose of opening the soul to its truth. In the presence of a skilled and caring woman, I plumbed my wounds, looking at the roots from which they rose, gradually finding my way toward healing. I gained help in naming and dismantling inner patriarchy and freeing myself from the old faces of daughterhood. The process assisted me to lay my hands on Big Wisdom and follow my thread. Most of all, it helped me forge a connection to my Feminine Self.

Sometimes my sessions were like therapeutic show-and-tell as I brought in written accounts of dreams I'd had, drawings I'd sketched and clay images I'd sculpted, writings I'd done, illustrations of the myth of Ariadne, childhood pictures, the deer antlers Sandy gave me. These and so many other small treasures became symbolic lenses through which my soul was brought into clearer focus.

One day I brought in a walking stick. I'd made it from a slender tree limb that had fallen from one of the branches in the circle of trees at Springbank. This would make a wonderful walking stick, I'd thought when I found it, and I took it home without a clue about how to make one. The next couple of weeks I sat night after night on the floor in the den, stripping off the bark with a little whittling knife until my thumbs were puckered with blisters. When I finished, I gathered up all the shavings of bark and saved them in a glass bottle. I varnished the stick and took it with me when I walked. It became a cherished thing.

Then one day I brought it with me to the solarium, and we talked about the process I'd gone through creating it. I began to see that it was not unlike the process I was experiencing, the blistering work of stripping away the old brittle layers in order to reach the beautiful grain of the female soul. The gathering up of the old fragments because transformation comes not by rejecting unwanted parts of ourselves but by differentiating then integrating them. And finally making the whole thing part of my walk.

I knew suddenly the ways of my journey. The impact and changes that my experience had brought slipped into focus. It was one of those moments of coming together.

When I teach creative writing classes, I always tell my students about what writer James Joyce calls the "epiphany" of a story. It's a moment of enlightenment or recognition when the character comes to realize something, to see something in a new light, and from then on the character's internal landscape is changed. It's worth noting, I tell them, that *epiphany* actually means a physical manifestation of something, so the character's internal realization comes through some tangible thing or outside action. In much the same way, the feminine journey is a story unfolding, and its epiphanies come through real things, through tangibles like walking sticks and dreams and deer antlers—all of which we might miss without taking time and space in Deep Being.

Of course, not every woman needs to be in Jungian analysis to travel a feminine journey, but we all seem to need at least one refuge of Deep Being where we have the ongoing freedom to tell our truth safely and truly be heard, where we can find the support we need to follow our thread, where the epiphanies can come. We need a place that will help us find the grain beneath all that bark.

We can accomplish it perhaps with a friend or special group, through a journal, through prayer, or through a creative work. The important thing is to find a process that works for you, that allows you to give yourself times of unconditional presence when you can attend your soul with all the acceptance and attentiveness you can muster.

THE PRACTICE OF MINDFULNESS   That winter while in a bookstore I picked up a book on mindful meditation by Zen master Thich Nhat Hanh. As I read it, I was drawn into the practice and discovered it to be another powerful experience of Deep Being.

Mindfulness is an ancient form of meditation in which one pays attention to the present moment and all that's unfolding in that moment, both within and around one. It's known also as conscious living because the person practicing it is forming an aware and intimate relationship with each moment.

I began to sit in a calm, accepting alertness for twenty to thirty minutes each day. I became attentive to my breath, noting the thoughts and feelings that arose, observing them the way the sky observes the clouds and lets them pass through. In this way I was able to bring attention to the content of my life as it was unfolding.

Mindfulness has been called a powerful form of self-healing by many teachers and practitioners.[57] How this process creates healing is part mystery and part grace. Somehow in a slow, hidden way, we're able to be with the depths of ourselves—our true natures, our souls—while at the same time observing our thoughts and feelings and not becoming caught up in them.

When practicing mindful meditation we aren't striving to do anything. We aren't grasping, struggling, thinking, expecting, or wanting but simply letting whatever is there be there and paying attention to it in a nonjudgmental way. We come to terms with reality as it is, bringing all our awareness to it, breathing with it, attending it.

This might sound easy; it's anything but. It took six months before I could sit for any length of time without traipsing off into the endless stream of thought and chatter in my head. I would realize suddenly that I'd completely lost my concentration, my awareness of the breath, any sense of the present moment, and I would have to call myself back a million times.

I like meditation teacher Jack Kornfield's analogy. He says when you start to meditate your mind is like a puppy you're trying to house-train. You place it on a piece of newspaper. "Stay," you tell it. "Stay." But does it stay? Of course not. It wanders off, and you have to bring it back. It doesn't help to punish the pup. The pup learns by being gently brought back over and over again.

From Thich Nhat Hanh I learned a way of being with my wounds while practicing mindfulness. He suggests that as feelings arise we acknowledge them. Yes, I'm feeling this. Then, he says, get even closer to the feeling. Rather than saying, "Go away, fear" or "anger" or "hurt," greet it, because banishing our feelings will not transform them.

He suggests we approach pain the way a mother tenderly picks up a crying baby. The mother represents your mindfulness, your true nature, the conscious, attending part of you. The squalling child represents your pain, the wounded part of you. When the pain makes itself felt, you can gently pick up the child and hold it.

All that winter and into the spring, I kept picking up the child during my meditation—all the personal and collective fear, anger, betrayal, and internalized sense of inferiority that make up the feminine wound—and holding her in my arms. It got to the point that when the wound made itself felt, I found myself naturally responding, "Oh, there you are again, I know you. Come on and I'll hold and rock you for a while." Eventually the baby stopped crying.

Once we get the baby quiet, we can begin to look deeply at the feeling. We begin to understand the attitudes, beliefs, and patterns that cause it. We start to see what keeps us stuck in our wounds and what we can do to transform them.

EARTH, WATER, WIND, FIRE   Nature can be one of women's most potent healers. Simone de Beauvoir believed that because women were excluded from culture, we turned to nature, finding transcendent experiences within it. I can't say I initially turned to nature for healing; I turned to nature because I discovered my connection to it and as a result found healing flowing back to me.

Can we say completely why nature heals? I doubt it. But the healing seems to happen more readily when we experience nature through moments of Deep Being. Shooting the rapids in a canoe or careening down a slope on snow skis all take place in nature, but they're not what I mean by being in nature. I'm speaking of being at the core of nature, vividly open to it, while at the same time being at the core of ourselves.

During this time I led a four-day women's workshop called "Women and Mother Earth." The last day I asked the women to go outside and walk silently in nature, walking with wonder, with beginner's mind, as if seeing everything for the first time. I asked them to put up their spiritual antennae and seek out something natural that spoke to them, then sit with it, trying to hear its message. Finally I asked them to bring back part or all of the object (only if moving it was possible and wouldn't be too disturbing to it or the environment).

We sat outside among the trees with the sea lapping not far away while the women spoke about their experience. What was remarkable was that all the objects the women encountered were healing for them in ways that fit their particular wounds. One woman, who told us that all her life she'd "silenced herself out of fear," brought back a hollow reed she'd found growing along the water. She told us that as she walked by it, she heard wind blowing inside the reed, a strange, intoxicating, flutelike sound. She heard herself saying over and over, "Make your own music," until there were tears pouring down her face. She felt herself newly freed to voice herself, for if this reed can pipe its song, she said, so could she. Another woman who'd been uncovering the feminine wound in her life told us about sitting beside a spider web and glimpsing the promise of wholeness that she could weave.

One of nature's most healing gifts to us, though, is its reminder to us to stay grounded and connected to the natural cycles of life. My moment of learning this came at the end of the workshop.

On the first day of the workshop I'd assembled the four elements and placed them on a table in the room to remind us of the sacred presence of nature. I'd filled a glass bowl with water, placed a candle there to hold fire, and laid a feather beside it to represent air. Then I'd gone outside and dug up a mound of earth. My pot was large, and I'd had to dig a fair-sized hole in order to fill it.

When the workshop was over I took the pot of earth back to the hole to fill it in. But a surprise awaited me. Sitting in the hole was a turtle. Since I now couldn't replace earth in the hole, I decided to sit there awhile and try to listen.

I saw how in living my life cut off from my female essence, I'd tended to stay "in my head" a lot of the time—thinking, planning, analyzing, relying on intellect, or else orbiting the high, heady places of spirit. Now here was this creature grounded on the earth, even *in* the earth, in the very hole I'd dug.

The turtle, moored in *my* hole, created a framework of meaning that took me by surprise. I recognized just how much I needed to find my berths in nature and stay grounded in them. For it is this that keeps us present in our own skin, whole and natural and awake with our feet on the earth and our hearts wild and free.

I emptied the pot of earth on the ground beside the turtle and left her in the hole. After that I sought new ways to connect to, to burrow down into, the earth's slow rhythms. I began to follow the cycles of the moon, to know at any given time when it was full, when it was dark. Every day I took some time outside where I forged new connections with the animals in my yard, including the spiders who came to spin at night, the plants, trees, and mosses, the sky shifting with the seasons. Such moments grounded me. They caused me to feel the slow rhythm of the earth, to surrender to it and to honor my own natural rhythms. And in such awareness there is always healing.

Ultimately nature heals because it reminds us that as humans, we *are* nature. We are earth, water, wind, and fire. The same cycles and rhythms that move the moon, drop the rain, and draw sap through tree veins operate inside us as well.

The Matryoshka Doll and the Motherline

The wise old crone came in my dreams one night. The first time she'd come was at the outset of my journey when she'd encouraged me to trust my own Feminine Source. Now, as usual with her appearance, this dream, too, marked a turning for me.

I am walking through a country where there has been fighting and oppression. Plants and crops are dying, and droves of people are walking along the road, leaving. I'm among them, exiting the old country that can no longer sustain life, when suddenly the Bishop appears. My old nemesis. He holds a stone tablet with the Ten Commandments carved on them and tries to hit me with them, but he's so weak and shriveled with age, he can't manage it. I grab the tablets away, stuff them in a paper bag, and walk on, leaving him behind.

I come to a new country where things are growing, then to one particular cottage with flowers making an arbor over the door. Inside I find the wise old crone propped on a bed, her lips fire-red, her hair long and white as the sheets. "Look in your paper bag," she tells me, all the while smiling as if she's up to something.

Peering inside, I notice the tablets are gone and in their place is a magnificent Russian nesting doll. As I lift the doll out of the bag, the old woman starts to sing an exuberant song about being a woman. About beautiful breasts and beautiful wombs. She holds up a mirror as she sings so I can see my image in it, and I'm struck by the beauty I see there. Then I notice I am also able to see *her* face blazing through the glass, too, giving a dual image of my face nested inside hers.

The dream signaled a healing transformation taking place inside me. Patriarchal law, represented by the tablets of stone, was being changed into a feminine doll. I recalled that Marie-Luise von Franz wrote that often a doll in a woman's dream could be a symbol of the divine Self. I thought, too, of the Russian story of Vasilissa, the girl who had been given a doll by her mother. Vasilissa kept the doll in her pocket. It acted as the voice of wisdom and intuition, helping her know which way to turn when she was uncertain. And the crone's song was a healing song, the mirror a symbol of reflection.

After that dream I began to envision myself differently, to experience the Feminine not as wounded, but as something beautiful, exuberant, wise, and unspeakably valuable. A gift from the wise mother.

Later, while browsing through a small shop in the mountains of North Carolina, I came upon a Russian nesting doll, painted red and yellow with inlaid wood. I admired it so long that the sales clerk said, "I see you like the Matryoshka doll."

"The what?" I asked.

"Matryoshka doll. It means 'mother' in Russian."

A warm, almost electric feeling flowed through me. I bought her, naturally. At home I opened her up and found another doll inside, then another and another. I kept opening until six dolls lay in a sloping line across the kitchen table and I came to the core of her, to the doll at the center.

Opening the Matryoshka doll spoke to me about the need to discover Herself—the Feminine Self, the feminine soul—deep inside and to open her layer by layer. It is uncovering the doll at the center that causes the exuberant healing song about being a woman to break out inside. Women, long denied the healing symbol of a Divine Being who is like ourselves, will find female wholeness forged in us as we peer into the mirror and see the real beauty of our feminine selves, which means seeing Herself's reflection nested in our own.

Healing came for me as I integrated images of a strong, powerful, compassionate Feminine Being, one who was creating the universe, creating Herself, birthing new life, and holding everything in being. For me this was the most significant factor in creating a restoration of feminine value, dignity, and power inside—seeing female as *imago dei,* the image of the Divine, revealed now through women just as it had been revealed all these centuries through men. It was the return of my feminine birthright.

Over the altar in my study I hung a lovely mirror sculpted in the shape of a crescent moon. It reminded me to honor the Divine Feminine presence in myself, the wisdom in my own soul. Sometimes when I peer in it I can see myself just as I looked in the mirror in my dream.

The Matryoshka doll found a place on my altar. Eventually, though, she came to represent not only the Divine Feminine at the core of a woman but also the line of mothers I came from. Poet Adrienne Rich has pointed out how little the mother-daughter connection has been emphasized in patriarchy. And as Carol P. Christ said, Christianity has celebrated the father's relationship to the son, even the mother's relationship to the son, but the story of the mother and daughter is missing.

The Matryoshka doll made me want to discover and celebrate my mother-daughter story. In my family it had always seemed to me that the line of father and son was paramount—the passing down of the male name, the male line. As the first child and only daughter with three brothers the importance of being a male was rarely lost on me.

My parents welcomed me as a girl and loved me, resoundingly so. Yet, strangely, I'd had vague feelings that on some unspoken level I'd been a disappointment by showing up as a girl, especially since I was the first child. So many times I'd heard people speak of the perfect family as having a boy first, then a girl. As a child in Sunday school, I'd soaked up Old Testament stories about the firstborn male receiving the birthright. That, along with the cultural negation of females in general and the historical imprint of preference for sons, formed an idea in me that while girls may be "sugar and spice and everything nice," boys were the most desired, especially as the first child.

The story I am about to tell relates a small thing, and yet it captures the subtle distinctions I felt growing up female. In my paternal grandmother's house were many treasures: several marble tables, an antique hat rack; bookshelves with glass panes, a marvelous old Victrola, and, treasure of treasures, a massive roll-top desk of oak that smelled like lemon seed oil. It was a desk with secret nooks and crannies that I loved to explore. I would find silver dollars and caramels and cans of Prince Albert pipe tobacco that smelled like my grandfather. For a girl who loved books and writing and secret places to put my words, the desk was an icon of the creative life, and I wanted it for myself.

One day I heard my grandmother talking about who would receive various things after she and my grandfather were gone. She named a couple of things designated for "the first male child," one who carried on the Monk name.

My heart sank a little, but then I thought, Aren't I the first female child? So I got up my courage. I crossed my fingers behind my back. "What about the desk?" I asked. "Who will get it?"

"That will go to the first male child," she said and seeing my disappointment added, "But don't worry, you'll get something special, too." She took me by the hand into the dining room and presented me with her antique hutch full of plates and platters.

That's when I knew for sure there was no such thing as the first female child.

That memory had always been strong in me, and it came back at times when I gazed at the Matryoshka doll on my altar. Here, I would think, looking at her, is an image that honors the motherline.

As Christmas came around, I went back to the shop and bought two more Matryoshka dolls—one for my mother and one for her mother, my ninety-five-year-old grandmother whose name, like mine, is Sue. I wrote each of them a letter to accompany the dolls. "Long ago you used to give me dolls for Christmas. Now I would like to give you one."

I wrote to them about our unfolding line of mothers and daughters. How we'd nested in one another and birthed one another. I told them we were connected not only through blood, tissue, and female likeness, but through feminine heart, memory, and soul. I spoke of the mystery of being inseparable but separate. I was thinking of the dolls but also of

Jung's words: "Every mother contains her daughter in herself and every daughter her mother and every mother extends backwards into her mother and forwards into her daughter."[58]

I also wrote about the endless renewal symbolized in the dolls, the ongoing transformation contained in us. I told them this doll even suggested the image of a Divine Feminine Source birthing and containing us all.

Several months after Christmas, I went to Georgia to visit my maternal grandmother Sue on her ninety-sixth birthday. She had broken her hip a couple of years earlier and didn't get around very well, but her mind and spirit were sharp. She took my hand and pointed to the Matryoshka doll I'd given her.

It had been opened so that each doll stood in a tilting line across the top of a table. "The first doll is Roxie," she said, naming her mother. "And the next doll is her daughter, which is me. And then my daughter, Leah, then her daughter, which is you, and then your daughter, Ann." One tiny doll remained. She picked it up and held it in her palm. "And this is the daughter who isn't yet born."

She was looking at me while she spoke, and it seemed to me she knew everything I'd ever felt about growing up female. She said, "When you were born, I looked through the nursery glass and I said, 'Oh good, it's a girl—a little girl!'"

I smiled, and she opened her arms to me.

I think when I'm very old, if someone asks me which moment of my life stands out as the most loving, I will tell about this one.

"It's a Girl!"

When I was in Crete I found myself in the Skoteino Cave, having an experience similar to the one with my grandmother.

As I wrote earlier, going into the dark of that cave, named for Skoteini, Goddess of the Dark, had been a parable of what it's like to grope our way into the unexplored gorge. But I learned other lessons as well after we blew out our candles and sat on the cave floor.

I was leaning against a huge stalagmite, seeing nothing, but I could smell the wetness in the air. The rocks beneath me were slick with calcareous water. The only sound was dripping, rhythmic as a heartbeat.

I was thinking how in ancient times caves were known as wombs of the earth, and I began to feel that not just I but all of us were gathered there inside Herself, waiting to be born in some new way.

Finally we lit our candles and moved back single file along the narrow passage of rock, climbing up and out. Because the rocks were slippery and the passage steep, the way was treacherous. In some places, for instance, we had to hug the wall and maneuver along skinny ledges, and in one downright awesome place we had to slide slowly on our bottoms along a chute of rock with a precipice on each side.

After a while I noticed the air grew lighter. Looking up, I saw a circle of light above, streaming in milky rays into the tunnel. Something about seeing the opening of that cave excited a burst of energy in me, and I hurried toward it.

A couple of others who'd already emerged stood at the entrance, and as I came out, they began to clap and exclaim, "Oh look, wonderful! It's a girl! It's a girl!" It became every woman's greeting as she emerged.

I stood there feeling infinitely welcome in the world. I was remembering, too, my grandmother who'd opened her arms to me and said nearly these same words. Only now it seemed the valuing of my feminine life was coming from the Great Mother Herself.

Two days later we visited two other caves. The first was known as the birthplace of Zeus. After winding through it, we found a private grotto nearby and made a small altar on one of the stones. According to the Greek custom, we poured water, wine, and milk on the altar. The milk, however, poured out in soured clots. Along the way it had spoiled. It prompted us to talk about the ways that "mother's milk" had gone sour in our own lives. We spoke about the difficulties, betrayals, and pain we'd experienced with our mothers.

Some of the women's experiences with their mothers were so decimating that these women had had terrible difficulty embracing the notion of a Divine Mother. As they told their stories, it became clear that when the idea of the feminine is mediated to daughters through mothers who uphold patriarchal values, who are severed from their own feminine ground, and who are driven by their own inner bishops, the daughters will have to redefine the feminine.

A mother may unconsciously inflict her inner bishop on her daughter, communicating the message that she's not good enough, capable enough, or pretty enough, driving her daughter toward perfection. At the same time the mother may be cautioning her daughter not to overstep conventional bounds, not to rock boats but to be a good patriarchal daughter. The mother is reflecting not a conscious feminine but a negative feminine that is reflected in passivity, inertia, inferiority, and dependency.

Others of us had not experienced such devastating relationships with our mothers while growing up, but instead, seeing the autonomy that was the prerogative of males, we had identified with our fathers and disidentified with our mothers.

Either way, it was only now as we made our journeys back to authentic feminine ground that we could appreciate and forgive their wounds and deficits, their aches and struggles to be themselves in a culture that was arranged against them.

Later that same day we entered the second cave, known as Trapeza. Here we sat in a small room and honored our motherlines. We called the names of our mothers, going back as far as we were able. The cave filled and echoed with dozens of female names. "I am Sue, daughter of Leah, who is daughter of Sue, who is daughter of Roxie, . . . " I said when my turn came, and I felt the connection to my mothers quicken inside.

The feeling was still with me a couple of days later as we hiked through the gorge at Zakros. It was steep, rocky terrain, and we went singing verses of a song called "Mountain Mother." Deep in the gorge we came upon a large stone that bore an uncanny resemblance to a great armchair with large, rolling arms and a wide, hollowed-out seat. Stopping beside it, I recalled the picture of the *Cartoon of St. Anne,* the dream of the *Pietá,* the image of the Great Lap. I felt I'd come upon the lap again, this time in Crete. The lap of the Mountain Mother.

One by one we sat in it. When it was my turn, I could think of nothing but the names of our mothers that we had recited in the Trapeza cave: Leah, Sue, Roxie, and all the others. There are moments when love moves out of the abstract and becomes a real thing, sudden in your chest, and I felt it there, sitting in the lap of the Mother and all my mothers. I felt healed.

Someone took my picture, which sits today on my desk. A dark-haired woman wearing a red baseball-style cap is beaming all over.

My mother knew I'd gone on a Goddess tour to Crete. Also, some time before departing, I'd given her a copy of an essay I'd written entitled "Going Back for Mary." The premise of it was that when the Goddess disappeared, Mary had in some ways carried on the Feminine Divine for us. The first time I saw my mother after arriving back home was Christmas. She handed me a small box wrapped in silver paper, then stood nearby watching as I opened it. Inside was a small pewter statue of Mary.

When I looked up, Mother was smiling. I carry that picture of her in my mind; it is the one I will always keep and cherish, because for the first time, I knew—I really knew—that she understood. It was as if she had given me her blessing. She was my mother, but she was also a woman like myself. I smiled back at her, and my eyes filled with tears.

TRANSFIGURING ANGER

Back during my awakening I'd learned to recognize my anger and allow it to have its place. I had stopped treating injustice against half the human population as a misdemeanor. Inside of me there had been a firestorm, and it had needed to be there for a while. It had opened my eyes, seared my heart, ignited my passion, and steepened my fierceness. But later, as I moved into other passages of the journey, especially the healing, I knew the anger would have to be healed along with other parts of me. It would have to be transfigured.

By transfiguring anger, I don't mean that we wave a placating wand and poof! anger disappears. Nor do I mean that anger is turned into sweet resignation. By healing or transfiguring it, I mean to imply, in Clarissa Pinkola Estés's words, that anger becomes "a fire that cooks things rather than a fire of conflagration."[59] A conflagration may embolden and impassion you for a while, but if you get stuck in it, it can burn you up. A fire that cooks things, however, can feed you and a whole lot of other people.

During my awakening, for a period of time the church had become a flash point for my anger. At the core of the feminine wound is betrayal, and the more we've trusted and invested in a relationship, the deeper the feeling of betrayal will be. When it came to the church, I'd trusted much and invested much. But gradually as episodes of healing took place, I began to move beyond reacting and blaming. Instead of simmering over patriarchal structures and wounds and acts of injustice, I started to respond creatively. I began to redirect the energy toward writing, imagining, speaking out, and empowering other women.

The transfiguration of anger is a movement *from rage to outrage*. Rage implies an internalized emotion, a tempest within. Rage, or what might be called untransfigured anger, can become a calcified bitterness. What rage wants and needs is to move outward toward positive social purpose, to become a creative force or energy that changes the conditions that created it. It needs to become out-rage.

Outrage is love's wild and unacknowledged sister. She is the one who recognizes feminine injury, stands on the roof, and announces it if she has to, then jumps into the fray to change it. She is the one grappling with her life, reconfiguring it, struggling to find liberating ways of relating. She is the one who never bores God or Goddess.

The summer I returned from England, that summer when feminist spiritual consciousness was dawning in my life, I went to speak at a contemplative conference at the Abbey of Gethsemani in Kentucky, the Trappist monastery where Thomas Merton had lived.

I'd not returned to a monastery since that visit years earlier when that "Father Sue" comment had caused such an implosion. Returning, I didn't know what to expect.

The first day was a vat of emotions. The place seemed to turn into a microcosm of the entire father-world, a world layered over with male entitlement, male language, and male-centrism. I relived the exclusivity and patriarchal underpinnings in the most vivid and sharpened way.

Most of all, I kept thinking about the balcony. The last time I'd been at the abbey, years before my awakening, I hadn't been allowed on the floor of the church because I was female (at least that was how the nice monk had put it), and I'd climbed the stairs to look down from the balcony. I told myself that at least I was on the premises; in some monasteries women couldn't even be retreatants at all, and I'd been turned away because of my gender several times. Even so, climbing the stairs on that first visit, I'd felt a vague sense of rejection and sadness. I had stood up there looking down, feeling quarantined so that no one would be infected with my femaleness but then dismissing that feeling as my own pettiness.

The memory of it now, however, made me seethe and ache. I thought of the balcony in the movie theater in my hometown, where blacks were sequestered during the segregation of the fifties. Balconies had long served as symbols of exclusion and unequal power.

That week at Gethsemani, the pain that patriarchal Christianity had inflicted in women's lives—the exclusion, the anger, the regret, the sense of betrayal—welled up and would not go away. But paradoxically, at the same time, I was touched by the beauty of the monastic chants, the honoring of Mary as Mother of God and Christ-bearer, the dissident female saints who often rocked the church and seemed everywhere around us, the nonviolent gentleness that pervaded the monks, the way the holy and the ordinary were blended into something seamless.

I realized that despite everything, strains of the deep song that played inside Christianity played inside me, too. Do you know what it's like to place your ear to a sea-beaten conch and hear a deep, mysterious whispering or to open a broken old music box and find the strains of a waltz suddenly escaping? It was a little like that—startling, strange, haunting, nostalgic.

What do I mean by the deep song within Christianity? I mean the music that plays beneath the patriarchal overlay. I'm referring to Christianity's inner life, the life of Jesus, the stories, the belligerent call to justice and compassion, the mysticism, the meditation, the saints, the art, the icons, the smell of wine in the communion cup.

There was the "balcony," yes, but there was also the resonance of this inner song. Probably that's what compelled me that week to volunteer, along with a few other women and a couple of men, to learn a liturgical dance, which we practiced every afternoon in the conference room.

One day, however, feeling the enormous tension inside, I went for a walk in the monastery woods. Following a little trail, I came unexpectedly to a life-sized bronze statue of Christ kneeling in agony, as he'd done in the garden of Gethsemane before his death. I sat on a log. I stared at it.

For a long while now I'd felt alienated from Father God. In my mind God as Yahweh, King, Father, had become associated with oppressive patriarchal power, with those who deny the feminine aspects of deity and women as equal participants. I felt the estrangement like a split, a deep crevice I could not bridge. I didn't know what I might do about it, but for the first time I noticed a small willingness to try to do something.

Our liturgical dance was going to be performed during a mass on the last day, but somehow it hadn't dawned on me that this would happen during the monastery's regular mass on the main floor of the church. (As far as I know, an unprecedented thing.) I felt nervous as I rose from my chair and began along with the others to move around the main altar, but I quickly lost myself in the dance, a feminine ballet filled with graceful arm movements, dips, and turns.

Then I happened to look up and see the balcony. I was so shocked at the sight of it, by the reversal of being "down here" and not "up there," I nearly stopped dancing. Look at me, I thought. I'm not up there. I'm here on the floor of the church, dancing. *I'm dancing because ultimately the feminine cannot be denied or shut away. It dances even here.*

The balcony, which had been such a symbol of exclusion and betrayal, seemed to recede, then dissolve, the bitterness it represented dissolving with it. I began to dance with my whole self lifted into it, feeling the presence of the Divine Feminine in my arms and legs, as if she were writing some new calligraphy in the monastic air.

An old monk sat on the front row in his black-and-white robe. I met his gaze, then turned. When I looked back, he was still watching me. He looked nearly transfixed by it all, his mouth parted like a child's, his eyes smiling, and I realized it was joy and love I was seeing on his face.

I was a *woman* dancing around the monastery altar—present, included, celebrated, loved. It was all there in the monk's face, and I knew even then that his face seemed to me the face of Father God. Suddenly I felt again the old, familiar presence.

That dance, which opened into unexpected healing, became my reuniting bridge. It evoked a *mysterium coniunctionis,* the unity of the divine symbol in which the Sacred Feminine and the Sacred Masculine began to come together in my life.

What is ultimately needed is balance—divine symbols that reflect masculine *and* feminine and a genuine marriage of the masculine and feminine in each of us. Meinrad Craighead in her book *The Mother's Song* refers to this. Her Catholic heritage and her deep foundation in God the Mother came together, she says. "The two movements are not in conflict, they simply water different layers in my soul."[60] Dancing at the monastery taught me what she meant.

FORGIVENESS

That dance was also a ritual of forgiveness.

Perhaps it's possible to forgive in one grand swoop, but I didn't experience it that way. I did it in bits and pieces, one stage at a time. The dance began the process.

You forgive what you can, when you can. That's all you can do.

To forgive does not mean overlooking the offense and pretending it never happened. Forgiveness means releasing our rage and our need to retaliate, no longer dwelling on the offense, the offender, and the suffering, and rising to a higher love. It is an act of letting go so that we ourselves can go on.

The circle of trees had represented many things to me—a refuge, a place to express my anger, a place to be supported, to heal, to encounter the Sacred Feminine, and to knit a way back to my soul. But eventually it also became the space of compassion. For in the end I knew: There is no healing without forgiveness, no forgiveness without love. Indeed, love is everything.

I was driving alone early one Sunday morning in Atlanta. I stopped at a traffic light beside a small brick Baptist church. I looked at it, then at a few daffodils blooming wild in a ditch nearby. They made me think of the daffodils I'd planted in the circle of trees at Springbank. I wondered if those were blooming, too.

Who knows what impelled me to do it—probably the need to finish and mark the forgiveness with a tangible act—but I pulled the car to the side of the road. I picked the flowers and tied them with a string, making a little bouquet of yellow. Then I walked to the church and left the bouquet at its front doors.

We can name the places in our lives where such offerings need to be left, places where the wounds have happened, and when we are ready we can mark them with the beauty of our forgiveness. The naming and the marking release us.

Driving away from the church that day, I felt I'd made my peace.

THE DANCE OF DISSIDENCE

After two years of grounding myself in Sacred Feminine experience, I realized I'd been creating a real, though unorthodox, spiritual path. It was a path all my own.

At first, for a short while, I'd thought of my experience as one of exile, but that wasn't it at all. My journey had created a deep, sustaining container for me, one that I could now rest within. My journey had also become an experience of unfolding, not something imposed on me from without, but the creation of my own feminine heart.

My vision of religious experience had changed and expanded considerably. My path included relating daily to the presence of the Divine; it included a web of rituals and a community of women; and it included various forms of prayer. There was the prayer at my altar when I lit a candle and asked for peace on earth and blessings for others, the prayer of turning ordinary moments into an experience of the holy, and the prayer of listening to the voice within, the voice of soul in the solar plexus that spins the thread of our own truth.

My path also encompassed sacred experiences in nature, relating to my inner life through analysis and dreams, using my creative work in the service of my vision, and struggling to act on behalf of love and justice. I had also begun to practice yoga in order to be aware of and honor my body, to practice Zen meditation and mindfulness in order to quiet my mind and awaken to my true nature.

Far from exile, my journey offered me a rich, multitextured, *feminine* experience of the sacred that flowed so deep and full inside that I could truly say, In my heart, I am home.

"My religion is kindness," says the Dalai Lama, and I think if I had to scrunch it all down into one word, I might say that, too. Except I can never say anything in one word; I don't seem to have enough spiritual simplicity yet to do that. So I would make it into a sentence and say, My religion is being in awakened relationship with all that is and doing so with a kind and pure heart, with an authentic feminine soul and a vision of justice. When I say my path is being in an awakened relationship with all that is, I'm referring to others, of course, but also to nature and earth, to myself, and to the One who holds us all in being.

So I made my own path. Sandy understood this, my children understood. But it was hard for some. When I tried to explain my spiritual path to those who asked about the changes in my life, I was sometimes met with puzzled, skeptical (yes, even alarmed) looks. Because they could not imagine it for themselves, they told me it was not a valid option.

I understand this. When we create paths that are utterly new and outside sanctioned models, paths that are native to the female soul, our paths are often dismissed or overlooked. "The new space," Mary Daly rightly observed, "has a kind of invisibility to those who have not entered it."[61] But if a woman has entered this journey, down deep she *sees* and *knows* the rightness of it.

I kept thinking about that familiar Zen saying: Before I was enlightened, I chopped wood and carried water. After I was enlightened, I chopped wood and carried water.

After the illusions are gone, after a woman wakes up, after she has become grounded in a new way and experienced healing and forgiveness, she continues on with her spiritual life, investing in church if she chooses it, but doing so with a world of difference. Now she can bring to it a whole new consciousness. She has a new heart, new vision, new soul, new voice, new knowing, and new grit. She has a whole new dance.

Some women say you must stay in the institution and try to change it. Others say women cannot stay in without being co-opted, that we can change things best remaining outside it. I say each woman must do what her heart tells her.

When I do attend church, it doesn't provoke the old feelings. Rather, I am there knowing who I am as a woman and allowing the church to be what it is. I find I can be connected to the community of people and honor the deep song that flows on.

Madonna Kolbenschlag suggests that if an awakened woman forgoes innocence and denial, if she refuses to make compromises with herself and defect to patriarchy, then her only option becomes deviance.[62] I chose deviance. I chose to be a loving dissident. To dance the dance of dissidence. This stance can be assumed from the inside or the outside. Whichever place we choose, the important thing is having the sustained will to be, act, and speak from the ground of our feminine souls, from the space inside the circle of trees.

You create a path of your own by looking within yourself and listening to your soul, cultivating your own ways of experiencing the sacred, and then practicing it. Practicing until you make it a song that sings you.

Turtle Song

Walking late one night along Edisto Beach in South Carolina, Sandy and I came upon a huge, domed shape emerging from the waves. I stopped, silenced. It was a giant sea turtle lumbering out of the sea to lay her eggs.

We turned off our flashlight and watched as she dragged herself toward the dunes. The moon hung full over the ocean so that she moved with an aurora at her back, as if rising up from some deep, shimmering mystery.

I'd never seen a creature work so hard to get anywhere. Turtles may be fluid as ballerinas in the water, but on land they take on the appearance of a toiling tractor, of Sisyphus rolling his great stone up the hill.

Easily three hundred pounds and five feet long, she left a three-foot-wide tractor-crawl behind her. She stopped beside a dune where the sea oats cast moving shadows across her shell. As we edged near enough to see but far enough to give her privacy, she began to dig. She flipped the sand into a pile behind her, working her flippers like tiller blades, making a bowl-shaped pit into which her great body sank, grounding herself, not unlike the way I'd tried to ground myself in the circle of trees. I listened to the sound she made until it took up residence in me like one of those radio tunes you cannot stop hearing—a whispering sweep of sand like chafes of wind, like the cadence of your mother's broom.

Then silence. She became still. A long while passed. Finally, slipping up behind her, I drew close enough to see the bluish white shells of the eggs. Here was female life moving through its rhythms. I sat down almost involuntarily, my legs giving way with the weight and beauty of the experience. I was thinking of the Chippewa healing song, "Great Turtle, I am sitting with you."

I thought back to the small turtle I'd come upon not so long ago, which had reminded me to stay grounded in the earth; then I went even further back to the night when my journey was first beginning, a night on a beach with another full moon. Women dancing around a sea turtle shell. That night, knowing how cut off I was from my female soul, I'd brushed my hand across the turtle's shell like a prayer.

Now I leaned over and laid my hand on the turtle's shell, and she turned her head and seemed to look at me. Something immense culminated for me in that moment. I came full circle.

I thought about the female-child who'd been conceived and birthed during my awakening, the potential that had been in me all along, the girl who would grow up to be a woman with her own soul. During my initiation experiences, this child had grown enough to cross over to a new womanhood. Now during grounding, she'd matured and begun to come into her own. Next, I imagined, she would, like the turtle, start to lay eggs of her own.

I could see in the turtle's act my own female soul moving through its rhythms, and they, too, seemed primal and beautiful to me. I felt a communion with her, and when I rose to my feet and saw the form of my shadow juxtaposed with hers on the sand, I was nearly knocked backward with love for my female life.

The turtle heaved herself up at last and began her slow crawl back to the ocean. I walked beside her, stopping when she stopped, moving when she moved, riding in the contours of her shadow. I went with her into the waves, over my knees, and watched till she was gone from sight.

"I took my lyre and said: Come now, my heavenly tortoise shell: become a speaking instrument," wrote the poet Sappho.[63] Sometimes I can still hear the song the turtle made in the sand that night as she dug her hole, and I imagine her like a great lyre that takes women's experience and turns it into a song.

PART FOUR

Empowerment

We are volcanoes. When we women offer our experience as our truth, all the maps change. There are new mountains. That's what I want—to hear you erupting. You Mount St. Helenses who don't know the power in you—I want to hear you. . . . If we don't tell our truth, who will?

Ursula K. Le Guin

This above all, to refuse to be a victim. Unless I can do that I can do nothing. I have to recant, give up the old belief that I am powerless. . . .

female character in Margaret Atwood's novel *Surfacing*

It had been nearly six years since my journey began, six years from the "Father Sue" visit at the monastery until the sea turtle crawled onto the beach. Several weeks after I met the turtle, I sat on the patio in my back-yard on an August afternoon. Our beagles, Caesar and Brutus, lay im-movable on either side of me like a pair of garden statues. I stroked their heads.

I thought of the turtle, the way she crawled out of safe waters onto a new, inhospitable, even hostile shore to lay her eggs in the world, and I wondered if that was where I was just now—emerging from natural feminine waters where I'd learned to swim, ready to come onshore and plant my journey in the world. I wondered if I could do that. What would it take?

COHESION OF THE FEMALE SOUL

During my life, as in most lives, I'd known individual moments of strength when I rose to the occasion, endured, showed some courage, ex-erted influence. Yet I had not experienced femaleness itself as a powerful thing. I had not carried an inner authority *as a woman* or experienced the abiding strength, resilience, potency, and substance that comes when a woman dwells in the solid center of herself. I had never dared things that required the kind of bravery that took my breath. Lay the eggs of this journey in the world? I didn't know if I had the—the what? The strength? The guts? Or, as a friend of mine says, the ovaries?

And yet, lately, I'd noticed a new and subtle something, a feeling, a knowing that I hadn't yet tried to articulate. I tried now to put words around it, at least in my mind. It was, I realized, an almost physical sen-sation of something coagulating inside me, coming together and solidi-fying. It felt like a new island formed after the volcano has erupted and poured its lava into the sea, so new it is still smoking with vapor and waiting for footprints. I felt like some great cohesion was going on, quiet and obscured. But what did that mean? Was it the natural and organic process of becoming empowered as a woman? Power. It was the thing I'd never claimed for myself.

I sat on the patio, trying not to think about power. A big squall of barking broke out as the dogs charged after a squirrel. Settled again in my chair, I found myself with a new thought. I was remembering poet Maya Angelou in a television interview I'd recently seen. The interviewer asked her what it took to be a writer. Three things, she said: something to say, the ability to express it, and, finally, the courage to express it at all. And it came to me all of a sudden that becoming empowered as a woman required three very similar things: a soul of one's own, the ability or means to voice it, and, finally, the courage to voice it at all.

First we need to find this soul of our own. We must wake up, journey, name, challenge, shed, reclaim, ground, and heal. We need to follow our Big Wisdom, the thread that spins out of our feminine core. And then, *then* we find the means—the authority, the solidity, the internal coagulation—that allows us to voice this soul.

In many ways female power is an organic thing. It grows and flowers naturally in us as we move through the passages of our journey, reconnecting with our feminine souls. It's just like Madonna Kolbenschlag writes, "Women, healed and whole, will find undreamed resources in themselves."[1]

Think of it like this. In the beginning we wake to find ourselves like transplanted saplings trying to subsist in an unnatural, unfriendly (patriarchal) ground. We discover ourselves becoming sapless inside, going dry in the place where feminine soul rises, animates, and nourishes our lives. We know that in order to save our lives as women, we have to find new ground. So we set off in search of the feminine ground inside the circle of trees. We put down roots. And if we are patient, if we are true to ourselves, if we are willing to see ourselves through the growing seasons, an inevitable thing happens. We become hearty women who have our own ground and our own standing, sturdy as oak after the winds. We become women who let loose our strength, whose truth, creativity, and vision fly like spores into the world.

The image that comes to me is a grove of cottonwood trees beside a friend's house in Albuquerque. While visiting her one June, as I walked among the trees a wind rose, shaking loose the downy cottonwood tufts filled with seed, turning the air into a blizzard of floating cotton. I think women who have found their feminine ground are like that grove. At some point their seeds fly with the wind.

That day in August I left the patio and went inside for my journal. I needed to write it all down, which is always my inmost craving, my way of making sense of things. So I wrote it all down, but I noticed that every time I wrote the word *power,* my pen would pause just a fraction of a second. This word was making me uncomfortable.

Now why was that?

AUTHENTIC POWER

Was it because I was uncomfortable with the concept of power *as it's practiced in our culture?*

It's hard to know what authentic power is; we've had so few examples of it. For so long power has been a matter of control and dominion, the thing that keeps some people up and others down, the blood that feeds the hierarchy.

The kind of power women need is not ruthless, controlling, self-serving, dominion-seeking power—power without benefit of love. It is not staying up by keeping others down. What we need is a potent, forceful power, yes, but one that is also compassionate, that enables others as well.

"The true representation of power is not a big man beating a smaller man or a woman," Carolyn Heilbrun writes. Nor is it a woman beating up on a man or finding a place in the hierarchy and mimicking the old patriarchal ways of entitlement, control, and command. Rather, Heilbrun says, power is "the *ability* to take one's place in whatever discourse is essential to action and the right to have one's part matter."[2]

That day, feeling the ripening sensation inside, the first impulse to lay my "eggs" in the world, I realized I'd come to a new passage of experience, to a time of empowerment when I must begin to truly own my experience, to feel the strength of it, to gather it up and put it "out there."

BUFFALO MEDICINE

One day that fall I went to the mailbox and found a letter from my mother. It contained a small, yellowed newspaper clipping, which she'd found "while going through some old things." As I sat at the kitchen table and read the clip, a long-lost story returned to memory.

I was three years old. The city zoo in a neighboring town was raising money to buy an American bison. "What's a bison?" I wanted to know. So my parents told me majestic stories about the buffalo of the plains. I had in my possession a prized nickel from my grandfather, and when I discovered a buffalo on it, it seemed fate had struck. Surely a *buffalo* nickel could buy a buffalo. I insisted on delivering the nickel to the zoo officials in person. I was so adamant about it, my mother finally drove me the twenty miles so I could give it to them.

The story ended up in the newspaper, and I somehow got the idea that with my fateful nickel I had single-handedly bought the buffalo myself. In my three-year-old heart that buffalo was mine.

My parents indulged this as a harmless notion, and I named the buffalo Billy. So began countless trips to the zoo to see "my animal." I would station myself at the buffalo exhibit, talking to him, rarely going to see the other animals. My attachment to him was the sort of love a child usually reserves for a first puppy.

Seeing the yellowed clipping of that story stirred up some of those long-ago feelings I'd had for "my buffalo"—the connection and love, my childlike reverence for it. I tacked the clipping above my desk. Over the next few months, I had a series of buffalo dreams.

In the first few, the buffalo appeared alone, female and white, a creature of awesome power. In the final dream she brought a Native American shaman on her back. He was adorned in a buffalo headdress and held a flaming arrow, which he shot at my feet. "From now on, you must take your buffalo medicine," he said. Whatever buffalo medicine symbolized, I knew it was important. I felt like I was being compelled to go back and reclaim something I'd left in my childhood, something the buffalo represented, and then take it into myself.

So off I went to libraries and bookstores. I read everything I could find about buffalo, especially in Native American spirituality. I discovered many things, among them that the white buffalo was terribly sacred and powerful and that its spirit was often considered to be a Divine Feminine presence. The Lakota Sioux tell the story of White Buffalo Calf Woman, a sacred spirit who came as a woman of mystery and power during a time of great hardship. She told the Native people about the value of the buffalo and gave them the sacred pipe and sacred teachings. She told them one day she would return. And when she walked away, she turned into a white buffalo calf. White buffalo cow societies, made up of powerful women, flourished among certain tribes.

I was intrigued by the connection of the white buffalo to feminine divinity and power, but I was also impressed by the buffalo's irrefutable persistence in surviving, even flourishing, despite the campaign that tried to stamp it out. In the early 1800s there were around forty million buffalo on the western plains; by 1900 there were fewer than a thousand. Today they are flourishing again, many roaming free, their numbers more than 135,000.

Gradually I came to see that taking "buffalo medicine" meant taking in this same kind of persistence and resilient strength. It meant standing firm and powerful, flourishing despite everything that would seek to limit or silence the feminine spirit.

Taking buffalo medicine meant following a path of female empowerment.

During a woman's retreat that winter I met a Cherokee woman and surprised myself by telling her my dream.

"A white buffalo," she said, eyes widening. "I suspect it has come to offer you a gift. It wants to make you a powerful woman."

When spring came, I visited my friend Terry in Colorado. Terry and I had known each other nearly ten years, but over the last few we'd become extremely close as we'd shared our spiritual journeys through marathon phone calls and letters and visits when we could manage them.

Before leaving home I'd gone to a coin dealer and purchased a buffalo nickel, 1937, one of the last years it was minted. I carried it as a reminder, and it was in my pocket one day as we were driving through the Rockies.

I was telling her about the buffalo in my dreams and its empowering symbolism. Her eyes started to gleam. "You won't believe this," she said, "but there's a spot up ahead where we might see some buffalo. It's unusual, but once in a while a herd comes in from the range to a place near the road."

A few minutes later we came to a sign pointing to the right that said "Buffalo Overlook," and Terry turned off.

There looking at us were twenty-seven massive, shaggy buffalo fifty yards from the road, cordoned off by a fence. I got out of the car and went to stand as close as I could. As the wind blew wildly and I burrowed down in my coat, I remembered the woman's words, that the buffalo wanted to give me a gift—to make me a powerful woman. I stood there a long time and tried to open myself to receive it.

Finally, as I turned to leave, a gust of wind lifted something small and brown on the other side of the fence and blew it inches from my feet. I squinted down at it. It was a tuft of buffalo fur.

I recalled from my reading that buffalo fur was considered by Plains Indians to be a carrier of buffalo medicine, and I took it into my hand as if it were the most sacred of gifts.

Like the child long ago, I wanted to offer my gift, too, so I dug in my pocket for the buffalo nickel. I left it on the ground inside the fence. And once again, by giving my nickel, I felt I was making this animal mine; I was enacting an intention to reclaim it, to reclaim the potential for power that I'd left behind.

Now I had this clump of fur, this symbol of female power, in my pocket, and something had to be done with it. I began to meditate on what it meant to take buffalo medicine. I began to understand that for me it meant a process of empowerment that involved three particular things: voicing the soul, finding and nurturing my inner authority, and learning to embody my sacred feminine experience.

VOICING THE SOUL

Back in the fall, before the buffalo dreams began, the wise old woman had returned in my dreams with the same long white hair and infinite wrinkles as before. Earlier, she had given me the Matryoshka doll, which had become a source of great healing. This time she came with a mandate. She raised her hand over my head. She said, "Your heart is a seed. Go, plant it in the world."

Sacred feminine experience can heal, make whole, season, and impassion women. It gives us a new and exciting context of spiritual meaning, vision, autonomy, strength, and integrity. And all that's a lot, but can we say it should end there?

Ultimately our experience needs to become a force for compassion and justice in the world. We must bear witness to what we have experienced.

Why is that important? Because what had been maturing in me— what matures in all women who undertake this journey—is something the world needs: feminine soul. The world needs a new ecological wisdom and the honoring of earth and body that the Divine Feminine implants. It needs to embrace the consciousness of we, the image of the web, the interconnection and interrelatedness that are central to women's experience and that Sacred Feminine experience only deepens. And finally, the world needs the vision and courage to dismantle hierarchies of power. It needs to be faced with its injustices, to hear voices that speak for the voiceless and powerless. It needs conscious women. Conscious men, too.

In order to voice the soul, we will have to balance our inner experience with an outer one. A mystic is a person who tends to have inward experiences of the Divine and who finds ultimate authority within that experience rather than in a source outside of herself. Prophets, on the other hand, are people whose spiritual energy moves externally into the world. They become voices, calling society to truth, justice, and equality. They go "out there" and struggle to bring about social and spiritual revolution. The point is, as authors Eleanor Rae and Bernice Marie-Daly suggest, we can no longer afford to be one or the other. Conscious women are both. As these two women tell us,

No longer must we be either mystics or prophets: now we can and must claim our experience both of God/ess and of the call to bring about justice as two interweaving threads of one common experience, the experience of the mystic/prophet. An introverted mysticism is a truncated mysticism, and a mere social reformer is no prophet at all.[3]

When I think of the fusion of the mystic and the prophet inside a woman, I think of the image the wise old woman brought me, of a woman planting her ripe heart in the world. Having had a transforming experience within, she begins now to find the impulse and the means to express it.

"Your heart is a seed. Go, plant it in the world" filled me with new inclinations and new bravery. For more than six years, I'd been more or less sequestered deep in my own experience. I'd spent a lot of time in the circle of trees at Springbank, literally and symbolically secluded in the woods. I'd needed that time to awaken, cross over, heal, and become grounded in a new place. That was my mystic self. Now there was the prophet to include.

As this was becoming clear to me, I went on my last retreat to Springbank. I walked about the circle of trees, knowing it was time to come out of the woods and bring the circle of trees with me. The last morning of my retreat, I stood where the path winds out of the circle and prayed for every woman who would ever come into that beautiful circumference. Then I left.

Women on the Loose

Coming out of the woods reminded me of a group of women I read about during the 1994 Winter Olympics at Lillehammer. Thirty-five Norwegian women skied down the slope, opening the giant slalom competition. In Norway this group is known as the *kjerringsleppet,* which roughly translated means "women on the loose."

The group formed back in 1989 when only men were invited to participate in the opening ceremony of Norway's Alpine Center. The women felt insulted and excluded, so these thirty-five banded together, waited in the woods until the appropriate moment, then shocked everyone by swooping out of the trees on snow skis, clanging cow bells and crashing the ceremony.[4] The country loved it, and the women became a fond symbol, so much so they were invited to the Olympics.

Back at the beginning of my journey, I'd recognized an array of daughter selves in my life: the Gracious Lady, the Church Handmaid, the Secondary Partner, the Many-Breasted Mother, the Favored Daughter, the Silent Woman. They were selves created from patriarchal blueprints. Now as I began to think about women's power, I speculated that I also had an array of empowered selves inside.

The *kjerringsleppet* were a marvelous image for the empowered self. A "woman on the loose" is a woman who leaves the woods where she has been growing strong all these years. She swoops out of the trees, ringing her bell. She is saying, I am here now. And I am not going away.

The motto that the women on the loose adopted is: "To improvise, surprise, and come uninvited." That's not a half-bad motto.

To *improvise* means to take whatever abilities and resources are available and to use them in whatever situation arises, often an unforeseen one. The women in Norway were presented with a situation in which they were excluded, so they improvised a way to challenge and circumvent it. As Sartre said, "Genius is the way one invents in desperate situations."

A woman of power becomes a genius in desperate situations; she is an improvisational artist. Rather than bypassing or shrinking from situations where her consciousness is needed, she speaks and acts, relying on something inside herself. All improvisational artists know that you must trust yourself. To improvise you must value your own knowing.

The rest of the *kjerringsleppet* motto is "to surprise and come uninvited," which means stepping out of the expected and becoming a daring and dissident presence. Powerful women are always surprising themselves, always getting a small gasp out of the world. I once saw Gloria Steinem on television, addressing women. She said, "In the next twenty-four hours do at least one outrageous thing in the cause of simple female justice." Of course, if we all did that, the world would turn on its head.

It reminded me of a woman who told the story of having to write a paper and submit it before an all-male board of seminarians in order to be approved for her ordination. The night before she was to turn in her paper, she was struck with the idea that she ought to rewrite it, taking out every masculine pronoun and putting a feminine one in its place. This was many years ago, when such ideas were appalling, and it was an enormous risk. But she did it anyway. Every masculine reference in scripture, every reference to God, every "universal *he*" was changed to *she* or *her*. When she appeared before the board, the men expressed the shock of reading something geared exclusively to the feminine. It stunned them with an awareness of what women experience. They said they'd felt religiously excluded for the first time in their lives. They applauded her courage and gave her her ordination. "When women speak truly, they speak subversively," writes Ursula K. Le Guin.[5] They refuse to be uninvited. They learn surprising ways to invite themselves.

From Silence to Lyricism

For a long while now I'd felt the need to walk away from my long career of inspirational writing and hurl myself in a new creative direction. I felt ready for it, but I hadn't yet leaped, and I wasn't sure why not. Fear of failure? Loss of security? Lack of focus? Resistance to redefining myself creatively? Was it just easier to plan to write fiction or to plan to write the uncensored truth about women's spirituality than it was to do it? My "cottonwood tree" felt full. What I needed was a stiff wind.

It came one day as I browsed through an art museum in a nearby city. I'd come alone to see an exhibit called "Telling Tales." According to the flyers, each painting contained a narrative, a story encoded within the canvas. As a writer, I was captivated by the mystery of a story nesting inside a single visual image.

I did the ritual you do in museums—stand before one painting a respectable amount of time, cock your head back and forth, then go stand before the next one. I'd viewed a half dozen without getting much of a story from them when I came upon a dark, brooding painting of a woman from ancient Greece, entitled *Sappho*. Unmistakably, it began to tell a tale.

It pictured the female poet of ancient Greece, sitting alone on a divan, her face in shadow, her lyre dropped to the floor and her arm dangling limply over it.

There was something painfully resonant about the image—the deserted lyre, the unspoken lament that flowed through the white bone of her arm down to the curl of her fingers. And worst of all, the silence. The painting touched the place in me where my own lyre lay dropped and silent.

I didn't know a lot about Sappho, but I did know she was a poet of ancient Greece and that her work had vanished into the trash can of history. There happened to be a library next door, so I walked over to see what more I could find out.

I found that during her life, Sappho was not silent at all but extravagantly lyrical. In Sappho, the Western world heard perhaps for the first time in written history the lush, creative voice of the female.

Her lyric voice graced the world with a power that was unsurpassed. While male poets of her day were writing and singing of war, politics, and worldly commerce, the lyric Sappho sang poems about love and suffering, about orchards and crickets and the moon in its roundness. At times her voice was joyful and sublime, other times insulting and ironic, but it was always fired with individual truth.

The silent Sappho came later, as her voice was condemned by patriarchy. In 350 C.E. the bishop of Constantinople ordered her writings burned wherever found. Today, of the more than five hundred poems she wrote, only seven hundred lines or fragments remain.

Sitting in the library, I speculated that both aspects—the silence and the lyricism—existed inside women.

As I left I wished for the lyric Sappho in myself. The next day I began to make arrangements to spend the summer studying fiction at Emory University in Atlanta.

For six weeks in June and July I made the commute twice a week. I immersed myself in learning a new craft, stockpiled books of literary fiction, and read and read like a thirsty sponge—all of this an initiation into a new creative path. Most of all, I began to write from a new place, a deeper place, from the circle of trees I was starting to carry inside. One of the first short stories I published told the story of a southern girl named Lily who struggles to find the strength of her feminine wings in a world that routinely clips them.[6]

That August on my birthday Sandy, who had heard my story about the deserted lyre, gave me a gift that I treasure as much as anything he has ever given me, including the deer antlers. It was a small replica of a fresco from Minoan Crete that pictured a woman playing a lyre made from two golden snakes. Sandy's card said, "Strum your heart out."

The lyric Sappho is another image of an empowered female self. She is the woman in us who takes up her *real* work, creates, sings her verses to the world. And she does so through the connection she establishes with her Deep Feminine instinct, a connection symbolized in the picture by the golden snakes.

To be empowered as women, eventually we must turn our snakes into lyres and strum our hearts out.

When I lament the loss of women's creativity through history, my friend Karen in Utah reminds me that women's creativity has always been there, but many times it was erased from history or stolen and used by men. Karen is a musician who has studied women composers. "They've always been there," she says, "but have been left out of dictionaries and catalogs, often by nineteenth-century men." Yet women's creativity has also been absent because of women's subordination and the denial of their value. Rather than creating ourselves, we've often been content to be muses to men, making their creativity possible. Sometimes when we have created, we've not used the mother tongue of our own soul but parroted patriarchal thought, turning out reframed versions of what we'd heard it saying. And as Karen points out, when we have spoken in our true creative voices, we frequently have been neglected, obscured, or overlooked.

I cannot tell you how many women I meet who say, "Oh, I'm just not creative." It breaks my heart, because every woman *is* creative in some way, and every woman's creativity is valuable.

Perhaps we think of creativity too narrowly. When a woman takes a cornfield and turns it into a woodland garden where women gather to talk and dance and feed their souls, like my friend Betty did, she is being a lyrical Sappho, creating out of her soul. When she develops an imaginative plan through which businesses can give a portion of their sales to abused women's shelters and environmental groups, like another friend of mine did, she, too, is strumming the lyre of snakes.

If someone should ask me, "What does the soul *do?*" I would say, It does two things. It loves. And it creates. Those are its primary acts.

The replanted, rewoven female soul sets loose a fecund spirit inside us. We grow fertile with new words, new ideas, new consciousness, new lyricism, new energy. Our journey deposits psychological or spiritual energy (empowerment) into our internal banks. As Mary Catherine Bateson points out, there is physical energy from finite resources, but psychic or spiritual energy—what might be called vitality—is something else entirely. "The energy to write this page is released by metabolized food," writes Bateson. "But the [psychic] 'energy' to write this page depends on my state of mind, and such 'energy' can come from a sunset or a remembered smile."[7]

The energy or vitality to create is engendered from the soul.

The first step toward lyricism is simply acknowledging our creativity. Second, we must explore it. Ask yourself, "What is my deepest passion, *really?* What moves me profoundly?" And let the answer float up from the truest, most vulnerable place in your heart. Greet this answer like it is your own newborn self being placed in your arms. Love it. Bond with it. Feed it. Don't push it aside, minimize, make excuses, and starve this thing of beauty, because this answer is the window into your creative life.

Third, we need to commit to our creative path. I don't mean to want to do it in our hearts or to make plans to do it. I mean to actually do it. When I teach at writers' conferences, I often meet women with books inside them they never write down. I meet women with all kinds of dazzling projects their souls have concocted that for some reason they never get around to manifesting.

I know this dilemma firsthand. For me it is often a lack of focus, allowing my energy to run out in dozens of directions—many of them silly tributaries of distraction—rather than setting priorities and funneling my energy toward the project at hand. Part of women's genius lies in our ability to make multiple commitments, to do many tasks, and to live with ambiguity and multiplicity. It's true that power can come from the flexibility of doing many things, but sometimes the multiplicity, the moving from one thing to another, is overdone and we diffuse our power. There are times it is best to dam up the tributaries and send the energy thundering in just one direction. All great things are launched on big rivers.

Closely connected is the matter of drawing boundaries. A retired woman came to me, miserable and frustrated, and said every time she set aside time to write, her husband would come into the room and launch into all sorts of topics or else stare at her "pitifully" until she stopped. She had not wanted to confront him, and her writing had practically ceased. I suggested to her that there comes a time when we have to put our foot down. Clarissa Pinkola Estés writes,

If we were to abuse our children, Social Services would show up at our doors. If we were to abuse our pets, the Humane Society would come to take us away. But there is no Creativity Patrol or Soul Police to intervene if we insist on starving our own souls.[8]

Empowerment involves learning to make boundaries and protect them. If it happens that my husband and college-aged children are home and I'm in the midst of a project that needs absolute focus, I close my study door. I tell them, "If there's an emergency—a *real* emergency and not, 'Have you seen my reading glasses?' or 'Is there anything to eat around here?'—knock twice. Otherwise, leave me be."

Another problem that keeps us from manifesting our creativity is a resistance to act. I'm not talking about being creatively idle. Sometimes I do my best creative work when I am spread-eagled on the grass with my eyes closed. Never lose that sort of sacred dawdling. The resistance to act is of a different sort. It is an odd contention that rises up inside and keeps us from beginning and then keeps us from following through. How are we going to live empowered lives if we don't lose that? "Better to strangle an infant in its cradle than nurse unacted desires," said William Blake.[9] A little strong, I think, but we get the message.

Often we like to dwell in the rapturous realm of imagination, passion, and ideas but hate to follow through with the leg work that brings those images, passions, and ideas into actual existence. I've had to learn this many times: Tapping the flow of the soul is only *half* the creative process; the other half is figuring out how to do commerce with the practical world. Maybe we have to learn how to use a computer or make a plan to market our idea or network with people or go out and find the place to hold the workshop. Being committed means learning what we need to know and doing what we need to do in order to make the voice of our souls heard.

And finally, to be empowered creatively we need to understand what to do when we move from lyricism back to silence. Inevitably I get discouraged and lose creative direction or passion—that psychic or spiritual energy I was referring to earlier.

When that happens, I've learned to drop down into the creative nothing. I do sacred dawdling. I turn to nature. I lie on the earth or dig in the dirt. I get still, go silent, rest, take herbal baths, listen to Bach's *Brandenburg Concerto* or James Taylor full blast. I buy flowers. I drink cinnamon tea, play with my dogs, meditate, and create rituals.

The main thing is to stop struggling and nourish yourself. When you nourish yourself, your creative energy is renewed. You are able to pick up your lyre again and sing.

FINDING INNER AUTHORITY

Empowerment also comes into a woman's life as she finds her inner authority. The word *authority* has lots of meanings, both positive and negative, but I like the meaning that comes from the Greek: "to stand forth with power and dignity."

Often we recognize or acknowledge this authority for the first time when our female backs are against the wall, when some challenge or opposition comes along and we feel our mettle being tested.

It happened for me in the spring of that same year when I was coming out of the woods and dreaming of buffalo. I delivered a speech on feminine spirituality and the ecological crisis at a mainline denominational conference. It was my first address on the suppression of the feminine within Christianity since becoming grounded in feminine spiritual consciousness, and I was feeling pretty nervous.

After I closed my speech, I remained at the podium for an open dialogue with an audience of a few hundred, about half men and half women. It was an audience, on the whole, wonderfully open to my message. But then a male clergyman rose to his feet, pointed his finger at me, and shook it as if scolding a rebellious child. "Young lady . . ."

I don't recall his words precisely, but basically he wanted me and the audience to know that traditions concerning women should not be tampered with, that women like me should cut this kind of stuff out.

He wanted me to know that he had daughters and he would never want them, much less the church, to hold outrageous ideas like mine.

There was a time when something like this would have blown me away, as the saying goes. His voice would have resounded as the authoritarian male voice, the voice of the patriarchal church, the voice of the culture, even the voice of Father God, and it would have left me unnerved, vulnerable, doubtful, afraid, wishing for a hole so I could disappear inside it, wishing I'd kept my mouth shut.

I remember standing there as he went on and on, waiting for my knees to buckle. But they didn't. Instead I found myself remembering a greeting card I'd purchased only a few days earlier with a quote on the front by poet Audre Lorde. It said, "When I dare to be powerful—to use my strength in the service of my vision—then it becomes less and less important whether I am afraid."

I almost smiled remembering it. It was like a big dose of buffalo medicine, and the feeling of solidity, which I'd been gradually sensing, was right there. I felt it like a hand slowly turning to fist inside my belly. It made me reposition my feet, plant them solid, and lift my chin. Funny thing, though, I didn't feel reactive. Not angry, not threatened, not the slightest need to defend myself. I merely felt firm, rooted in some kind of new power. In fact, I was so caught by the surprise of these feelings, I rather lost what the man was going on about.

When I refocused my attention on him, I thought how admirably he represented patriarchy. I kept thinking that here is a frightened man reacting. And so when he finished, there seemed nothing left for me to say that he had not already unwittingly demonstrated. "Obviously we have very different visions about women," I said, and then I went on.

I think that's when I first realized that feminine journeys really do yield empowered female lives, that new authority issues out of our experiences.

Sometimes, though, people tend to mistake female authority for female bullishness. For instance, in a small group during a women's retreat, as we were discussing female empowerment, a woman told us that she was a strong woman like her mother.

"We don't take anything from anybody," she said.

The more she talked, the more it became apparent that like her mother she ran the house, ran her husband, ran the show. What she thought of as female power was really being overbearing and opinionated, controlling, and argumentative—enforcing one's will in a driven way.

Running the show is hardly female authority. To stand firm with power and dignity has little to do with ordering people around, constantly uncorking a lot of strong opinions and judgments, controlling things, or spouting off when someone pushes your button.

Eventually the woman recognized that like the rest of us she and her mother had their own wounded feminine life inside, that they, too, had been severed from their feminine souls and because of that had learned to mimic the ways of patriarchy. What they mistook for female strength and authority was recycled patriarchal power.

We find genuine female authority within when we become the "author" of our own identity. By taking the journey to the feminine soul, we "authorize" ourselves.

Ann Ulanov, professor at Union Theological Seminary, writes that a woman who has found her authority "is securely and consciously anchored in her own feminine being."[10] As a matter of course, this woman begins to experience the internal solidity I was beginning to notice, the change in substance. She comes to the solid center of herself and finds her own ground to stand on. And she stands there with her own authority.

Rather than needing to control and enforce things, she stands, steady and dignified, in this authority, with a knowing that is barnacled to her insides, that gives her the gumption and the enterprise to act in behalf of her vision and her soul. It's what allows her to do intrepid things— sometimes being gentle, sometimes fierce, sometimes waiting, sometimes leaping. But always knowing who she is.

The One-in-Herself Woman

As summer came, I read physician Esther Harding's book on feminine psychology, coming upon a train of thought that at first baffled then intrigued me. Harding spoke about a woman who may be married and have children or may have much sexual experience but is a virgin. Naturally, I wondered how a woman manages a thing like that.

Harding points out that in ancient times the word *virgin* had a different meaning than it does now. It didn't mean being chaste or physically untouched. Rather, being a virgin meant belonging to oneself.

Being a virgin, she says, refers to "a *quality*, a subjective state, a psychological attitude, not to a physiological or external fact." For a woman it means she is uncaptured or, as Harding puts it, she is "one-in-herself."[11]

In that context, a married woman, a mother, or any sexually experienced woman can be a virgin. It means that while she may relate fully to her partner, she does not give herself away to him or to patriarchy. She gives herself to her own soul. She is her own mistress, her own authority, her own woman.

Once when I tried to explain this to someone, she thought I meant that in being a virgin we would have no need for anyone else. But that wasn't it at all. By now I knew how intricately connected I was. If anything, as I belonged more and more to myself, I was able to relate more deeply and truly to those in my life. The relationships became something I chose, not something I felt dependent on or trapped in.

Being one-in-myself wasn't an aloof containment but a spiritual and psychological autonomy. It meant being whole and complete in myself and relating to others out of that soul-centeredness.

The journey to Crete, which I've referred to many times, took place the following fall. Before departing, I read about an ancient rite performed by the prepatriarchal Goddess Hera. The myth said every year she would return for a ritual bath in the Kanathos spring in Greece to renew her virginity, or her quality of belonging to herself.[12]

While in Crete, our leader, a scholar in women's spirituality and Goddesses of the ancient Mediterranean, mentioned that ancient women took part in these same baths, immersing themselves three times in the sea, in order to reclaim their virginity.

So one free afternoon in the village of Mochlos, I swam out into the sea with my friend Terry, the same Terry who'd led me to the buffalo in Colorado. A few hundred yards out in the water was a tiny, deserted island that contained nothing but scruffy brush and some ancient Greek ruins. We planned to spend the afternoon there.

Behind us in the water we pulled a child's inflated, plastic boat, which we'd purchased in the village. It was loaded with supplies Terry had brought from home to make masks—rolls of plaster of paris, scissors, Vaseline to protect our faces from the plaster, towels, bottles of water. It had been her idea to make a mask here, to capture an image of ourselves to take back home and paint.

As we dragged our little boat up onto the shore, I couldn't help but think of Naxos, the island where Ariadne had been deserted by Theseus. The thought stayed with me as Terry and I went exploring and finally came to part of a ruin at the water's edge. It was a low rock wall with some kind of basin cut into the stone, maybe part of an ancient house or temple. We spread out our supplies, filled the ageless basin with seawater, and cut the plaster into strips.

Then we picked our way barefooted over the stones, down to the sea. We waded out waist high and immersed ourselves three times. I remember most the shock of coldness as I went under, the rhythmic, almost mesmerizing immersion down and under, down and under, the gauzy light sifting under the water, and then the way the sun spattered on the surface when I came sputtering up the third time. I remember the rinsed look of everything, the determination in my chest, the power in my belly.

After drying off, I spread a towel on the ground inside the ruin and lay down. Terry spread the plaster of paris strips over my face, covering everything but my eyes and nostrils. "You have to be perfectly still," she said, "until it dries."

Lying silent in the Greek sun, the plaster tightened and seemed to dissolve into my skin, becoming part of me. Earlier when we'd talked about which aspect of ourselves we wanted the mask to symbolize, I'd thought of Ariadne. Now I replayed her story again—how after Ariadne had been abandoned on Naxos, she turned inward, finding her own resources. On Naxos she'd become one-in-herself.

Just a few days earlier, the tour bus driver had pointed to the craggy brown island of Naxos sitting out in the Aegean. Lying now on the Mochlos island, drowsy with sun and meditation and myth, I could easily imagine it as Naxos, the space of becoming One-in-Herself.

Finally Terry lifted away the dried mask and put it into my hands. Gazing at my cheeks, chin, forehead, nose, lips, I remembered this face going into the sea three times. The mask represented the face of the woman who came up out of the water. It registered in me as the image of an empowered self. It made me think of the female authority that comes when we start to belong to ourselves, to our own souls.

Back home I painted the mask green. On it I glued rocks, feathers, and shells from Crete, a brass labyrinth, and a coil of the string that my friend Betty and I had followed that night we moved through the woods, learning how to follow our thread.

Today the mask of the One-in-Herself Woman sits on a stand in my study. When I look at her, I feel the solid knowing in my belly. I remember who I am and who I hope to be. I smile at her a lot.

Iron-Jawed Angels

I flipped the channel to PBS one night and landed in the middle of a program about the suffragettes. I tuned in just in time to see policemen taking women away from the front of the White House where they had stood holding signs that asked, "How long must women wait for liberty?" The women were hauled away to jail, but then another handful of women came with the same determined look in their faces and held up the same signs.

They were taunted by passing men but also by other women, a thing that seemed incredulous on first glance. I mean, how could these other women believe they should not have the right to vote? Unless—and now suddenly I wasn't thinking only about women in 1920—they'd become so conditioned to subordinate experience and so used to being denied their rights that they'd normalized it.

I pondered what caused one group to support the system that subordinated and wounded them and the other group to believe their rights as women were worth fighting for. Looking at those two disparate groups of women, the things I'd learned during my awakening had never seemed more true—that women internalize the feminine wound or feminine inferiority so deeply, there's little or no female authority and esteem to fall back on. So they seek it by adopting and pleasing patriarchal standards. And my heart went out to these women, too, despite their blindness, because once upon a time, I'd been there.

I watched as the suffragettes stood, unflinching, through all the derision. The police came again and took the second group of sign holders away.

Inevitably, the authorities decided the women with their signs were getting out of hand, so they stepped up their intimidation, interrogating them in jail. The women responded by going on hunger strikes. The authorities insisted they eat. The women refused. The authorities brought in gastric tubes and force-fed them. Still the women refused to open their mouths to eat. They were, as one sympathetic bystander called them, "the iron-jawed angels."

In the end the women couldn't be broken, so they were released. They went back to their signs and their exhausting work of standing firm with power and dignity. And in the end they won us our right to vote.

Having never thought much about these women until I saw that program, I was unprepared for the rush of feeling I had for them, the love, gratitude, and awe for these ordinary women who took on husbands, fathers, government, church, and the entire weight of cultural tradition for the sake of justice. I sat on the sofa awhile after the program ended and asked myself about fifty times whether I could have done something like that.

The image of the iron-jawed angel became another representation of the feminine power I hoped to nurture: the self inside who, carrying her own sense of authority and esteem, can exhibit an uncommon resilience and inner toughness, especially when opposition comes.

Women who struggle for justice in religious structures, who dare to save the Divine from exclusive masculinity, who seek truth instead of defending dogma need every bit as much of the brawny-hearted strength those iron-jawed angels had. For opposition nearly always comes. I had my moments of it, some large, some small. But remember: *At the time it's happening, all opposition feels large,* and even when it's quite small, you still have to reach inside for the same unwavering grit.

I'm thinking of a phone conversation with a male priest friend who was uncomfortable with my transformation. He said, "Sue, as a priest I must tell you, by not being faithful to the church as you once were, you're setting the wrong example for your children. They'll be the ones to suffer." Translation: I am a spiritual authority. I, therefore, know what's best for you. What's best is for you to get back in line. And I will try to get you there, if necessary by raising the specter of bad motherhood—the ultimate leverage.

When someone tries to put you back into a box from which you've already escaped, you might recall a line from the Indian poet Mirabai. She said, "I have felt the swaying of the elephant's shoulders and now you want me to climb on a jackass? Try to be serious!"[13]

Still, hearing opposition as I did from my priest friend can be a mild shock, especially in the beginning. You may have to lay the phone down for a few seconds and breathe. When you finally comprehend what is happening, you may feel the iron-jawed angel wake up inside. You may hear yourself tell the person on the other end of the line that he shouldn't worry, you're your own authority now.

Sometimes the more public the opposition, the larger it may seem. Once when I spoke before a large audience on the feminine spiritual journey, a woman in the back stood up during the question session, raised her Bible, and cried out, "What you're saying is an abomination!"

After having her say (and what a say it was!), she marched out, inviting others to follow. Fortunately, only one other woman went, but it was high drama, moments I watched in still-frame, half-believing. Meanwhile the full realization about the opposition that's out there came crashing down like a piece of the sky.

What I did was to stand there and remember every iron-jawed angel I could think of.

One I often recall is the old grandmother in the movie *Strictly Ballroom.* Her granddaughter, along with a partner, wants to dance a daring new dance that breaks with convention. They face a barrage of public opposition because of it, so much that they are about to back off. At this moment, the old grandmother steps forth, sets her iron jaw, looks into her granddaughter's eyes, and says, "A life lived in fear is a life half lived."

I try to take that old woman with me at all times.

In the end, refusing the fear is what gets us through oppositional experiences. Refusing to half-live our lives means going out there and daring our dance.

Atop the Acropolis in Greece is a building known as the Erechtheum. The roof on its south porch is supported by the caryatids, six columns sculpted in the shape of women. While I was in Greece, the sight of the caryatids holding up that large ancient roof was the most inspiring thing on the Acropolis, even more than the Parthenon. The caryatids formed the stirring image of strong women bearing up, and I stood there thinking of all the women I knew who had borne up under enormous weight and opposition and in doing so made a space, a shelter, something of beauty for the rest of us.

A friend stood nearby, also gazing at them, and her thoughts must have paralleled mine, because she said, "Now *there* are some strong-necked women."

I liked her description. Strong-necked women. Just another way of saying iron-jawed women. Either way, it was the group I wanted to belong to.

EMBODYING SACRED FEMININE EXPERIENCE

Female empowerment is not only about emerging to voice our souls and finding a new inner authority as women. It is also about something far more simple—embodying our Sacred Feminine experience. This means bringing it home, so to speak, to our work, play, and relationships. The more we enact our feminine consciousness in our ordinary lives—living out the truth in our souls, the convictions in our hearts, and the wisdom in our bodies—the more empowered we become and the more capable we are of affecting the world immediately around us.

Becoming the Circle of Trees

In Crete we visited a mountaintop shrine called Kato Symi, where thousands of years ago the Great Mother had been worshiped. An ancient tree grows there. The inside of its massive trunk has been hollowed out, and one side of it has worn completely away, leaving a crescent-shaped wall of bark that rises into the sky. The space inside the tree is so large, all fifteen of us women were able to gather inside it.

Standing inside the tree, surrounded by tree trunk and the smell of gnarled bark, I suddenly realized that I was not in a circle of trees but inside the circle of a single tree. Perhaps it was the deepest circle yet. From this unique perspective I had the feeling of being taken into the tree, of being part of the tree, part of the trunk and roots and branches.

The moment affirmed to me all over again that *having* Sacred Feminine experience wasn't enough. It wasn't enough to have a sacred place, to go to a circle of trees in the woods. I needed to *become* the circle of trees, to be the sacred place wherever I went, to dwell so deeply inside my experience and have it dwell so deeply inside of me that there was no separation between us.

Embodiment means we no longer say, I had this experience; we say, I am this experience.

You have seen women like this, women who carry their feminine consciousness, their spiritual wisdom, their knowing, so fully and naturally that it is written all over them. I've known powerful women like this, and I find myself wanting to be in their presence and drink deeply. They are mentors, wise women, women whose transfiguration has settled deep inside them. Walt Whitman in his preface to *Leaves of Grass* seems to be describing the very quality these women embody: "Reexamine all you have been told in school or church or in any book, and dismiss whatever insults your own soul; and your very flesh shall be a great poem, and have the richest fluency, not only in words, but in the silent lines of its lips and face and between the lashes of your eyes, and in every motion and joint of your body."[14]

In Margaret Atwood's novel *Surfacing,* one of the characters says, "I lean against a tree. I am a tree, leaning."[15] When I read that I felt it was describing the shift to embodiment. For a long time we lean against the trees in the circle and they hold us up. But there comes a time when we realize that we must become the tree in the circle, able to hold the leaning of others.

A Spirituality of Naturalness

One particular way we can embody Sacred Feminine experience in our daily lives is to embrace a spirituality of naturalness. Like springwater, this spirituality arises out of our nature, our feminine nature. It's native to us, not artificial or manufactured or piped in from some other place. Very simply, this spirituality is true to who we are as women; it comes from within us and flows out.

The spirituality we've inherited from patriarchy is laced with a denial of the natural. Patriarchal spirituality becomes a flight from earth, flesh, temporality, and the present. But Sacred Feminine consciousness seizes us by the shoulders, looks in our eyes, and tells us with passion and simplicity: If you don't get anything else, get this. This is your life, right now, on this changing earth, in this impermanent body, among these excruciatingly ordinary things. This is it. You will not find it anywhere else.

A natural (and feminine) spirituality tends to incorporate three very organic, basic, but overlooked things into our sacred experience: the earthly, the now, and the ordinary.

THE EARTHLY   I live only a few hours from the ocean, and I try to get there as often as possible. The last time I was there, on a September morning, I took my scarf, a wild purple thing with gold fringe that I'd bought in a used clothing store in New Mexico, and I went down to the shore with my flashlight just before the sun came up, when no one was around, not even the crabbers. I took my scarf and danced in my bare feet in the breaking light, on and on along the waves that had by then all turned to harps. The wind whipped my scarf, whipped through me. I was living out my freedom. I was paying my respects to Herself, rejuvenating my connection, pulling myself like a thread through the shoreline. On that morning I felt that I was one of the ten thousand broken shells tumbling in the surf or one of the pelicans, with her belly skimming the ocean, open-billed, gulping in the mystery firsthand. I told myself: This . . . *this* is my spirituality.

To dance with waves, sand, birds, and shells, to immerse ourselves in these earthly things, whether in jubilation at the earth's beauty or sadness over her ruin, or to simply participate in earth's small, unceasing, familiar rhythms is to embody a spirituality of naturalness. When we do these things, we are stitching ourselves into the tattered fabric of the earth. We are learning, as the Lakota Sioux say, "to live well in the natural world."

Cut off from nature, we get sick inside. We lose our sense of belonging to the earth. This belonging fuels the core of energy inside us that sustains our activism. And when we lose that, we lose drive and power. We are not able to be the tree that holds the leaning. The more we draw the earthly into our spirituality, the more responsive we become, and our responsiveness calls forth the responsiveness of others.

The afternoon after my early morning dance, I walked along the beach, picking up trash. Soon Sandy came to help, then two people, perfect strangers, joined us. Further down the beach a few children came to help. Before it was over I'd handed out half a box of garbage bags. Sandy joked that I was the pied piper of beach trash. That evening I realized that what had happened in the afternoon was not at all separate from the connection I'd felt to the earth early that morning as I pirouetted along the waves.

THE NOW A spirituality of feminine naturalness not only teaches us that the earth is our true home but that *this moment* is our true home. "You cannot step twice into the same river," wrote Heraclitus, "for other waters are continually flowing on." This river is your life, and it is different every moment. The important thing (the sacred, empowering, natural thing) is to step deeply into it every single moment and be there as fully as you can, seeing as clearly as you can.

Being fully in the now implies a certain acceptance of what is. When my children were small, I read them Winnie the Pooh, who, as you may know, is an exceptionally enlightened bear. One thing Pooh says is, "A fish can't whistle and neither can I." When the enlightened Pooh says this, he's accepting "the clear reality that Things Are As They Are," says the little book *The Tao of Pooh*. "That doesn't mean we need to stop changing and improving. It just means that we need to recognize What's There."[16]

When we do this, we start to come home to the now. We accept where we are standing in the river right now, and we enter the immediacy of it, even when it's painful, because by doing so we are being present to our lives. We are attending to them, living them with awareness. If you think about it, how else can we be fully alive?

As we become alive and awake to the present moment, we start to "look deeply into things and see how we can change ourselves and how we can transform our situation."[17] And gradually, as we change, things around us change. We may not realize it, but by being present and looking deeply, we are becoming activists. We start to see that the roots of injustice, the oppression of the feminine, and the planetary crisis are after all linked to how we shop and dispose of our garbage and react to the morning news and ignore our bodies and teach our children and swallow our anger at our mates.

Without this deep looking at the present unfolding of our lives, we tend to perpetuate the old ways. Indeed, one reason that great social movements, including the feminist movement, sometimes hold within them pockets of unresolved anger and hostility is their failure to be present. Their members tend to live trapped in old patterns of seeing, reacting to the past rather than focusing on the transforming potential of now.

THE ORDINARY The really important question is, What does the Sacred Feminine have to do with how we go through an ordinary day? In a way all sacred experience and all journeys of soul lead us to the smallest moment of the most ordinary day.

Yesterday I woke too early and lay there listening to the dogs snoring beneath the bed. I watched Sandy's unshaven face lying on the pillow-case, the same face I have waked to for twenty-six years. And the same light as always was expanding across the room, falling in like bright water, making me want to stay there and watch how it flowed over us, illuminating a continent of small things—my glasses beside the bed, my journal, piles of books, Sandy's terry cloth robe coiled around the bed-post, the ficus plant in the corner grown large from all the watering. There were the children's pictures framed on the dresser—babies then, gone away now. I noticed the place beside the closet where Mother and I hung the wallpaper crooked. I felt my flesh pressed against the sheet, pressed upon this moment. From the bathroom I heard the faucet dripping, then the murmur of my breath moving in and out of my nostrils, and behind it all the pendulum clock in the distance, clicking like a metronome atop a piano, creating the domestic cadence against which this morning and all other mornings played.

I rose to make the coffee. I walked to the door and paused. When I looked back, I saw my life shining within every ordinary thing. And I was seized by the same feeling I get whenever I see the ocean—the feeling that it is all too much to behold, too beautiful, too much to bear—and I was filled with an aching love for it.

In the next instant the moment was gone, and I was climbing down the stairs, walking into the kitchen, into a day of small, humble, distracting things, and somehow nothing seemed more holy to me than just being there, naturally myself, in the midst of it.

Such moments are not as common for me as I might wish. But when they come, they leave me with a willingness to relate to my ordinary space—my work and family and friends and all the mundane duties—more authentically. I want to be in my feminine center in the midst of those plain places and to tell the truth and be the truth.

I heard a story about a man who went about the countryside asking people how they would spend their last day on earth. He came upon a woman who was out hoeing her garden, surrounded by her children and neighbor women. He decided he might as well ask her, too, even though he didn't expect much of an answer. "Woman," he asked, "if this were your last day on earth, if tomorrow it was certain you would die, what would you do today?"

"Oh," she said. "I would go on hoeing my garden and taking care of my children and talking to my neighbors."

The woman knew that there is nothing more important than being fully where we are, in the plain, ordinary events, day in and day out.

When what we have learned and lived during our journey begins to flow into these places—into our garden hoeing and our child rearing and our relationships with our neighbors—then we begin to affect the world around us in the most intimate, natural, and profound ways.

I think women understand that we create change as we live out the experiences of our souls in the common acts of life.

DAUGHTERS, THE WOMEN ARE SPEAKING

When I went to Crete, my daughter, Ann, was a senior in high school. One day browsing in a shop in Heraklion, I saw a small statue of Nike, and I wanted Ann to have it.

Nike was known as the Goddess of Victory, she who gives the power to prevail and then celebrates with us when we do. Within her, two things are brought together: womanhood and power. In ancient times Nike was the one who came and placed the laurel wreaths on the heads of Olympic winners. The Nike statue in the shop held a wreath in her outstretched hand, and she was standing very erect, proud, strong, and stalwart, like a tiny reflection of embodied female power, as if she were announcing, "Okay, world, here I am." When I gave the statue to Ann, I told her about Nike, about the Feminine Divine. Ann already knew much about the journey I'd been on for the last few years, but now I told her even more.

Ann turned the statue over in her hands. By giving her that gift, I was trying to tell her what was possible, because there's no female journey without someone to show us what's possible. I was trying to say: Your female soul, your deepest Self, is a thing of deep beauty and power, a thing to be embraced and celebrated. It is there for you if you choose it.

The wise old woman had come in my dream saying, "Your heart is a seed. Go, plant it in the world," yet where I most wanted to plant it was in my own daughter's life.

Ann put Nike on a little chest in the corner of her room. We didn't talk about her again. Months went by, and then, too suddenly, it was time for Ann to go to college.

I did not sleep very well the night before she left. It's odd the things you think about. I remembered her, five years old, bursting into the house to tell me the magnolia had a flower on it or that there was a cloud over the neighbor's house that looked like a bear sitting on a mushroom and I had to come see. I remembered her a hundred different ways at a hundred different times, and I said good-bye to the little girl. I was saying good-bye to myself, too, to all those mothering years of my life when I would go outside and stand for an inordinate amount of time trying to picture a bear on a mushroom.

But at the same time, beneath the sadness of the ending, I felt the kind of exhilaration that comes after you have invested much for a very long time and finally see the results. I knew joy, not sadness, was the thing that would last—the joy that she had arrived at this astonishing place where she was on her own.

I had bought a card with a turtle on the front, which I intended to give her the next day. I opened it now in the late hours of the night and sat thinking about what I wanted to tell her. In the end I wrote what a gift her life was to me then scrawled one bit of parting wisdom, condensing it all down to this: "Whatever else you do, listen to your Deepest Self. Love Her and be true to Her, speak Her truth, always."

The next day we drove to the college and began to unpack Ann's things in her new dormitory room. She unzipped a suitcase and to my surprise lifted out Nike. "Where should I put her?" she asked.

Just that, Where should I put her? But so much more was going on than that simple question. As I watched her place Nike first on the top of the desk, then on her dresser, the moment grew more and more transparent to me. Some kind of transmission was taking place, a transmission of female wisdom from my life to hers, a passing on of consciousness, of the potential for sacred poetry that lives in the feminine soul. All this was symbolized in the little statue with the laurel wreath. The gift was going with her into the world.

"The daughters of your daughters of your daughters are likely to remember you, and most importantly, follow in your tracks," writes Clarissa Pinkola Estés.[18]

"I like her here," Ann said, staring at the dresser, tilting her head a little.

"Yes," I said. "I like her there, too."

As I left, I propped the card containing my message beside Nike, then held my daughter close for a long time.

On the drive home, I remembered these lines from a favorite poem by Linda Hogan:

> Daughters, the women are speaking.
> They arrive
> over the wise distances
> on perfect feet.
> Daughters, I love you.[19]

As Sandy drove, I leaned my head against the car window, wanting to weep at the wonder of taking a feminine journey, of daughters receiving the precious thing we bring back from our journey.

We take our journeys and bring back the gifts. We find our hearts and we plant them. We do it as we voice our souls and find our authority, and we do it also in the quiet enactment of a natural spirituality. We do it for ourselves but also for all the daughters, all the women, all the men, all creation. We do it out of love for the women we are becoming, out of love for the earth. We do it because *we* are the change the world is waiting for.

THE STORY

Sandy and I drove a long time in silence. I was lost in reverie, thinking about my experience, following the threads of memory all the way back to the beginning, aware suddenly how much I had changed. A woman is transfigured into being by a long collection of events and moments. And it can start any sort of way.

"You sure are quiet," Sandy said.

I smiled at him. "Just thinking."

"About what?"

"Oh, about the slow, hidden way a woman's life changes."

"Hidden how?"

"Well, let's say there's this woman, this Everywoman, and one night she has a dream about giving birth to herself. She doesn't realize it, of course, but she's about to be pregnant with a new feminine life. And sure enough, she starts to get wake-up calls—an odd slip of tongue, maybe, in which she hears herself putting the word *Father* before her own name. The next thing she knows, she's uncovering the feminine wound—hers and the church's and the whole world's. She tries to run away from the whole thing, but before she gets too far, she finds herself on a beach with dancing women, celebrating an experience of female soul she can't even comprehend but that down deep makes her long for the mysterious thing she's lost."

He looked at me. "And this woman decides to find it."

"Yes, but first she decides she has to look honestly at her female life. When she does, she starts to see what a good daughter to patriarchy she's been, how she's created her life by blueprints that aren't even her own. Then she looks at the church, her marriage, the whole culture, the way it *really* is, the way women have been devalued and excluded, how the feminine has been suppressed and left out, and she knows for the first time that the absence of the Divine Feminine has left a hole in her.

She says, No more. She gets angry—no, make that furious. But she's real scared, too. She feels stuck, so lodged in 'the way it is' she can't imagine anything else. Until one day she goes into a drugstore and sees her daughter on her knees before these men who are laughing at her subordinate posture, and something happens to this woman."

The car slowed a little as Sandy grew more absorbed in what I was saying. I realized he was hearing the unbroken tale of my journey, albeit the ultracondensed version, for the first time, and in a way I was, too.

"So the woman decides to go away and reassess, to follow her own wisdom, which is starting to trickle down to her. She decides to let her old life collapse at her feet, to risk everything."

"I bet her husband remembers that part real well," he said.

"Okay, so it's hard on them both. But it's worth it. Because in the end, they find a whole new marriage. Plus, the woman finds this circle of trees, this space of Sacred Feminine experience unlike anything she's ever known, and deep inside her something says, *home*. She learns to dance in that circle, to create rituals, to open herself to the unknown. She discovers a myth, or maybe it discovers her, and it tells her what she needs to know about rebirthing as a woman. She faces off with the patriarchal voices she's internalized, buries the patriarchy in a shoe box, buries her old female self."

I paused. It was the oddest thing, the way the story was forming as I spoke, all the pieces—the trivial and the terrible—falling out of my mouth into this little pattern of meaning. It awed me as much as if a child had spilled a jigsaw puzzle on the floor and it had fallen into a picture. *This* is my story, I thought.

"Go on," said Sandy.

"Then she opens her arms to the Divine Feminine, discovering her in ancient places and traditional places, but mostly inside her own self. And she loves this presence with all her heart. Her consciousness starts expanding. She discovers she's not separate from anything—that earth, body, and mother are all divine, and this knowing changes everything. She discovers there is fire in her, a passionate struggle for women.

"She starts to heal, too. She moves deep into nature, into relationships with female friends, into herself. She comes upon a Matryoshka doll, and it teaches her to honor her feminine legacy. She goes to Crete and finds healing. She goes back to the monastery and dances around the altar and learns to forgive. And one night on the beach she sits with a sea turtle and is overwhelmed with love for her female self.

"All this causes her to give up the idea she's powerless. She starts to feel her strength, her own authority as a woman. She dreams about buffalo, and even they help her reclaim her power. Then, of course, she finds out that she has to bear witness to all this, that she has to plant her heart out there in the world. She decides to be brave, to play her music on a whole different lyre. More than anything, she wants to be a one-in-herself woman, to have her Sacred Feminine experience become a natural part of her life.

"And then one day she's sitting in the car beside her husband, having just taken their daughter to college, thinking of all these things."

There was silence in the car. He reached over and covered my hand with his.

My life had been miles and miles of reconstruction, but sitting in the car that evening, I felt glad for it. I was even glad for the miles and miles of my life *before* the reconstruction. For a time I'd thought of that part of my life as wrong. But our earlier lives aren't wrong, they are just pre-construction, that's all. Our lives are meant to unfold, to evolve, and that's good. The only wrong thing, perhaps, is permanently hesitating on the verge of courage, which would prevent this process from taking place.

It's a process that doesn't really end. That's why after eight years on this journey, I cannot write an ending and the story I told Sandy in the car keeps forming. I am still waking up, still crossing thresholds, still healing, still grounding, and always scraping up the bravery to plant my heart in the world.

Nothing happens neatly on journeys such as this. There is no one-two-three program. There are no guarantees, and no two journeys unfold the same way. Every woman's story of finding the Sacred Feminine brims with its own unique events, risks, complexities, pains, and rewards. And every story is a luminous thread that becomes part of a larger fabric, a fabric we are weaving together for the whole world, and this fabric is a thing of immense importance and beauty.

I look back now and I am grateful. I recall that whenever I struggled, doubted, wondered if I could pull my thread into this fabric, someone or something would always appear—a friend, a stranger, a figure in a dream, a book, an experience, some shining part of nature—and remind me that this thing I was undertaking was holy to the core. I would learn again that it is all right for women to follow the wisdom in their souls, to name their truth, to embrace the Sacred Feminine, that there is undreamed voice, strength, and power in us.

And that is what I have come to tell you. I have come over the wise distances to tell you: She is in us.

NOTES

INTRODUCTION

1. Nisa, "From Nisa: The Life and Words of a !Kung Woman," *The Norton Book of Women's Lives,* ed. Phyllis Rose (New York: W.W. Norton, 1993), 637.

2. Etty Hillesum, *An Interrupted Life: The Diaries of Hetty Hillesum 1941–43* (New York: Washington Square Press, 1981), 35.

PART ONE: AWAKENING

1. Maxime Kumin, "The Archeology of a Marriage," *The Retrieval System* (New York: Viking, 1978).

2. Toni Morrison, *Song of Solomon* (New York: Alfred A. Knopf, 1977), 149.

3. Jenny Joseph, "Warning," *When I Am an Old Woman I Shall Wear Purple,* ed. Sandra Haldeman Martz (Watsonville, CA: Papier-Mache Press, 1979), 1.

4. Clarissa Pinkola Estés, *Women Who Run with the Wolves: Myths and Stories of the Wild Woman Archetype* (New York: Ballantine Books, 1992), 10.

5. Carolyn G. Heilbrun, *Writing a Woman's Life* (New York: Ballantine Books, 1988), 20–21.

6. Madonna Kolbenschlag, *Kiss Sleeping Beauty Good-Bye: Breaking the Spell of Feminine Myths and Models* (San Francisco: Harper & Row, 1979), xiii.

7. Quoted in Peggy Taylor, "Rediscovering the Wild Woman," *New Age Journal* (Nov.–Dec. 1992), 63.

8. See Lyn Mikel Brown and Carol Gilligan, *Meeting at the Crossroads: Women's Psychology and Girls' Development* (New York: Ballantine Books, 1992).

9. Statistics from Lori Hesse, World Watch Institute, and the United Nations Report on the Status of Women, as quoted in Christiane Northrup, *Women's Bodies, Women's Wisdom* (New York: Bantam Books, 1994), 5.

10. Sue Monk Kidd, "Sleepwalking," *South Carolina Collection* (Fall 1991), 40–48.

11. For a discussion of the mother tongue and father tongue, see Ursula K. Le Guin, *Dancing at the Edge of the World: Thoughts on Words, Women, Places* (New York: Harper & Row, 1989), 147–63.

12. Elizabeth A. Johnson, *She Who Is: The Mystery of God in Feminist Theological Discourse* (New York: Crossroad, 1993), 27.

13. Carol P. Christ, *Diving Deep and Surfacing: Women Writers on Spiritual Quest* (Boston: Beacon Press, 1980), 13.

14. Anne Wilson Schaef, *Women's Reality: An Emerging Female System in a White Male Society* (San Francisco: Harper & Row, 1981), 27.

15. See Peggy Orenstein, *Schoolgirls: Young Women, Self-Esteem, and the Confidence Gap* (New York: Doubleday, 1994).

16. Polly Young-Eisendrath and Florence Wiedemann, *Female Authority* (New York: Guilford Press, 1987), 2.

17. Quoted in Alice Ostriker, *Writing Like a Woman,* Michigan Poets on Poetry Series (Ann Arbor: Univ. of Michigan Press, 1983), 126.

18. C. G. Jung, "On Psychic Energy," *Collected Works,* vol. 8, par. 100 (Princeton Univ. Press, 1978), 53–54.

19. Christiane Northrup, *Women's Bodies, Women's Wisdom* (New York: Bantam, 1994), 4.

20. Naomi Wolf, *Fire with Fire* (New York: Fawcett Columbine, 1993), 141.

21. Mary Daly, *Beyond God the Father: Toward a Philosophy of Women's Liberation* (Boston: Beacon Press, 1973), 4.

22. *Children's Letters to God,* compiled by Eric Marshall and Stuart Hample (New York: Simon and Schuster, 1967).

23. Le Guin, *Dancing,* 151.

24. "A Self of One's Own: An Interview with Alice Walker," *Common Boundary* (Mar.–Apr. 1990), 17.

25. Northrup, *Women's Bodies,* 19.

26. Barbara Walker, *The Women's Encyclopedia of Myths and Secrets* (San Francisco: Harper & Row, 1983), 603, 610.

27. This story is related in Sue Monk Kidd, "Going Back for Mary: A Protestant's Journey," *Daughters of Sarah* (Fall 1991), 28.

28. Referred to in Carol P. Christ, *Laughter of Aphrodite: Reflections on a Journey to the Goddess* (San Francisco: Harper & Row, 1987), 130.

29. See Heilbrun, *Writing a Woman's Life,* 11–31.

30. Gerda Lerner, *The Creation of Patriarchy* (New York: Oxford Univ. Press, 1986), 12.

31. See Le Guin, *Dancing,* 157; Kolbenschlag, *Kiss Sleeping Beauty Good-bye,* 23.

32. Sylvia Brinton Perera, *Descent to the Goddess: A Way of Initiation for Women* (Toronto: Inner City Books, 1981), 12.

33. Quoted in Heilbrun, *Writing a Woman's Life,* 109.

34. Lerner, *Creation of Patriarchy,* 5.

35. June Singer, *Boundaries of the Soul: The Practice of Jung's Psychology* (New York: Doubleday, 1972), 240.

36. Sherry Ruth Anderson and Patricia Hopkins, *The Feminine Face of God: The Unfolding of the Sacred in Women* (New York: Bantam Books, 1991), 184.

37. Virginia Woolf, "Professions for Women," *Women and Writing,* ed. Michele Barrett (San Diego: Harcourt Brace, 1990), 59.

38. Jong, quoted in Judith Warner, "Fearless," *Mirabella* (June 1994), 42.

39. Gail Godwin, *A Southern Family* (New York: William Morrow, 1987), 51.

40. Muriel Rukeyser, "Kathe Kollitz," *No More Masks: An Anthology of Poems by Women,* ed. Florence Howe and Ellen Bass (New York: Doubleday, 1973), 103.

41. Schaef, *Women's Reality,* 4.

42. Jane Wagner, *The Search for Signs of Intelligent Life in the Universe* (New York: Harper & Row, 1986), 18.

43. Anne E. Carr, *Transforming Grace: Christian Tradition and Women's Experience* (San Francisco: Harper & Row, 1988), 136.

44. Schaef, *Women's Reality,* 162–63.

45. Elizabeth Dodson Gray, *Patriarchy as a Conceptual Trap* (Wellesley, MA: Roundtable Press, 1982), 19.

46. Carol Gilligan, *In a Different Voice: Psychological Theory and Women's Development* (Cambridge: Harvard Univ. Press, 1982).

47. For instance, an article in my local newspaper on Jan. 27, 1995, reported that researchers at the brain behavior laboratory at the University of Pennsylvania have found several dimensions of brain function that correspond to differences between men and women. They found the brains of men and women identical except in the region that deals with emotional processing. The part of the brain controlling action-oriented responses was more active in men, while the part controlling more symbolic emotional responses (like words) was more active in women. It is not known, however, whether we develop brain chemistry because we act a certain way, or we act a certain way because of brain chemistry.

48. Margaret Starbird, *The Woman with the Alabaster Jar: Mary Magdalen and the Holy Grail* (Sante Fe, NM: Bear, 1993), xix.

49. Quoted in Joanna Macy, "Awakening to the Ecological Self," in *Healing the Wounds: The Promise of Ecofeminism,* ed. Judith Plant (Philadelphia: New Society Publishers, 1989), 202.

50. Rosemary Radford Ruether, "Motherearth and the Megamachine," in *Womanspirit Rising: A Feminist Reader in Religion,* ed. Carol P. Christ and Judith Plaskow (San Francisco: Harper & Row, 1979), 48–49.

51. Elaine Pagels, *The Gnostic Gospels* (New York: Random House, 1979), 63.

52. Carr, *Transforming Grace,* 46–48.

53. Cullen Murphy, "Women and the Bible," *Atlantic Monthly* 272, no. 2 (Aug. 1993): 41–42.

54. Johnson, *She Who Is,* 26.

55. Nelle Morton, quoted from the film of her life, *Coming Home.*

56. Heilbrun, *Writing a Woman's Life,* 15.

57. Joy Harjo, "The Blanket Around Her," in *That's What She Said: Contemporary Poetry and Fiction by Native American Women,* ed. Rayna Green (Bloomington: Indiana Univ. Press, 1984), 127.

58. Henrik Ibsen, *A Doll's House, The Wild Duck, The Lady From the Sea,* trans. R. Farquharson Sharp (New York: E. P. Dutton, 1958), 68–69.

59. Estés, *Women Who Run,* 13.

60. Elizabeth Cady Stanton, *The Woman's Bible* (New York: European Publishing, 1895).

61. May Sarton, *The House by the Sea* (New York: W. W. Norton, 1977), 224–25.

62. Anne Sexton, *The Complete Poems* (Boston: Houghton Mifflin, 1981), 255–58.

63. Kabir, *The Kabir Book,* trans. Robert Bly (Boston: Beacon Press, 1977), 41.

PART TWO: INITIATION

1. Carter Heyward, *Touching Our Strength* (San Francisco: Harper & Row, 1989), 29.

2. Penelope Washbourn, *Becoming Woman: The Quest for Wholeness in Female Experience* (New York: Harper & Row, 1977).

3. Karen A. Signell, *Wisdom of the Heart: Working with Women's Dreams* (New York: Bantam, 1990), 75, 40.

4. May Sarton, *The Reckoning* (New York: W. W. Norton, 1978), 90.

5. Jean Shinoda Bolen, *Crossing to Avalon: A Woman's Midlife Pilgrimage* (San Francisco: HarperSanFrancisco, 1994), 108.

6. Christin Lore Weber, *Womanchrist: A New Vision of Feminist Spirituality* (San Francisco: Harper & Row, 1987), 36–37.

7. Nelle Morton, *The Journey Is Home* (Boston: Beacon Press, 1985), 153.

8. Starhawk, *Truth or Dare: Encounters with Power, Authority, and Mystery* (San Francisco: Harper & Row, 1987), 67.

9. The picture can be found in Erich Neumann's *The Great Mother* (Princeton: Princeton Univ. Press, 1963), 332, plate 180.

10. Naomi Wolf, *Fire with Fire* (New York: Fawcett Columbine, 1993), 23.

11. Carolyn G. Heilbrun, *Writing a Woman's Life* (New York: Ballantine Books, 1988), 92.

12. Jean Baker Miller, M.D., "What Do We Mean by Relationships?" *Work in Progress,* no. 22 (Wellesley: The Stone Center Working Paper Series, 1986), 3.

13. Riane Eisler, *The Chalice and the Blade: Our History, Our Future* (San Francisco: Harper & Row, 1987), 31.

14. Charlene Spretnak, *Lost Goddesses of Early Greece* (Boston: Beacon Press, 1978), 17–38.

15. Joseph Campbell, *The Inner Reaches of Outer Space: Myth as Metaphor and as Religion* (New York: Harper & Row, 1986), 55.

16. Heilbrun, *Writing a Woman's Life,* 62–63.

17. Bolen, *Crossing to Avalon,* 163.

18. See Robert Graves, *The Greek Myths* (Baltimore: Penguin Books, 1955), 1:293–95 and 2:400.

19. Buffie Johnson, *Lady of the Beasts: Ancient Images of the Goddess and Her Sacred Animals* (San Francisco: HarperSanFrancisco, 1988), 296.

20. Sylvia Plath, *The Journals of Sylvia Plath,* ed. Ted Hughes (Garden City, NY: Dial Press, 1982), 176, 177.

21. Etty Hillesum, *An Interrupted Life: The Diaries of Etty Hillesum, 1941–1943* (New York: Washington Square Press, 1981), 222.

22. Starhawk, *Truth or Dare,* 66.

23. Marian Woodman, with Kate Danson, Mary Hamilton, and Rita Greer Allen, *Leaving My Father's House: A Journey to Conscious Femininity* (Boston: Shambhala, 1992), 31.

24. Cynthia Eller, *Living in the Lap of the Goddess: The Feminist Spirituality Movement in America* (New York: Crossroad, 1993), 202.

25. Charlene Spretnak, "The Unity of Politics and Spirituality," in *The Politics of Spirituality,* ed. Charlene Spretnak (Garden City, NY: Anchor Books, 1982), 351.

26. Joseph Campbell, with Bill Moyers, *The Power of Myth,* ed. Betty Sue Flowers (New York: Doubleday, 1988), 150.

27. From the discussion of entelechy in Edward C. Whitmont, *Noetic Sciences Review,* no. 31 (Autumn 1994): 11–18.

28. Louisa May Alcott, *Little Women* (New York: Macmillan, 1962), 394.

29. Jean Shinoda Bolen, *Gods in Everyman* (San Francisco: Harper & Row, 1989), 260.

30. Nancy Qualls-Corbett, *The Sacred Prostitute: Eternal Aspects of the Feminine* (Toronto: Inner City Books, 1988), 73.

31. I have ambivalent feelings about the inner masculine in a woman's life, because it has come to be defined so stereotypically. I've seen it written, for instance, that if a woman asserts herself in the world, it's not her own feminine self doing this but the masculine within her, suggesting that the feminine has no attribute of assertion and autonomy but must go through the masculine to get it. I do not accept this view, but I do acknowledge a masculine aspect within women, one that can be both positive and negative. When negative, it criticizes, judges, limits, undermines, and oppresses a woman. There was an undeniable connection between my struggle to speak, create, and act and the images in my dreams of crippled or tyrannical men. When the inner masculine in a woman is positive, it supports her and helps her manifest her vision, voice, and soul into the world. But I don't see the positive inner masculine as her intellect, her logic, her spunk, her independence, her authority, her strength, or her ability to have an opinion. I see all of these things inherent in her feminine self. Her positive masculine is a conduit, an enabler that helps to manifest these things.

32. George B. Hogenson, "The Great Goddess Reconsidered," *San Francisco Jung Institute Library Journal* 10, no. 1 (1991): 24.

PART THREE: GROUNDING

1. See Marija Gimbutas, *The Goddesses and Gods of Old Europe* (Berkeley and Los Angeles: Univ. of California Press, 1982), *The Language of the Goddess* (San Francisco: Harper & Row, 1989), and *The Civilization of the Goddess: The World of Old Europe* (San Francisco: HarperSanFrancisco, 1991).

2. In addition to Gimbutas, *Civilization of the Goddess*, see historian Gerda Lerner, *The Creation of Patriarchy* (New York: Oxford Univ. Press, 1986); art historian Merlin Stone, *When God Was a Woman* (San Diego: Harcourt Brace Jovanovich, 1976); art historian and professor Elinor Gadon, *The Once and Future Goddess* (San Francisco: Harper & Row, 1989); scholar and attorney Riane Eisler, *The Chalice and the Blade* (San Francisco: Harper & Row, 1987).

3. Ntozake Shange, *for colored girls who have considered suicide / when the rainbow is enuf* (New York: Macmillan, 1976), 63.

4. Janda J., *Julian: A Play Based on the Life of Julian of Norwich* (New York: The Seabury Press, 1984), 99.

5. Sallie McFague, "God as Mother," *Weaving the Visions: New Patterns in Feminist Spirituality*, ed. Judith Plaskow and Carol Christ (San Francisco: Harper & Row, 1989), 141.

6. Anne E. Carr, *Transforming Grace: Christian Tradition and Women's Experience* (San Francisco: Harper & Row, 1988), 140.

7. Paul Tillich, *Theology of Culture*, ed. Robert C. Kimball (New York: Oxford Univ. Press, 1964), 53–67.

8. Carr, *Transforming Grace*, 141.

9. Nelle Morton, "The Goddess as Metaphoric Image," in *Weaving the Visions*, ed. Plaskow and Christ, 116.

10. Mary Daly, *Beyond God the Father: Toward a Philosophy of Women's Liberation* (Boston: Beacon Press, 1973), 19.

11. McFague, "God as Mother," in *Weaving the Visions*, ed. Plaskow and Christ, 139–40.

12. McFague, "God as Mother," in *Weaving the Visions*, ed. Plaskow and Christ, 141.

13. Nelle Morton, "Goddess as Metaphoric Image," in *Weaving the Visions*, ed. Plaskow and Christ, 111.

14. Sogyal Rinpoche, *The Tibetan Book of Living and Dying*, ed. Patrick Gaffney and Andrew Harvey (San Francisco: HarperSanFrancisco, 1992), 164.

15. Carol P. Christ, *Laughter of Aphrodite: Reflections on a Journey to the Goddess* (San Francisco: Harper & Row, 1987), 100.

16. Morton, "Goddess as Metaphoric Image," in *Weaving the Visions*, ed. Plaskow and Christ, 111–12.

17. This story was published in a slightly different form in Sue Monk Kidd, "Reclaiming Lost Altars," *Encore* 2, no. 5 (Jan. 1995): 35–36.

18. Stone, *When God Was a Woman*, 1.

19. Elizabeth A. Johnson, *She Who Is: The Mystery of God in Feminist Theological Discourse* (New York: Crossroad, 1993), 47.

20. Rosemary Radford Ruether, "Sexism and God-Language," in *Weaving the Visions*, ed. Plaskow and Christ, 154.

21. Ruether, "Sexism and God-Language," in *Weaving the Visions*, ed. Plaskow and Christ, 153.

22. References to Wisdom/Sophia can be found sprinkled throughout the Bible, especially in Proverbs, Ecclesiastes, Job, and two apocryphal works, Sirach and Wisdom of Solomon. For amplification, see Susan Cady, Marian Ronan, and Hal Taussig, *Wisdom's Feast: Sophia in Study and Celebration* (San Francisco: Harper & Row, 1989). Also, a good summation can be found in *Feminine Aspects of Divinity* (Wallingford, PA: Pendle Hill Publications), pamphlet 191.

23. Proverbs 8:22–23, 27, 30.

24. C. G. Jung, *Answer to Job* (1958; reprint, Princeton: Princeton Univ. Press, 1969), 86.

25. Cady et al., *Wisdom's Feast,* 44–45.

26. Cady et al., *Wisdom's Feast,* 45.

27. See Elaine Pagels, *The Gnostic Gospels* (New York: Random House, 1981).

28. Pagels, "What Became of God the Mother?" in *Womanspirit Rising: A Feminist Reader in Religion,* ed. Carol P. Christ and Judith Plaskow (San Francisco: Harper & Row, 1979), 109.

29. Pagels, "God the Mother," in *Womanspirit Rising,* ed. Christ and Plaskow, 110.

30. Pagels, "God the Mother," in *Womanspirit Rising,* ed. Christ and Plaskow, 110.

31. Ruether, "Sexism and God-Language," in *Weaving the Visions,* ed. Plaskow and Christ, 153.

32. Johnson, *She Who Is,* 4.

33. Deepak Chopra, *Perfect Health* (New York: Harmony Books, 1991), 132.

34. Beatrice Bruteau, "Deep Ecology and Generic Spirituality," *Silence in the Midst of Noise: An Ecumenical Approach to Contemplative Prayer,* ed. Beatrice Bruteau and James Somerville (Pfafftown, NC: Philosopher's Exchange, 1990), 105.

35. Sallie McFague, "God as Mother," in *Weaving the Visions,* ed. Plaskow and Christ, 143.

36. Nancy Passmore, as quoted in Charlene Spretnak, "Toward an Ecofeminist Spirituality," in *Healing the Wounds: The Promise of Ecofeminism,* ed. Judith Plant (Philadelphia: New Society Publishers, 1989), 129.

37. Susan Griffin, *Woman and Nature: The Roaring Inside Her* (New York: Harper & Row, 1978), 227.

38. This experience was published in a slightly different form in Sue Monk Kidd, "Weeping with Dolphins," *Pilgrimage: Psychotherapy and Personal Exploration* (May–Aug. 1993).

39. Griffin, *Woman and Nature,* 219.

40. This story is adapted from Kidd, "Dolphins," 7.

41. "Everyone Is a Closet Mystic: An Interview with Andrew Harvey," *Inquiring Mind* (Fall 1994), 8.

42. "Closet Mystic," 9.

43. Jean Shinoda Bolen, *Crossing to Avalon: A Woman's Midlife Pilgrimage* (San Francisco: HarperSanFrancisco, 1994), 39.

44. From an interview with Thomas Berry in Mark Matousek, "Reinventing the Human," *Common Boundary* (May–June 1990), 34.

45. Hildegard of Bingen, *Mystical Writings,* trans. Robert Carver, ed. Fiona Bowie and Oliver Davies (New York: Crossroad, 1990), 91–93.

46. Sue Woodruff, *Meditations with Mechtild of Magdeburg* (Santa Fe: Bear, 1982), 42.

47. Janet Frame, *An Autobiography,* vol. 2, *An Angel at My Table* (New York: George Braziller, 1991), 188.

48. Judges 19.

49. Phyllis Trible, *Texts of Terror* (Philadelphia: Fortress Press, 1984), 81.

50. Maya Angelou, *The Complete Collected Poems of Maya Angelou* (New York: Random House, 1994), 163.

51. Susan Griffin, *Woman and Nature,* 188.

52. Johnson, *She Who Is,* 5–6.

53. Tillie Olsen, "I Stand Here Ironing," *Tell Me a Riddle* (New York: Dell Publishing, 1956), 12.

54. Annie Dillard, *Pilgrim at Tinker Creek* (New York: Bantam Books, 1974), 35.

55. Daly, *Beyond God the Father,* 51.

56. Isak Dinesen, quoted in Hannah Arendt, *The Human Condition* (Garden City, NY: Doubleday, 1959), 175.

57. For reading on mindfulness see: Thich Nhat Hanh, *Peace Is Every Step: The Path of Mindfulness in Everyday Life* (New York: Bantam Books, 1991); Thich Nhat Hanh, *The Miracle of Mindfulness: A Manual of Meditation* (Boston: Beacon Press, 1976); Jack Kornfield, *A Path with Heart* (New York: Bantam, 1993); Joseph Goldstein, *The Experience of Insight* (Boston: Shambhala, 1976); Joseph Goldstein and Jack Kornfield, *Seeking the Heart of Wisdom* (Boston: Shambhala, 1987); John Kabat-Zinn, *Wherever You Go, There You Are: Mindfulness Meditation in Everyday Life* (New York: Hyperion, 1994).

58. C. G. Jung and C. Kerenyi, *Essays on a Science of Mythology,* Bollingen Series 22 (Princeton: Princeton Univ. Press, 1963), 162.

59. Clarissa Pinkola Estés, *Women Who Run with the Wolves* (New York: Ballantine, 1992), 364.

60. Meinrad Craighead, *The Mother's Song: Images of God the Mother* (New York: Paulist Press, 1986), vii.

61. Daly, *Beyond God the Father,* 41.

62. Madonna Kolbenschlag, *Lost in the Land of Oz: The Search for Identity and Community in American Life* (San Francisco: Harper & Row, 1988), 81.

63. *Sappho: A New Translation,* trans. Mary Barnard (Berkeley and Los Angeles: Univ. of California Press, 1958), poem no. 8.

PART FOUR: EMPOWERMENT

1. Madonna Kolbenschlag, *Kiss Sleeping Beauty Good-bye* (San Francisco: Harper & Row, 1979), 196.

2. Carolyn G. Heilbrun, *Writing a Woman's Life* (New York: Ballantine, 1988), 18.

3. Eleanor Rae and Bernice Marie-Daly, *Created in Her Image: Models of the Feminine Divine* (New York: Crossroad, 1990), 101.

4. The story with photograph was reported in *USA Today,* February 24, 1994, 8E.

5. Ursula K. Le Guin, *Dancing at the Edge of the World* (New York: Harper & Row, 1989), 159–60.

6. See Sue Monk Kidd, "The Secret Life of Bees," *Nimrod: International Journal* 37, no. 1 (Fall–Winter 1993): 21–30.

7. Mary Catherine Bateson, *Composing a Life* (New York: Plume Penguin Books, 1989), 169.

8. Clarissa Pinkola Estés, *Women Who Run with the Wolves* (New York: Ballantine, 1992), 318.

9. Cited in Brenda Ueland, *If You Want to Write: A Book About Art, Independence and Spirit* (St. Paul: Graywolf Press, 1987), 40.

10. Ann Belford Ulanov, *Receiving Woman: Studies in the Psychology and the Theology of the Feminine* (Philadelphia: Westminster Press, 1981), 118.

11. Esther Harding, *Woman's Mysteries: Ancient and Modern* (New York: Harper & Row, 1971), 102, 103.

12. Charlene Spretnak, *Lost Goddesses of Early Greece: A Collection of Pre-Hellenic Myths* (Boston: Beacon Press, 1978), 87.

13. Mirabai, "Why Mira Can't Go Back to Her Old House," in Robert Bly, *News of the Universe* (San Francisco: Sierra Club Books, 1980), 256.

14. Walt Whitman, *Leaves of Grass* (New York: Heritage Press, 1936), xxvii.

15. Margaret Atwood, *Surfacing* (New York: Fawcett Crest, 1972), 17.

16. Benjamin Hoff, *The Tao of Pooh* (New York: Penguin Books, 1982), 39, 43.

17. Thich Nhat Hanh, *Peace Is Every Step: The Path of Mindfulness in Everyday Life* (New York: Bantam Books, 1991), 112.

18. Estés, *Women Who Run,* 460.

19. Linda Hogan, *That's What She Said: Contemporary Poetry and Fiction by Native American Women,* ed. Rayna Green (Bloomington: Indiana Univ. Press, 1984), 172.

PERMISSIONS

1. Mary Barnard. *Sappho: A New Translation.* Copyright © 1958 by The Regents of the University of California; copyright © renewed 1984 by Mary Barnard.

2. Elizabeth A. Johnson. *She Who Is: The Mystery of God in Feminist Theological Discourse.* Copyright © 1992 by Elizabeth A. Johnson. Reprinted by permission of The Crossroad Publishing Co., New York.

3. Cullen Murphy. "Women and the Bible." *Atlantic Monthly,* August 1993, vol. 272 no. 2, 41–42.

4. Anne A. Simpkinson. "A Self of One's Own." *Common Boundary,* March/April 1990, vol. 8, no. 2.

5. From *Selected Poems,* published by Bloodaxe Books Ltd., Newcastle-upon-Tyne. Copyright © Jenny Joseph 1992.

6. Excerpted from "The Archeology of a Marriage" as published in *The Retrieval System.* Used by permission of Curtis Brown, Ltd. Copyright © 1978 by Maxine Kumin.

7. From "Why Mira Can't Go Back to Her Old House" in *News of the Universe* by Robert Bly. Copyright © 1980 by Robert Bly. Reprinted with permission of Sierra Club Books.

8. "The Blanket Around Her," in *Moon Drove Me to This?* by Joy Harjo. Reprinted by permission of the author.

9. "The Women Speaking," in *Daughters I Love You* by Linda Hogan. Reprinted by permission of the author.

10. Excerpts from *Woman and Nature: The Roaring Inside Her* by Susan Griffin. Reprinted by permission of HarperCollins Publishers, Inc. For additional territory, please contact the author: 1027 Merced Street, Berkeley, CA 94707.

11. Naomi Wolf. *Fire with Fire.* Copyright © 1993 by Fawcett Columbine. Reprinted with permission of Random House, Inc.

12. From *And Still I Rise* by Maya Angelou. Copyright © 1978 by Maya Angelou. Reprinted by permission of Random House, Inc.

13. May Sarton. *The House by the Sea.* Copyright © 1977 by May Sarton. Reprinted by permission of W.W. Norton & Company, Inc.

14. From "Kathe Kollwitze," by Muriel Rukeyser, *A Muriel Rukeyser Reader,* W.W. Norton, New York. Copyright © 1994 by William Rukeyser.

15. Excerpt from "Professions for Women" in *The Death of the Moth and Other Essays* by Virginia Woolf. Copyright © 1942 by Harcourt Brace & Company and renewed 1970 by Marjorie T. Parsons, Executrix. Reprinted by permission of the publisher.

16. From *The Kabir Book* by Robert Bly. Copyright © 1971, 1977 by Robert Bly. Reprinted by permission of Beacon Press.

17. "Everyone is a Closet Mystic: An Interview with Andrew Harvey." *Inquiring Mind,* Volume II, No. 1.

18. From "Reclaiming Lost Altars." First printed in *Encore Magazine,* Vol. II, No. 5. 604 Pringle Ave., #91, Galt, CA 95632.

19. From Sue Monk Kidd, "Weeping with Dolphins." *Pilgrimage: Reflections on the Human Journey,* May/August 1993. 135 Sequoyah Ridge Rd., Highlands, NC 28741.

20. Judith Plaskow and Carol P. Christ, eds., *Weaving the Visions: Patterns in Feminist Spirituality.* Reprinted by permission of HarperCollins Publishers, Inc.

21. From *for colored girls who have considered suicide / when the rainbow is enuf* by Ntozake Shange. Copyright © 1975, 1976, 1977 by Ntozake Shange. Reprinted with the permission of Simon & Schuster.

Awakening

1. It frequently takes a series of wake-up calls or collisions with the truth to jolt a woman into a deep awakening to the Sacred Feminine. What experiences have served as wake-up calls for you?

2. What was your childhood church or culture of faith like? How did it become part of your internal geography? Did you identify with Kidd's memories of being a young girl in school and church, thinking God was male?

3. "The truth may set you free," Kidd writes, "but first it will shatter the safe, sweet way you live." Has your awakening been difficult and challenging? Was there internal and external resistance to it? Did you experience any part of it as shattering? Dangerous? Freeing?

4. If Jesus was a feminist in that he preached a gospel of liberation and mutuality and treated women as equal, why were women excluded for so long from leadership in most churches and forbidden from having authority over men? Where does your tradition stand on women's positions in organized religion? Are there ways in which we support the very structures that wound us?

Initiation

5. Kidd writes about her need to find a "circle of trees," her metaphor for the container that would hold and nurture her as she began the process of reconnecting to her feminine soul. How and when has it been important for you to find a contained space where you could really face and tend what was happening, where "the green shoot of your feminine soul could have its hothouse"?

6. The author writes candidly of her husband's initial resistance to her process. Men's resistance to Sacred Feminine awakenings often

grows out of their fear of change, fear that women's gain may be their loss. Kidd suggests that men need to become aware, but that blaming them doesn't help, it only polarizes the two sides. How can we negotiate through the resistance that might arise in a marriage? How can men become aware? How can they be invited into the struggle and made part of the quest?

7. Do you remember the first time you encountered a Divine Feminine image? Do you recall the first time you heard prayers using "she," "her," and "mother"? How did these things affect you?

8. How do you feel about the importance of rituals? In what ways have they shifted things for you? Have you had moments in which you felt you had truly crossed a threshold into a new landscape of feminine spiritual consciousness from which there was no turning back?

Grounding

9. How do you respond to the word *Goddess?* Does it create anxiety in you? Why? Do you think it helps to break the lock that patriarchy has on divine imagery?

10. Kidd concludes that since images, symbols, and words for God are necessary, they should be balanced and equitable. Do you agree with her that imbalance in our pictures of God perpetuates imbalance in our societies? In what ways does our world suffer from this imbalance? What impact does it have on the psychological and spiritual unfolding of girls and boys, women and men?

11. The Divine Feminine symbol creates a feminist spiritual consciousness that includes a passionate struggle for women's dignity, value, and power. When Kidd looked at the horrors women have suffered through the ages, she embraced their struggles as her own. How has the church helped women in their struggles for safety and full personhood? How has it undermined these struggles?

12. Are there times when it may be necessary to leave one's religious tradition (e.g., in order to protect and "birth" one's feminine spiritual consciousness)? Have you ever been in a dilemma about whether to leave or to stay? How do you feel about women who believe they need a brand new model that exists outside their tradition, and women who attempt to create new models within their tradition?

13. As Kidd immersed herself in the feminine spiritual experience, she was initiated into her body in a deeper way. Women's experience of body has historically been immersed in shame. What messages did you

receive about your body as a child? As an adult? Are we still affected both subtly and unsubtly by ancient taboos and attitudes that are associated with women's bodily functions such as menstruation, pregnancy, childbirth, and lactation?

14. How do fear and silence cut off your journey? Did you identify with the image of a "lovely, quiet girl, no trouble at all"? Do you have a negative voice inside that cages or restricts the natural or spirited part of yourself?

15. The Russian Matryoshka doll became for Kidd a symbol of the "mother line"—the unbroken line of grandmothers, mothers, and daughters—and the feminine wisdom that can flow through this connection. The nesting doll reminded her of the ways we've nested within one another and birthed one another. How do you feel about your mother line? In what ways did your mother express the Sacred Feminine? In what ways did she uphold patriarchal values and caution you not to step outside conventional boundaries or to rock the boat?

Empowerment

16. What does the word *empowerment* mean to you?

17. In a dream, a wise old woman told Kidd: "Your heart is a seed. Go, plant it in the world." How are you compelled to plant your heart in the world? What deep impulse in your feminine soul needs to be expressed? What holds you back?

18. "All journeys of soul lead us to the smallest moment of the most ordinary day." What does it mean to embody Sacred Feminine experience in your daily life? How can it become a seamless part of how you relate, work, play, and go about your life?